DANCE BEAT

Selected Views and Reviews 1967–1976

Deborah Jowitt

MARCEL DEKKER, INC.　　　New York and Basel

The articles contained in this book were originally published in other sources. Acknowledgment to these other sources is given in the text. Permissions have been granted as follows:

Reprinted by permission from the *New York City Dance Calendar* (published by Association of American Dance Companies for the Theatre Development Fund).

Reprinted by permission of *The Village Voice.* Copyright © The Village Voice, Inc., 1967-1976.

Reprinted by permission from *Art in America* (May-June 1971).

© 1971/72/73/74/75 by The New York Times Company. Reprinted by permission.

Marcel Dekker, Inc.
270 Madison Avenue, New York, New York 10016

Library of Congress Catalog Card Number: 76-44564
ISBN: 0-8247-6506-0

Current printing (last digit):
10 9 8 7 6 5 4 3 2 1

Printed in the United States of America

This book is dedicated to Baird Searles,
Letitia Kent, and my husband, Murray Ralph—
all of whom made me a dance critic in spite
of myself.

PREFACE

I usually tell people that I became a dance critic by accident—that I was pushed into it, or fell into it, that it wasn't my idea at all. All of which is true. Nevertheless, I notice that I now seem to be addicted to writing about dance. The ephemeral nature of the art exasperates and excites me. Record films, videotapes, notation scores of dances aren't usually available to the general public (and if they were they might prove misleading or incomprehensible). I often feel as if I'm pursuing a dance with words—sprouting far more adjectives and adverbs than a good writer should—in an attempt to define precisely what struck me as important or interesting about that work. Often the dance in question evades my analysis, but occasionally a few words or phrases stick to it; I like to think this helps to evoke the experience again or perhaps provides those who enjoy thinking and talking about dance with new fodder for argument.

That I didn't stop choreographing and performing when I began to write criticism has disturbed other critics, but dancers don't seem to find it particularly odd. Perhaps they know that while fair-mindedness can be achieved, objectivity is a fallacy. Perhaps, too, having seen me sweat and heard me curse, they know that—however my taste may differ from theirs—I can never forget how much thought, care, and work goes into the making of a dance. That is, I'm interested in thinking about bad dances—although I'd rather think about great ones—rather than simply stomping on them and sweeping them under the rug.

My appreciation of a dance seems to operate on a sliding scale, and I occasionally worry that this is confusing to readers. I may complain, for instance, about a Balanchine ballet and rejoice over a small work by a new and relatively unknown choreographer; it doesn't mean that I think this artist outranks Balanchine, but only that he or she pleased me in a way appropriate to the scale and concepts involved, and that Balanchine failed to top himself this time. I've noticed too that I'm more sympathetic to fairly interesting "experimental" art than to low-grade traditional art.

Since late 1967, in addition to freelancing for a number of publications (principally *The New York Times*), I've written an article almost every week for the *Village Voice*, and consider myself extremely fortunate to be working for a paper that gives its writers large amounts of freedom and space to shrug around in. I've also worked with enlightened and perceptive editors, in particular Diane Fisher at the *Voice*, who first encouraged me to write about movement (isn't that what dance is all about?) and Seymour Peck of *The New York Times*, who was interested in topics that interested me, even if they weren't always such hot news.

While choosing articles for this anthology, I've been overwhelmed by the sheer numbers of choreographers and dance companies this country has accumulated since I started writing criticism. There are many choreographers and companies who are considered important and/or whose work I admire who aren't represented in this book: Murray Louis, Paul Sanasardo, Cliff Keuter, Rod Rodgers, Multigravitational Experiment Group, Lar Lubovitch are just some of the significant omissions. I wasn't particularly taken with what I'd written about their work. A critic, like a choreographer, like a dancer, is capable of producing a fair amount of duds. Still I hope I've managed to convey some sense of the liveliness and variety of the New York dance scene over a period of nearly nine years.

Deborah Jowitt

CONTENTS

Ballets—Mostly New

The Third Generation: Mostly Rebels

Ballets—Mostly New

Original (?) Swan

The Village Voice, December 19, 1968

Although we are forever hearing that American Ballet Theatre is teetering on the brink of financial ruin, its repertory still goes about in diamonds and sables. In this age of smart, sparse decor, ABT lugs elaborate painted backdrops and sturdy furniture around on its tours. Somewhere along the line, this pioneer of American ballet has decided to be a stronghold of classicism. Points in favor of this: 1) someone has to preserve the classics; 2) much of the American public has never seen said classics; 3) ABT has always been more impressive in dramatic ballets than in pure dance ones.

So now the company has "Giselle" and "Coppelia" (just acquired), and "Swan Lake." Ballet Theatre's "Swan Lake" was purchased, an act at a time, from David Blair of England's Royal Ballet. The Royal Ballet (in its early Vic-Wells incarnation) has been taught the work by Nicholas Sergeyev who had toted scores and notation straight from the Maryinsky Theatre where the 1895 version was first performed with choreography by Marius Petipa (Acts I and III) and Lev Ivanov (Acts II and IV). There have been a lot of other versions—then, now, and in between. If over the years the choreography has metamorphosed as much as the story, I can't say for sure whose ballet I really saw bursting the seams of the Brooklyn Academy stage the other night. (For example, in the earliest version of the scenario, the Swan Queen's grandfather has hidden her away at the bottom of the lake to keep her from the destructive wrath of her sorceress stepmother; he changes her and chums into swans by day as a favor, in order to let them get a little fresh air and exercise.)

ABT's add-a-pearl "Swan Lake" raises a few questions about how to resurrect a classic. Blair is credited in the program with revisions in some of the dances. Unfortunately, he was not tempted to insert a little dancing or genteel acting in place of the pantomime sections. It's not that ABT principals don't perform this codified mime well; they do. It's simply that the passages of repetitious, mute dialogue stop the action and give the characters a slightly dim-witted air ("Me no speakum English, but me lovum anyhow").

Acts I and III of "Swan Lake" teem with people—peasants and nobles on a spree in Act I, courtiers and royalty and entertainers in Act III. I don't care for Blair's direction of them, although he has draped them prettily about. The people were very ho-ho animated until anyone started

3

some serious dancing; then they relapsed into vigilant, appraising stillness. Little in the supposedly festive first act (including Ted Kivitt's good, quietly bouncy dancing in the pas de trois) could match the stunning entrance of Bruce Marks as Prince Siegfried, all princely happiness and arrogance and holding a sleek Great Dane by the collar. (I mean a real dog—not Erik Bruhn).

The plot of "Swan Lake" is shaped to give plenty of hooks to hang dancing on, and, as everyone knows, the ballet has its choreographic attractions: the gentle, moonstruck pas de deux in Act II; the hard, flashy grand pas de deux in Act III; the sexy czardas; the white girls, docile in their perpetually symmetrical formations. The ballet also radiates that mysteriously satisfying quality of fairy tales: a froth of sugar and cream, satin and good breeding covering some darker, crueler myth of transformation, resurrection, and violent death. When daylight begins to leave Act I's jolly fete champetre and Benno points out the flight of swans to the Prince and they both dash off, crossbows in hand, there is a sudden, inexplicable chill in the air. ABT milks this atmosphere grandly with Oliver Smith's drops of ruined turrets over the lake and, later, the gloomy stone interior of Prince Siegfried's castle. Jean Rosenthal's lighting and a smoke machine contribute good things too.

There is something touching and infuriating about the characters in "Swan Lake." They behave as if slowness on the uptake were an integral part of the romantic condition, or a prerequisite for nobility. Benno dashes with his bow right into the center of a cluster of swan maidens, who dutifully finish their variations before they cower. The Prince searches distractedly among the ladies for his beloved, even though he ought to know by now that her tutu is a good 12 inches shorter than anyone else's. Oh, they're all so pretty and hapless. Their predicaments brush against you ever so delicately—moving you, if at all, by the death of your own romantic fancies, rather than by their deaths, which are as painless and monochromatic as dream.

I thought that Bruce Marks made a splendid Siegfried. Despite a vile makeup job, he looked young and dashing, but had enough melancholy restraint to make his involvement with a bird-girl believable. Most important, he's a fine dancer, with a particularly noble carriage of the head and upper body. Toni Lander was better as Odile than she was as Odette, by virtue of her strength and brilliance. She was certainly skillful in the white acts—softening her formidable attack and phrasing very delicately at times. But she was always centered, always on balance, always so very sure, and she lacks flexibility in the back. All this made her very much the well-bred princess, but did not permit the wildness and the vulnerability that I like to see in the bird parts. Enrique Martinez, Lucia Chase, and Richard Gain play respectively—and very well— the foolish old tutor, the Prince's mother, and the wicked sorcerer. It's good to see a von Rothbart who can really flap around in his death throes.

What about full-length story ballets anyhow? Well, I'm for going the whole hog, if you're going to do it at all. I'd rather yawn through the dull parts than see disembodied second acts and characterless snap-crackle-and-pop pas de deux. The idea of authenticity is intriguing, but I'll bet the original "Swan Lake" has long since been blurred in its hand-to-hand passage. The question remains: would a really free and swinging version make the story seem ridiculous, or would it release the spirit of the original "Swan"?

It strikes me now that when I wrote this piece either I still harbored the modern dancer's view of ballet as charming, but hopelessly old-fashioned, or else I was playing the role of intransigent young critic to its slangy hilt. Eight years later, I see no point in updating classics and have become fond of mime passages in ballet. No matter how drastic the situation, everyone waits his turn to "speak," and I enjoy the rich, polite leisureliness of that.

Sour Notes in the Ballet Season

The Village Voice, August 12, 1971

I can understand why Bela Bartok in 1918 might have found Menyhert Langyel's libretto for "The Miraculous Mandarin" provocative enough to spin some really splendid music around. I cannot understand why so many choreographers—including now the young Swede, Ulf Gadd— have been drawn to it. The scenario is all but unplayable, but perhaps some copyright law demands that music and libretto not be separated. I cannot quite understand why Ballet Theatre chose to mount Gadd's version, except that it is a good vehicle for a strong male actor-dancer like Erik Bruhn, who danced in it on opening night.

Here is the story: three thieves employ a prostitute to decoy the men that they plan to rob. Two prospective victims—a drunken sailor and a young boy—escape. Enter the Mandarin. According to the program, the girl arouses his "savage nature," and no matter how the three gangsters beat him up, choke, and stab him, he refuses to die until she crawls into his arms. According to the press release, she falls in love with the Mandarin at the last moment and is forgiven for her life of sin. Strong stuff.

According to the *ballet*, however . . . well, I just don't know. Everything is a little illogical. Some actions take disproportionately long; others are accomplished in the wink of an eye. The three robbers are far too randy to make efficient pimps; they'd wear the girl out before she could get started. The drunken sailor stays drunk for about eight bars, then bangs the girl competently and escapes the three toughs with absolutely no trouble. The program says that they chase him away because he has no money, but I don't think this happened either. They just make ineffectual grabs at him as he whisks into the wings and then climb sulkily back up their ladder. (I should mention that the ballet set by Hermann Sichter is a splendidly forbidding grid affair that looks a little like a boom-town skyscraper.) The young boy is too tender and sweet to take quick advantage of the girl, but after the thugs let him escape too, they unfairly beat her up. Another example of what inefficient pimps they are. However she makes another attempt. The Mandarin is mysterious from the start; he just stands there in profile while she does a long tired solo around him. Once he opens his jacket at her, showing her a handsome chest and an even more handsome blue-sequined lining. In this ballet, he doesn't get much chance to show how savage his nature is, because the three thieves for once pull themselves together and attack—even though this one obviously knows a bit of karate. Well, they really maul him, carry on in a most unpleasant manner. And each time they leave him for dead, he slowly rises and heads for the girl. The most persistent erection in stage history. After a while, this stops being ghoulish and starts being funny. Anyway, naked and cuddled up to the girl, he finally dies. So does she, I think.

This production aims at being modern. The costumes are rather German expressionist, with bald head-pieces for the thieves and the Mandarin. And at the end, a host of black-robed figures holding white masks assembles to stare at the collapsing prostitute. The style of the dancing is flashy, muscular "modern ballet" with explicit sex stuff. The cast I saw consisted of Royes Fernandez as the Mandarin, Diana Weber as the girl, David Coll as the Sailor, Warren Conover as the Young Boy, and Alexander Filipov, Ian Horvath, and Gaudio Vacacio as the Three Gangsters. They all did their best, but the work is not really choreographed to show you these characters; instead it seems as if Gadd wanted to make sure that you would know that they were dancers. The poor, weary, beat-up whore is never too tired to jump up and whip off another pirouette. How, given this approach, can Diana Weber convince you that she is anything but a superbly lithe young athlete who could probably knock out all three of her bosses with one well-aimed kick? And these three, by the way, do a lot of their threatening and mugging in controlled unison passages. Interesting that in 1760 Noverre wrote that in a scene d'action "symmetrical and formal figures cannot be employed without transgressing truth and shocking probability, without enfeebling the action and chilling the interest. There, I say, is a scene which should offer a ravishing disorder . . ."

Ballets like "The Miraculous Mandarin" obviously bring out the worst in me.

Some of the elements I was sniping at in this ballet are discussed more fully in an article on p. 64, titled "The Hybrid: Very Showy, Will Root in Any Soil." However, in that article too, I never came right out with the problem, which I now think has to do with a dance technique becoming an aesthetic in itself, instead of simply a means to express something else.

Playing Around with Time & Space

The Village Voice, August 5, 1971

What Antony Tudor did in his 1943 "Romeo and Juliet," now revived by Ballet Theatre, makes it one of the most brilliant and interesting of recent ballets. In particular, he has worked with the structure of the play so as to situate it in the kind of Renaissance time and space with which Shakespeare's work has so many affinities.

As Wylie Sypher pointed out in his "Four Stages of Renaissance Style," the plot of "Romeo and Juliet" is an essay in symmetry and proportion. Capulet is weighed against Montague, Romeo's passion against Paris's suitability, love against hate, night against day, rashness against prudence, etc. Time is compressed into 42 hours; space is defined and confined by the walls of Verona's chambers, gardens, piazzas, There is none of the depth, irregularity, or ripeness of the later "Hamlet" or "Macbeth."

Tudor has set his version of this sad and lyrical equation in what might be compared to a continuous Botticelli frieze. There is an emphasis on elegant, agitated, fastidiously sensual flow rather than on volume. It is as if Tudor had speeded up the heartbeat of the play, so tremulous is one's reaction to it. His space, like Botticelli's, is almost more medieval than Renaissance: depth is created by temporary hierarchies, events separated in time can coexist in space. When Romeo and Juliet wind through the pillars of the piazza in an ecstatic return from their wedding, they are small upstage figures, seen through the minor bustle of the square. When Juliet, enveloped by the Nurse, weeps over Tybalt down left, their figures are balanced by those of Romeo and Friar Laurence consulting hastily down right. And the two tableaux are separated by a temporary "wall" formed by two watching women. Tudor's use of these women is another odd detail. They witness the action from different positions, like those little faces in the corners of certain medieval paintings.

7

The effect of all this compression on the spectator is fascinating. There is no blood, thunder, bombast; the action is drawn lightly over you like a veil while you sit in a state of almost febrile tension. Events, briefly sketched, flow out of each other; even what Tudor has chosen to show or not show is revealing. Nothing seems to have any preliminaries. The Montague boys' decision to attend the Capulet ball is conveyed by Mercutio's brusquely beckoning finger, while the powerful effect of the lovers' first meeting on Romeo and his friends is shown more fully. Letters are not delivered, potions are drunk, marriages are arranged at high speed and with pictorial clarity.

Eugene Berman's marvelous pillars, archways, and porticos hold and shape the action, add to the morbid delicacy of atmosphere. When a curtain is drawn to reveal the ball in progress, the dancers first appear cramped, too large for the space they inhabit—another painterly touch. Tudor's choice of excerpts from Delius is extremely unusual. The music meanders along its own path—painting a lush, summer atmosphere that is neither dramatically nor rhythmically assertive, but full of feeling. Often it creates a curious tension between its dreamy flow and the action of the play. For instance, the insistent little tappings and steppings of the court dances begin to be almost ominous against the inconclusive music.

Since nothing in this ballet ever really stops, pauses for large scale "dance numbers" would have been unthinkable. Tudor has built the dancing out of gesture so subtly and naturally that you are not aware of anything but the continuous unfolding of this lyrical disquisition on action. There is a ball scene, of course, quietly and slowly built-up. There is no grand pas de deux for the balcony scene: alone on the stage floor, Romeo bursts into an exulting stammer of leaps and postures and wide-flung gestures, while Juliet on the balcony above returns his passion with slow and happy stretchings and curvings of her body and arms. Even the morning-after-the-wedding scene turns into a dance imperceptibly through a series of muted rushings, claspings, near-swoons.

Because nothing seems calculated, no particular moments of dance can be easily isolated. Pointework has a special expressive function. Juliet steps up onto pointe as if some delicate emotional balance were at stake, or as if she were on unfamiliar ground. In some of her steps, she might be swooning upward.

I saw only one of the two casts—John Prinz and Natalia Makarova rather than Ivan Nagy and Carla Fracci. Prinz was a surprise—impetuous, hot-eyed, he looked caught in an affair he couldn't fathom. Except for some overflung arabesques as he exited, he was splendid. Makarova presented some problems. Strong and sensitive, holding herself in admirably, she still didn't seem quite spontaneous. Her modesty, expressed by a head thrust forward and down, had something calculated about it.

Perhaps she has been trained to think of ballet acting as a series of attitudes that can be easily formulated. She's not helped by an ugly wig that's a shade too carroty and makes her look hard. Dennis Nahat made a bright and flippant Mercutio. His death, as Tudor conceived it, is wonderful—poignant, a waste, over before you know it; like the ballet, it speeds through time, while seeming suspended in space.

Thornless Rose and Other Vagaries

The Village Voice, July 20, 1972

American Ballet Theatre is a restless, nervy kind of company. The management, confident about the varied repertory and the fine dancers, is often daring: company members like Dennis Nahat and Michael Smuin create new works; revivals are mounted of unusual ballets, like Antony Tudor's morbidly beautiful "Romeo and Juliet"; "modern" choreographer Alvin Ailey is asked to choreograph one—now two—new productions. Some of these pay off in spades, either commercially or artistically or both.

ABT is also in the hot property market, and one of its ongoing problems is finding roles for its small bevy of charismatic European ballet stars who can't, won't, or shouldn't make their company debuts in "Rodeo" or "Les Noces" or "Pillar of Fire." The glossiest new attraction is Paolo Bortoluzzi, the Béjart superstar, and ABT is offering him up in a revival of Michel Fokine's "Le Spectre de la Rose" (staged by André Eglevsky, who was assisted by Annabelle Lyon).

"Spectre," as everyone probably knows, is a delicate, understated pas de deux, suffused with the kind of willful Romantic thinking that prefers its heroes and heroines to loll about (or even race about) yearning after the unattainable, rather than working toward the possible. In this ballet, the dreamer is a Young Girl just back from a ball. Overstimulated, she dozes off in a large armchair with a rose in her hand, and the Spirit of the Rose suddenly thrusts itself through the window of her safe, white room and dances for her and with her. More courtly and undemanding than any real young man might be (the one who gave the rose, for example), he leaps out of the window and leaves her alone.

In "Le Spectre de la Rose," the Romantic aesthetic has been divested of possible wildness and covered with sugar, white tulle, and rose petals. It's pink and white, sweet and cozy—a proper dream for any jeune fille. Yet what I find intriguing about the ballet is that the role of the Rose was made for Vaslav Nijinsky—by all accounts a brilliant jumper, heavy-muscled and somber, with an almost feline sensitivity. Performed by him, the image of sexual power, thinly disguised by the flower image of the Young Girl's safe dream, must have been arresting. Several years ago, at Jacob's Pillow, I saw Edward Villella perform the role (with Lone Isaksen); he was careless of his line, impetuous with the jumps, handsome and unruly. He didn't wear the rose-suit.

Paolo Bortoluzzi is a very different sort of dancer from Villella, from my picture of Nijinsky, from Eglevsky and Youskevitch, who used to dance the role for ABT. He's a slight man, dapper and elegant. Jumping is not his thing; he has none of the weighty, elastic pouncing of the big jumper. Instead, he excels in achieving a faultless line in brief, lightweight flights. His Spirit of the Rose is just that—an otherworldly and quite asexual being. His rapid, neat leg beats, his broken-wristed gestures, his politeness with the girl impart a tame charm to the ballet. In the pink tights and petal-strewn leotard and gauze helmet, he looks like the Pease-blossom from an art nouveau "Midsummer Night's Dream"—alert, sweet, helpful. What could be the harm in having such a lover around all the time?

However, I think that audiences will love his perfection, love the prettiness of the idea, and love Carla Fracci's Young Girl. She contrives to look happily sleepy most of the time, drooping confidingly against him, faltering lightly as he guides and leads her, a girl who is easily tired by real exertion—just the sort of girl, in fact, who would have this sort of a fantasy. Perhaps the Rose was never meant to have thorns . . .

Another revival of the current American Ballet Theatre season at New York State Theatre is a more recent foray into Romanticism: Eliot Feld's lovely "Intermezzo." Feld has worked at making a kind of visual emblem for the impetuous pulse and bittersweet coloring of a series of Brahms intermezzi. Some of his dance phrases are tender, suspended, questioning; some are tumbling, marked by dashing accents of heel, hand, head. The three couples are dressed for a ball. There is a piano on the stage. Some of the time, they actually seem to be at a ball; the rest of the time, they are in a countryside made only of music and feeling and the large shadowed space. The young men and women are by turns formal with each other, tender, absent-minded, daring. Two of them, although holding hands, almost lose each other in the Romantic mist through which they have chosen to grope.

Feld's now defunct company used to dance "Intermezzo" with the vulnerability and slight awkwardness that was part of its charm (and one of its problems). The dancing in ABT's production is much silkier and gives the work a darker, richer, tone. (Pianist Howard Barr is an important part of this.) Cynthia Gregory uses an almost reckless amount of space when she dances, but has a suppleness and a poise usually associated with tamer attack. Mimi Paul has a touch of strangeness about her, is cool but extravagant, Ivan Nagy is smooth, elastic, courtly. Jonas Kage has more of a darting quality. Of the original cast, only Christine Sarry and Feld himself are left. Sarry is as extraordinary as ever. She appears never to finish phrases, but instead to arrest them on the way up. This gives her an almost incredible lightness and a restless, clever look. Surely no one else can make fast dancing look so fast. When Feld first took over one of the male roles from David Coll, I was distressed. In trying to set the right tone of passion and daring, he became what I thought was too rash. Everything he did looked hasty and misjudged. When he hurled Sarry up in the air in one of his most surprising lifts, I felt worried instead of excited; she looked ready to die for him, but did it have to be right now? This season, Feld dances more fluently, without having lost any of his impetuosity. In that same lift Sarry now reaches the peak with a paradoxical slow rush, seems to hover there for a second, then turns in the air and plunges into his arms. The symbolic peril is more thrilling than what used to look like real danger.

During ABT's first week, I saw two performances of George Balanchine's "Theme and Variations" with two different sets of soloists: Natalia Makarova and Ted Kivitt; Eleanor D'Antuono and John Prinz. When I saw the work last season I was struck by the warmth and liveliness and precision of the way ABT's dancers perform it compared with the elegant nonchalance of Balanchine's own company. This time I was first struck all over again by the brilliance of the choreography—by how the brief, polite theme really does engender all the variations that follow, by how inventive those variations are, by how much diversity Balanchine can suggest even though he uses the space in an absolutely symmetrical manner almost all the time.

Then I became fascinated with the differing approaches of Makarova and D'Antuono. Makarova finds ways of emphasizing what must strike her as odd or unusually beautiful about the movement. On supported arabesque turns, she begins very quickly and with erect carriage (as I remember), and then is able to show you a great sweep of leg opening into position. On a sprightly diagonal progression, there is a moment when the toe starts to take the weight, then doesn't, then does. She makes it look clever and almost treacherous by actually putting quite a lot of weight on the toe before she lifts it, thereby creating an elegant little stumble in the rhythm of the phrase. She is careless, wanton even, with time, as if she were more concerned with interesting ways of filling the larger musical units than with being precise about beats. With this approach, she can, and did on this occasion, actually finish her variation early. Her partner, Ted Kivitt, looked (was it my imagination?) slightly harried by her unruly splendor, but rose to the challenge. It was his doing as much as hers, that in one of the lifts she appeared suddenly hung on him as if she had been inadvertently caught up in his progression and carried along.

In comparison, D'Antuono is very well-behaved. She is musically accurate, and many people who were in the audience both nights preferred her to Makarova in this role. Certainly she has developed a proud and sparkling manner, but she keeps to herself—that is, she is never very daring with space or time or her own weight. She dances tastefully, as if she were trying to smooth out or de-emphasize the same choreographic irregularities that Makarova celebrates.

Maybe next time I see "Theme and Variations" I'll get around to speculating on the male role. Comparative viewing is the only thing I envy the daily critics for.

An Exclamation Shot Into Space

The Village Voice, November 10, 1975

Maybe this whole business of Bicentennial dances isn't going to be such a bore after all. The way that choreographers respond, and the choices they make are revealing. Eliot Feld's "Excursions" traffics not with nostalgia, but with theatrical stylizations of ideals. The four sections of his ballet (set to Samuel Barber's music of the same name) are forays into an American moral landscape—a paean to clarity, speed, great distances, vigor, plain manners, work.

"Excursions" is like Balanchine's "Western Symphony" in its formality and abstractness, but the manner is very different. "Western Symphony" is a Petipa ballet with a vernacular twang, a boisterous, but well-regulated kingdom whose courtiers are disguised as cowboys and dancehall girls. But in Feld's sharp, pristine open spaces, even such vague roles as these rarely appear.

Feld builds his dance out of brilliantly distorted stereotypical gestures but never lets the dancers stop to indulge in them. The air on stage seems abrasive; the light sharp enough to burn flesh.

Christine Sarry is the leader. She scouts the dance territory for everyone else. Shrugging, prancing, grinning, reckless, but precise, she reminds you of Christine Sarry in "Rodeo." But that's inescapable; she's not that woman. Give or take a few gestures, she could be a surrogate for Feld himself. And this is one of the ballet's most bracing—and most formalizing—devices: that most of the time the six women and men in the cast share common dance material. Pale, delicate Michaela Hughes and Linda Miller bounce through the same jutting, broncobusting phrases as the men. Edmund LaFosse (who partners Sarry when there's partnering to be done), Jeff Satinoff, and Patrick Swayze shimmy their shoulders when the women do. Alone together they all squat, chin in hand by imaginary campfires, straddle horses.

The first section bursts out as an elated surveying of space. Oh what a beautiful morning! And the dancers shiver in mid-jump, snort up air that is palpably fresh. In the second dance, a whiff of blues in the music invades the dance. Sarry, twisting her leg, is for a second recognizably stubbing out a cigar(ette?), but the gesture, perfectly rendered as to intent and focus, is still not pointed up as a gesture; it's introduced as a motif. This is the part with the most (the only, as I remember) male-female byplay. Hints of a cheerful honky-tonk lustiness.

Part Three is a loping, saddle-easy affair. The image of the dancer as combined horse and rider harks back to "Oklahoma!," "Rodeo," and "Billy the Kid." But, as I said, Feld doesn't dwell on such things. He embeds them in such intricate, unusual, smartly paced dancing that your eye has to grasp them on the run. And actions like chest scratching (men only), mid-air bucking—seen as pure, vigorous dancing, instead of as moves in a contest between brawny men and flouncing girls—become newly useful thematic material instead of sentimental references. Part Four presents the deeds and behavior of Part Three wound up into a breath-taking celebratory tempo. It ends with all hands in a comradely pose as if on a corral fence, while one breathes out "Sheeit!"

In this razor-walking choreographic feat, Feld has sacrificed some of the cameraderie between dancers which he usually creates, in order, I think, to avoid the possible banality of the roles usually associated with the movements he's chosen as a springboard. The dancers travel through a space, but their dancing doesn't mold it. Despite their high spirits, the landscape seems as vast and barren as the moon; and, although Sarry is superbly, unsentimentally warm, the ballet has something of the cool audacity of a man shattering the silence of Grand Canyon by shouting "Hello!"

Mazurkas Speed Inside the Soul

The Village Voice, October 27, 1975

I think that "Mazurka" may be the most individual ballet that Eliot Feld has ever choreographed. The entire work, a formal suite of Chopin mazurkas danced by four couples, seems to articulate the tensions that exist between lovers. Feld makes you terribly aware of the forces that make bodies spring away from other bodies or coil in toward them, that proclaim who shall lead and who follow and who sidestep.

Feld has based the structure of his ballet on accounts of the dance as it was performed in 19th-century Poland: an opening procession, a series of showy solos and duets and ensembles, a closing group dance.

The dancers (Christine Sarry and Richard Fein, Elizabeth Lee and John Sowinski, Helen Douglas and George Montalbano, Naomi Sorkin and Edmund La Fosse) have been elegantly dressed by Rouben Ter-Arutunian in dark costumes, the men flaunting one dashingly asymmetrical white collar-point. But, for the most part, "Mazurka" doesn't appear to be taking place at a gathering. You don't envision a place or a society; for the dancers, the "place" is inside the music or inside the soul, the "society" the person closest. There is very little changing of partners. And there are no onlookers.

The form of the mazurkas defines the dancing. Perhaps that's why the ballet makes you sense motions and emotions pressing and shifting to fulfill themselves within severe limits. Almost every dance takes off with three repetitions of its opening phrase. Steps and gestures proper to the mazurka recur everywhere—folded arms, stamps, small side-traveling hops with one foot lightly beating the other. Bold, weighty moves often give way to a sputter of small, rapid, almost irritable ones.

All the dances are passionate, but whether brooding, or exultant, or flashing, the dancers never stop to indulge in anything; the momentum of the mazurka pulls them along. "Mazurka" isn't ingratiating. It's too fast and too difficult for that. All that is strange and harsh and devious in those lovely somber melodies has gotten hold of Feld. The dances are full of unrest: The dancers reverse directions seemingly in mid-air; while the impetus is carrying them one way, they somehow muster their weight to pursue a new path. In one group section, all the dancers take up a devilish pattern begun by Sarry and Fein in which the partners rush past each other, and the next instant you see them they're standing on one leg, grasping each other by one hand. In a remarkable solo, Helen Douglas opens her arms from overhead, lifts one leg to the side, and bends her other knee slightly; but something unusual about the lean of her body, the focus of her head makes the gesture look irresolute—a ballet position canted off balance by the pressure of emotion.

There are passages in "Mazurka" as beautiful as astonishing as anything I've ever seen. And in some way, the speed of the ballet does make the complexity more dazzling. Perhaps one of the reasons the ballet seems so complicated is that Feld has kept partners dancing so close together. These days when quite a few male choreographers—think of John Neumeier—have ironically responded to women's-lib by creating pas de deux in which the woman is no more than a pliable statue to be hefted around, Feld's patterns are unusually, strikingly, companionable. Partners often dance side by side in unison or in teasing counterpoint, with the man occasionally slipping his arm around the woman's waist or something so that she can fly briefly off the floor—as a natural, if heady extension of what she's already doing. In the duet for Douglas and Montalbano, she soars into slow leaps, supported almost invisibly by her own hand pressing down on one of his. What big lifts there are are memorable, partly because they don't happen every second, and partly because the dancers don't play them up by gritty preparations. Christine Sarry, following Richard Fein off stage, suddenly—in the middle of doing something else—bounds into the air, turns, and is caught and carried away. While our breathing stops.

I imagine that what will happen now with "Mazurka" is that Feld will allow pianist Peter Longiaru to slow a few dances down (unlikely) or that he will lash and cajole his superb dancers until they can achieve and maintain the speed of lightening (more likely).

New Company

The Village Voice, November 23, 1967

We've all been wondering for some time now what the Harkness Ballet would be like. We've read about Renaissance patroness Rebecca Harkness refurbishing a little palace for it in New York, summering it in Watch Hill, opening it in Cannes, touring it around the world, weeding, pruning, and watering it. Parenthetically, I wish more people with money to spare would follow Mrs. H's example.

The company ended its first New York engagement at the Broadway Theatre on November 19. I've seen the pieces that were formerly in the repertory of the Joffrey company and some of the new pieces, and I have a few first impressions of what the Harkness is all about. To begin with, it's a big company. None of this business about alphabetical listing and everyone getting his chance to shine. There's a corps, and then there are soloists.

It's a lavish company: any dance that needs costumes and scenery gets them—sometimes to the point of almost wanton luxury. The repertory seems unnecessarily huge and hence is bound to be of uneven caliber. Despite its limber, clean-limbed, American-trained dancers, the Harkness comes on like a European company. It's hard to pin down the reason. The overall rhythms, pacing, spatial design, the way the ensemble is used are oddly old-fashioned. Some of the choreographers seem modern only in that they are willing to make use of distorted design and loveless sex. Many of the themes are neo-Romantic—maybe as opposed to Balanchine-classic—and the movement fits these themes: it is movement that directly expresses emotion, rather than movement as a metaphor for feeling.

15

"Monument for a Dead Boy," by Dutch choreographer Rudi van Dantzig, generated quite a lot of excitement despite its dated, almost Wedekind-like Sturm und Drang. In an atmosphere suffused with passion, a boy (Lawrence Rhodes) and his younger self (Warren Conover) relive the ordeal of his passage from adolescent heterosexuality to homosexuality to despair and spiritual death. Van Dantzig worked out his theme in movement of wracking intensity; the characters literally haul and tear at each other. This is especially true of the boy's parents—hateful puppets in '40s garb, grimacing out a lust ugly enough to turn the most stalwart adolescent against women. Except for a sloppy and gratuitous chorus of fright-wigged ladies, billed as "Darkness," this dance is all of a piece. It has the sincere force of autobiographical expiation.

Some of the most beautiful moments that I saw during the run occurred in John Butler's "A Season in Hell," inspired by Rimbaud's work of that name. I couldn't follow the exact relevance of the three principal dancers' actions to the Rimbaud-Verlaine relationship (implied in the program) but it didn't matter. The dance began with a fine solo for Lawrence Rhodes as the poet protagonist, against a starry backdrop and under some gleaming metal rods that Rouben Ter-Arutunian designed. Then Rhodes and Brunilda Ruiz performed a duet that is Butler at his best—twining around each other in a remorseless lust to discover and experience everything. Very Rimbaldien. Sated, I wanted the dance to end much sooner than it did.

This genius of Butler's for sculptural dance becomes a liability when he applies it to the corps de ballet. In his "Landscape for Lovers" he had six couples in unison repeating almost exactly the very personal erotic movement that the prinicpal couple had just performed. He used the same device in "Season," where it has more motivation, but is still odd. All of a sudden, a lesson in gang-banging. And in such passages, Butler doesn't like to use space; it's as if he has a "camera eye" hang-up from doing so much TV and has to plunk each dancer or couple into a square yard of stage and keep them there.

Every ballet company, it seems, must have its quota of formal pas de deux and pas de trois. No matter what gimmick a choreographer gives them, their purpose is to show off the dancing, to provoke gasps and roars. At best, such a dance becomes a kind of metaphor for a 19th century relationship. All that courtly handling. I saw a sensitive, young, romantic one by Richard Wagner called "Youth" that kept its fancy-work subdued, and Brian MacDonald's flashy "Canto Indio." MacDonald evidently knows that be it "à la turque" or "à la espagnol," a pas de deux is always ballet. His dance made its bow to Mexico with a Carlos Chavez score, costumes of Imperial Russian Inca, and a few quaint folk steps and flexed feet scattered among the arabesques. The steps were hard as hell and fun-looking, and Elisabeth Carroll and Helgi Tomasson made brilliant whoopee out of it all. From the way she looks at the audience, you can tell that she knows what a pas de deux is all about too. A pas de trois is a pas de deux with complications. Someone always has to wait his turn. And an element of polite rivalry is added: one boy has nice buttery turns, but look at the way the other twiddles his feet in the air! Brian MacDonald's "Zealous Variations" is an inventive exercise in this form. It makes you wonder, though, about dance audiences. If a painter today painted in the style of Corot or a musician composed echoes of Schumann, he'd never survive, but it seems de rigeur for a ballet company to lard its repertory with clever new variations on 19th century motifs. This is bad enough when the work in question is good, but when it's like MacDonald's massive, vulgar, jewel-encrusted "Tchaikovsky," one really longs for a contemporary point of view. (The program note for this monster says, "If Peter Ilich Tchaikovsky had been entertained at Newport just before the turn of the century, it might have been at a gala such as this." What an infuriating "if"! What was good enough for the Tsar is quite good enough for us.)

This dance was probably designed to show off the dancers. They shine in spite of it, and in fact one of the strongest impressions made by the Harkness Ballet is that it has a remarkably fine group of principal dancers. Lawrence Rhodes and Brunilda Ruiz are especially sensitive and dramatic; they seem able to bring off everything with distinction. Elisabeth Carroll is a technical whiz. Helgi Tomasson and Finis Jhung are both fine, smooth dancers with great presence. Lone Isaksen is lovely in a cool fragile way, and although I saw Annette av Paul only once, I thought her strong and charming.

Mercifully, I haven't talked about all I saw, and I haven't begun to see all of the Harkness's big shiny repertory. Maybe now the company will make a practice of dropping in on New York from time to time.

This article was written about the original *Harkness Ballet, or the just-ex-Joffrey ballet. This was the first appearance of the company in New York, after Rebekah Harkness elected to withdraw her financial support from the Robert Joffrey Ballet and branch out on her own. Not knowing the full story—or perhaps knowing too many sides of the same story—I was prepared to give this latter-day Renaissance princess the benefit of a doubt. Especially since many of the dancers had been with the Joffrey.*

Atomic Circus

The Village Voice, March 14, 1968

Gerald Arpino's new ballet, "The Clowns," for the City Center Joffrey Ballet is no merry circus romp; it is a delicate, but chilling little parable of the cyclic destruction and rebirth of mankind. The ballet is preceded by sounds of an explosion, and the curtain opens on a heap of white clown bodies. More (these are dummies) fall from the sky. One who has survived (Robert Blankshine) carefully piles all the bodies on the heap. While he is dancing and miming a combination of despair and elation, one girl clown comes to life and dances with him—a silly, happy duet punctuated by little kissing noises. In a macabre parody of growing plants, the other clowns come alive, and the hero welcomes them joyfully. They put on brightly colored ruffles, false noses, wigs, baggy pants, ribbons. They're turned on—doing a lifetime of tricks, all the standard gags: double takes, pratfalls, flat-footed jumps, collisions, acrobatic feats. Hershy Kay's music, with some of the wind instruments miked, becomes nastily, stridently gay. Hurdy-gurdies and calliopes out of tune. The action gets a more and more disorderly and unchoreographed look. The clowns get hold of some plastic pillows with long obscene nozzles. If a clown falls on a pillow, the nozzle inflates. Bang, you're dead! The hero enters walking in a long plastic tube that trails behind him like a discarded cocoon. It too becomes a weapon; the others turn on him and try to strangle him with it. A still more formidable plastic shape looms upstage. It fills with air, becomes a huge bubble, beyond control. The clowns are drawn into it and trapped inside. Although the hero has been flung right onto the top of the bubble, he rises again—still alive—as the plastic contracts and crushes to the floor the clowns flailing about inside it.

Gerald Arpino has chosen the clown symbol wisely. If you want to show the human race coming alive, you are stuck with the problem of how to dance "life" without resorting to balletic clichés for labor, love, repose, etc. But when clowns come to life, life is represented by what they do best: clowning. The cliché is so obvious that it acquires a kind of dignity and depth. Also the clown figure trails behind him a cloud of metaphors, not only the romantic concept of the breaking heart behind the grinning mask, but—grimmer and older—the central figure of the Saturnalia. Isn't it the fool, after all, who is ritually murdered and resurrected in the winter solstice mummers' play—as Tammuz, as Dionysus, as Christ?

So the hero is mankind; the others are men. The clown that Blankshine plays so well seems somehow a cut above his fellows, because Arpino has given him the strangely beautiful weeping eyes, the elegant and futile hand gestures, the innocent silliness of a classic Pierrot. Also because he "dances." The others are real circus vulgarians—brash, sloppy, lovable, cruel. He is the ideal clown, they the mob of manifestations. And here is the third point in favor of the clown metaphor: this innocent Pierrot is an ideal "man" for ballet—as a heroic, muscular figure may be for sculpture or a questing intellectual for literature. Ballet cannot properly show a Noah chosen for moral rectitude. This hero rides out the flood through sensitivity, gallantry, skill, and beauty. Each artist must deal with the holocaust in his own way.

I've always considered this ballet a fine example of what, I believe, Arlene Croce was the first to term "pop dance." It is alluring and sleekly theatrical—topical in its subject matter and trendy in its materials. The first time I saw it, it produced a powerful and instantaneous high and left me with some images I still cherish. But its impact lessened slightly with each viewing. I should have known better. After all, you don't usually re-read detective stories, even those you loved.

The Glamor Trap is Closing . . . Run

The Village Voice, October 24, 1974

I think that when Gerald Arpino began to work on "The Relativity of Icarus" for the Joffrey Ballet, he meant to make a sincere and positive statement about homosexual love. Perhaps he took on too much in attempting to relate this idea not only to the Icarus myth, but to the Oedipus one, and to the many cosmic ramifications of both these stories. Perhaps he was simply beguiled by his own skill at devising unusual sculptural poses. Whatever happened, the resultant ballet has little to do with Icarus or Oedipus, nor does it seem to be a real or moving exploration of homoeroticism. All of Arpino's ideas seem trapped in glittering and static displays, and this makes them look not so much sensual as pornographic.

The curtain goes up on a small tower, which has giant mirrored vanes that open in irregular ways. A light reflector. Big and bright enough to give the whole audience a tan. But first, all you see is the girl, Ann Marie DeAngelo, in a nude body stocking, painted with rainbows that ripple down her flanks. She's not the sun, she's a very young version of the intruding bitch that always breaks up good relationships between nice young men in modern ballets. She's also a contortionist, or at least, a capable acrobat; stroking herself and leering meaningfully at the audience, she suddenly grabs her leg and pulls it up behind her in a Harriet Hoctor attitude. Not a sympathetic character, this Sun, and about as warm as a window pane in winter.

After her solo, she sits down and starts to reel in a long white rope that she found in the labyrinth. The mirrored vanes begin to spin and fan open, and there on a raked, oval deck crouch Daedalus and Icarus. Scantily clad, Daedalus (Ted Nelson) has prominent arm and shoulder muscles and therefore can lift Icarus (Russell Sultzbach, who is a little slighter in build). This is what distinguishes "father" from "son." Many of the lifts involve Nelson's lying down and using his arms and legs to press Sultzbach up into spreadeagled positions that suggest flying. One of the mirrors isolates a view of Nelson's buttocks opening and closing. Oh, Daddy, nobody else can do me like you do. And, held aloft, Sultzbach creates another meticulously sculpted pose as he leans down to lay his cheek on Nelson's codpiece.

When the two men descend from the platform and increase the scope and daring of the lifts (Nelson standing instead of lying), DeAngelo begins to snake around them with two rainbow scarves. Suddenly, in a brief scuffle, drama and motion enter the ballet. Nelson lifts DeAngelo and tries to get her out of the way; he tries to keep Sultzbach from getting close to her. The two men embrace, struggle. Sultzbach finally grabs the white rope and commits patricide in the tradition-approved manner: Daddy gets it in the neck with the piece of umbilical cord Mommy's been saving for years—waiting to slip it to Sonny until his jockstrap filled out. But with Daedalus dead, Icarus can't "fly" anymore; he plunges over into a despairing headstand by his companion's body, while the Sun climbs triumphantly into the labyrinth and jabs her pointe shoes into its floor.

There is little tenderness in any of this. Just before the murder, the two men cling to each other on the floor, but it's too late in the ballet for Arpino to try to express all their old love and mutual dependency as well as one's attempt to go and the other's attempt to hold him back. Perhaps Arpino meant to say that some people never realize they need each other until it's too late, but he didn't leave himself space or time to deliver his message eloquently.

It's hard for me to explain, or even understand, why I find the dance almost pornographic. Perhaps because the poses, and the rubbing of body against body to get to the next pose, are so joyless, so calculatedly beautiful. Also, there is no motion in the dances; the characters don't fly, or struggle, or fall. They assume poses that suggest these activities tidied up and frozen by a sculptor or a photographer. Nowhere in the ballet could I find images of growth or change or movement that would tell me that this thing I was watching was, in fact, a dance. During the first duet, each lift and embrace was isolated so meticulously from every other one that I began to feel as if I were flipping rapidly through a striking photo essay in "After Dark," experiencing only a vague semblance of motion.

Interesting to remember Lucas Hoving's "Icarus"—a dance that would seem almost drab beside this one. Hoving's Sun was a remote goddess—ignorant of evil, innately magnetic, pursuing her own course. And, especially when Hoving played Daedalus, that "Icarus" suggested not only the relationship between a son and a stern, loving father, but the one existing between a young dreamer and a disillusioned one, between a poet and a practical man, between two lovers. Hoving's dance was modest, but it conveyed much. Arpino's ballet is an elaborate trap that throws his ideas back at him, distorted by a new kind of hall of mirrors—one that makes everything horrifyingly glamorous.

Gerald Arpino has firmly denied that he was trying to make a homosexual ballet. There is always the possibility of a discrepancy between what a choreographer intends to make, what he makes, and what another perceives him to have made.

White Petticoats and Sailor Suits

The Village Voice, March 12, 1970

I remember seeing John Cranko's "Pineapple Poll" when the Sadler's Wells Theatre Ballet toured the United States in 1951. It fitted easily and happily into my somewhat limited concept of ballet and theatre: limited because, in the first place, I grew up in Los Angeles, and, in the second place, for years I was taken to nothing that had the remotest chance of giving me nightmares. So, theatre to me meant Sigmund Romberg, Gilbert and Sullivan, Fokine, and Massine—maybe Shaw and Noel Coward for weightier stuff. I thought "Oklahoma!" the height of realism until "Streetcar" and "Death of a Salesman" came to town and knocked me for a loop.

"Pineapple Poll" has been reproduced by David Blair for the City Center Joffrey Ballet, and I have inserted the foregoing tedious background material on myself—rather than on the ballet—to explain the ambivalence of my reaction toward it. I smiled often, laughed outright, felt perfectly comfortable. I also sympathized completely with the girl slouched down in front of me with her eyes closed and my husband, restless and appalled, polishing his watch.

"Poll" is an old-fashioned ballet bouffe, and it might as well have been composed in 1921 as in 1951. The music is a Sullivan potpourri arranged by Charles Mackerras, and the plot is loosely based on "The Bumboat Woman's Story"—one of Gilbert's "Bab Ballads." The scenery by Osbert Lancaster is several canvas views of a charming, colorful, pollution-free London dockside. The sailors and their sweethearts are as working class as the leisure classes could bear to see them for the purposes of art: handsome, hearty, and very clean. This wholesome British crew rollicks through symmetrically arranged sequences that are similar in shape to the sung choruses in Gilbert and Sullivan operettas. The girls hop yearningly after Captain Belaye for, say, four bars; the sailors haul them back by the waists for four bars; the sailors threaten Belaye for four bars; during the last four bars, everybody returns to position to repeat the whole sequence. Hardly brain-tickling stuff. And since Cranko was considerably less tricky with movement than he is now, there is a lot of lively dancing, but little that is exciting or unexpected.

The plot is blessedly easy to follow and concerns the unrequited love of Poll, the Bumboat Woman (a bumboat was a small boat that carried provisions to ships anchored in a harbor or dockside), for Captain Belaye, who is quite happy with his dizzy fiancée. Jasper, a potboy, loves Poll unrequitedly, so everything works out. Poll is not the only girl to be smitten with Belaye, and at one point all the girls dress up as sailors in order to sneak on the ship to be near him. Where they got that many small sailor suits in such a short time is no one's concern. This is a ballet bouffe, remember. Nor should you expect that Belaye will think it at all odd that one of his sailors is wearing pointe shoes.

Anyway, I think Sullivan was one of the great pop musicians of all time, and his jolly tunes keep the ballet bouncing, and fortunately Cranko also kept things jigging along. The Joffrey company did dance it splendidly. The boys playing sailors seemed to take special pleasure in their combination of fist-clenching, sweetheart-cuddling, and tours en l'air. Chartel Arthur was nicely woebegone as Pineapple Poll. I like her droopy bourrées and a way she has of pouting that makes her face look as if it were melting. The most genuine pleasure of the evening came from Edward Verso's characterization of Captain Belaye. His dapperness and dash came not just from his bearing or his swanky costume, but from a marvelous suavity in his dancing—an assurance absolutely unmarred by effort.

My father used to say that he loved those early musical comedies that opened with a lot of pretty girls in very short skirts hanging out laundry and singing like mad. Well, nobody does any washing in "Pineapple Poll," but they do a lot of what usually followed the singing in those musicals: the girls all run into a huddle with their heads together and their tails out—swishing their white petticoats and giggling. Judging from the audience reaction, someone could probably make a pile with a few Victor Herbert revivals.

Celebration

The Village Voice, May 29, 1969

Once in a while you see a ballet that is so eloquent, so true to itself that the critical eye is confounded. There is no resisting it; just sit back and let it wash over you. Jerome Robbins's "Dances at a Gathering," now in the repertory of the New York City Ballet, is such a work. It is so transparent that through this one dance's complex simplicity you seem to understand what Dance is all about.

"Dances at a Gathering" is a very quiet ballet; everything about it, every possible meaning is whispered—as if it were happening in such clear air that sound carries a great distance. The ballet does, in fact, appear to be taking place out of doors; the enormous New York Theatre stage is bare, and Thomas Skelton has projected some barely discernible tracery of what might be foliage onto the blue cyclorama. A non-specific "place," yet clearly one with particular meaning for the dancers who pass through it. Edward Villella's opening solo—performed for a good part of its duration with his back to the audience— marks off the space and, in a sense, consecrates it.

The dancers are friends, lovers, people who dance with each other and only incidentally for the audience. Whoever they are, whatever they are celebrating. They dance to a continuous flow of Chopin—mazurkas, waltzes, etc.—that Gordon Boelzner probes sensitively out of a piano on the far side of the stage apron. The dancing is Polish only in the way that the music is: a suggested rhythm, fragment of melody, a quick gesture transformed by an individual creative intellect. You see a pair of hands on hips or behind the head, male hands clasping arms, feet stamping—but they are gone almost before you notice them. The vocabulary is balletic, rich and immensely clever, but made to look simple by Robbins's beautiful way of shaping phrases. Preparations are never obtrusive; girls rise almost invisibly onto pointe, as if such an action were the natural consequence of drawing breath. Contemporary ideas about art have freed Robbins to be romantic in a way that choreographers contemporary with Chopin were not ready to be. Not for them the irregularities, asymmetries, open forms that give "Dances at a Gathering" its air of naturalness and inevitability. There seems almost to be an invisible wind on stage—one of those gentle, but exhilarating winds—that pushes the dance along. One of the most memorable movement motifs is just a smooth run, forward or backward.

Some of the dances are clearly personal, like a lovely solo for Violette Verdy or a passage in which Allegra Kent attaches herself insouciantly to each new man who dances through, liking her, but on his way somewhere else. Other sections are social dances—like, yet unlike, dances you have seen or done at parties. In one, for example, three girls are handed down the line of their partners. The first man slides each girl in turn along the floor in a half split, launches her into the second man's arms; he twists her gently and tosses her on to the third. She is then free to begin all over again or start something new. Certain sections reflect encounters of individuals through customary dance encounters, as when Villella and Anthony Blum circle each other in a duet that is both comradely and challenging.

Robbins has used some of the company's best dancers, and they perform marvelously for him. Some of them even look like different people. The women are Kent, Leland, Mazzo, McBride, Verdy; the men are Blum, Clifford, Maiorano, Prinz, Villella.

"Dances at a Gathering" is very long, and I like that. It has the exhausting beauty of certain celebrations. At the end, the dancers all gather to watch something moving far in the distance behind the audience. A falling star? A bird? It doesn't matter.

Happy Birthday, Dear Igor

The Village Voice, June 29, 1972

One of the many fine things about the New York City Ballet's Stravinsky Festival was that it was like old times at City Center, albeit on a more magnificent scale. Each night of the week, the State Theater was packed with knowledgeable and wildly excited balletomaniacs; hopeful gate-crashers panted in the Plaza; the dancers, who had had to learn up to 20 new ballets and polish up some old ones, challenged their own mental and physical fatigue by dancing with a bold and feverish confidence. The week was full of surprises, unexpected beauties, dance jokes, and a kind of camaraderie between the audience and the company that the grandeur of Lincoln Center usually doesn't encourage.

The audience played one-up games with each other: "I didn't see you last night. You missed the 'Duo Concertante' then? It was incredible, just incredible . . . " Some people, unwilling or unable to store up too many impressions, raced through intermissions trying to get ratifications for their own opinions so that they could clean out the closets of their minds before they got too full: "Wasn't that beautiful?", "Did you hate that as much as I did?" I only went twice, and my mind is bursting.

It was fascinating to see how the different choreographers involved approached the vitality and rhythmic complexity which make Stravinsky's music so splendid to dance to. Two of the company's fledglings,

Richard Tanner and Lorca Massine, tried to keep up with Stravinsky's wiles by contriving difficult movement or complicated patterns. Tanner approached the "Concerto for Two Solo Pianos" in the Balanchinian manner; he created a neo-classic dance concerto, but grafted spikes and angles and thorny partnering onto the basic vocabulary, just as Balanchine often does when he choreographs Stravinsky. Tanner's flexed-foot positions, turned-in knees were more blatantly displayed, however, and this gave his work a coarser texture. Also, in this ballet, he followed the broad gestural shape of the music, rather than any of its inner parts. For a time, the dancers had to perform movements that looked as they should have been done twice as fast, and toward the end the ballet began to feel thick and shapeless, even though its basic structure was obvious.

Lorca Massine's "Ode" blunted Stravinsky in a different way. Massine is a neo-Romantic, turn-of-the-century French in sensibility. Long, churning diagonals of dancers; vague, but intense emotion; a continual flutter of arm gestures; everyone moving differently, moving all the time. The hectic, undirected activity and lack of repose were linked to the most obvious ingredients of the music, so that after a while Stravinsky's music began to sound as cluttered as the dance looked. Christine Redpath and Colleen Neary danced excellently for both Tanner and Massine, and so did everyone else. Robert Maiorano's muscularly poetic looks were ideal for his odd-man-out part in Massine's work.

Todd Bolender has always been capable of wittiness, both as a dancer and as a choreographer. Jerome Robbins, eclectic and unpredictable and sometimes magnificent, can always deliver a good number—so sleek, so clever, so beautifully paced and directed that Broadway producers must be going crazy trying to lure him back to choreographing musicals. On Friday evening, Bolender and Robbins offered light, slightly outrageous, very loveable ballets—sparked by the fragments of ragtime, jazz syncopations that Stravinsky often inserted so wittily into his music. Bolender's "Piano-Rag-Music" was a romp made wholly out of John Clifford's brash, but likeable style, the serene and happy whorishness that Gloria Govrin can summon up, and the odd-couple look of these two together. The gags were, of course, predictable: the small, aggressive Clifford being effortlessly lifted out of the way by Big Gloria, and so on. What made the ballet worthwhile was that the jokes popped quickly and casually in and out of a texture of fast and intricate and friendly dancing.

Robbins's setting of the "Dumbarton Oaks" concerto surprised everyone—horrified some—with its irreverent treatment of the music. The curtain went up on an elegantly trellised garden tennis court. The corps of six-and-six skipped on, looking ready to do "The Boyfriend," but with a sweetness and modesty that kept the ballet from being just another clever '20s parody. Robbins shaped the ensemble passages into meticulous unison phalanxes with an occasional impetuous solo twist, or clear-cut antiphonal contests between the sexes. There were even a couple of high kicking chorus lines. Allegra Kent and Anthony Blum circled the stage in a light, busy-footed couple dance full of silly, suddenly-we're-in-love charm, which ended with a sportsmanlike handshake and a retrieval of tennis rackets. For their second entrance, the men and women put on soft, heeled shoes so that they could patter out intrepid little rhythms, emphasizing crannies in Stravinsky that we might have missed. I sometimes feel that Balanchine is excited mainly by creating—by the training of those tall bodies he likes, by making movement for them. But Robbins, I think, is excited by the process of direction, by being able to make a step look a certain way according to how it is performed. The dancers in "Dumbarton Oaks" looked especially stylish, well-rehearsed, and—considering the idea of the piece—remarkably free from overt camp or aggressive performing.

The other ballet of Robbins's which I saw, "Scherzo Fantastique," was interesting chiefly for his way of (when he wishes) making you see more space on stage and between the dancers than actually exists. The dancers in "Scherzo" used rapid birdlike port de bras and a sharp, but soaring way of punctuating the music. Gelsey Kirkland's tireless, unstrained brilliance has a reassuring effect on an audience, and Bart Cook has a warm lithe quality; I liked them together. I also like the way Robbins chooses young dancers from the company and makes you look at them and like them. Suddenly in this dance, Bryan Pitts, Stephen Caras, and Victor Castelli emerged as interesting, distinctive, men to be remembered and watched for again.

Then, a special joy, two new Balanchines: "Symphony in Three Movements" and "Violin Concerto." Here again was the wonderful sweep and formal clarity of the great Balanchine-Stravinsky collaborations. Here again the fresh teams of agile, clever bodies in practice clothes—spelling each other in Balanchine's delicate contentions with the music. I can't say that every single moment of both works excited me, but the broad impact of both was thrilling.

"Symphony" employed rather ornate versions of the basic Balanchine-for-Stravinsky vocabulary that I mentioned earlier. I was more than usually aware of those alternately rising and pressing-down arm gestures, the pussycat paws, flexing feet and wrists, those brief turned-in positions with the weight on one foot which remind you of World War II cheesecake. I sometimes don't enjoy the movements per se, but accept them as Balanchine's way of forcing Stravinskian angularities into his long, straight classic line. On the other hand, "Symphony" also employed a few surprising space patterns—unusually unbalanced and tugging for Balanchine. The basic plan involved the manipulation of 16 women, 10 secondary couples, and three principle couples (Sara Leland and Edward Villella, Helgi Tomasson and Linda Yourth, Marnee Morris and Robert Weiss). Although the ballet began with Tomasson dancing extravagantly in front of regrouping diagonals of the 16 women, and although he and Yourth were especially prominent in the first movement all of the soloists kept popping in a very asymmetrical way and getting mixed with the 10 couples. The effect was both spacious and complex, but occasionally one of those easily graspable Balanchine space games would crop up to reassure everyone—like pairs of girls leaping in a counterclockwise circles while Leland spun a clockwise chain of turns that split through each pair. The second movement duet for Leland and Villella was gently tricky and featured many isolated twinings of heads or arms or feet. Even the finale was less symmetrically stacked than usual with the group suddenly snapping into an end pose straight out of a high school yearbook.

The effect of "Violin Concerto" was lighter and less complicated than "Symphony." Four soloists, Karin von Aroldingen, Kay Mazzo, Jean-Pierre Bonnefous, and Peter Martins, took turns leading on little squadrons from the corps—first the opposite sex, then the same sex (or vice versa?). Interesting to watch the way the different dancers approached the tricky steps. Martins, for instance, is so nobly erect that you feel every deviation from a centered position is a triumph for him, while Bonnefous, mobile, almost sly, swings dangerously from one of those fallen-away Balanchine poses to another without even appearing to pass through center. The duet for von Aroldingen and Bonnefous was jazzily acrobatic, while that for Mazzo and Martins was ample and tender with some lovely leaning poses outlined with looping, embracing arm gestures. Both duets, oddly, ended in oblique, questioning positions—bodies arched back or upside down.

The Balanchine-Robbins-Berman-Stravinsky-Pergolesi "Pulcinella" was a great sloppy, bawdy concoction that must have been fun to perform and certainly was fun to watch. There seemed to be hundreds of Pulcinellas, roistering around in red caps, white floppy suits, beaked-nosed masks. The principal one was Edward Villella, who lumbered splendidly, and some were very small children. The commedia dell'arte escapades appeared to involve a welching on a contract with the Devil (Francisco Moncións) who kept appearing in drag (Shaun O'Brien) but with horns showing. Violette Verdy appeared as a kickable peasant girl and reappeared later looking very spicy and did a long sprightly solo that was the only "ballet dancing" in the work. I liked a funeral procession of pall-bearing Pulcinellas who abandoned their job by twos and threes, returning just before the corpse crashed to the ground. I also liked an insane surfeit of spaghetti that threatened to cover the stage and did in fact entrap the Devil. (The baby Pulcinellas munched with

27

contagious glee.) Oh, and in the middle of an elaborate final celebration, Robbins and Balanchine marched on as two beggars, pretended to thwack each other with big sticks, did a fumbly dance, and generally thrilled the fans.

One night I also saw a nice little sweet-16 duet for Sara Leland and John Clifford, choreographed at the last minute by Balanchine to a fragment of early Stravinsky which Madeleine Malraux had ferreted out and which she played with great style. I also saw the Robbins-Balanchine "Firebird," in which Karin von Aroldingen stalked about in a stiff white costume like a pea-hen and Peter Martins ran around after her in awe. I was awed too and thought almost longingly of the earlier version (which I never liked much either) in which Maria Tallchief spun around in a mini-tutu in a red spotlight and Francisco Monción had one hell of a time holding her down.

So what started out as a loving tribute to a splendid composer and a shrewd publicity gimmick for a splendid company turned out to be a little treasure trove of new works, many of which will be taken into the repertory in the fall. And then we can start all over again.

When I saw "Symphony in Three Movements" later, I cringed at my image of the dancers forming a "high-school yearbook" pose. What I had remembered was a tableau of kneeling men and standing women. But the men are squatting tensely as if waiting for the starter's gun, and the womens' arms branch up and out stiffly. This inaccurate description is a good (bad) example of what happens when you take in pattern and don't notice focus or dynamics. At the second performance, I wondered how I could have missed so much of the violence that pervades the ballet.

Re-reading this article now, I notice something else: I never mentioned that Stravinsky was dead. As Balanchine said in his opening night speech, we were celebrating Stravinsky's 90th birthday—and his genius— and Stravinsky himself had simply taken a "leave of absence." Only after that week was over did I fully appreciate the wisdom and the gallantry of that dancing against death.

Wings in a Cardboard Mansion

The Village Voice, February 8, 1973

I went up to the New York State Theater to see Balanchine's "Harlequinade" because he's been tinkering with it again and I thought I should be up-to-date. I also thought it would be fun, and it was.

Rouben Ter-Arutunian's first-act set is a large-scale version of those little painted paper theatres you can buy and then fold and tab together.

It looks like a giant toy, and pretty soon I begin to think of the characters in this commedia dell'arte tale of romance and chicanery as being little cardboard dolls who slide on and off stage in grooves. The way Balanchine has organized the ballet heightens this illusion. Action is always happening elsewhere. The puppet-dancers dash offstage to accomplish chases and searches, to hide from chases and searches. Some, like the three Sbires, hired by Columbine's father, Cassandre, to capture Harlequin, seem to be in perpetual, sneaky transit. Groups of dancers replace each other as if one were being pulled off as the other rolled on. A large group of gaudily dressed merrymakers with paper lanterns appears from nowhere to perform a pretty, if cramped tarantella. They disappear in a body into the night (unfortunately leaving a small debris of lanterns behind), and the Scaramouches, four courting couples elegantly dressed black silk, suddenly occupy the stage.

The tale itself has traces of coarse humor, of eroticism, of violence. The sequence in which Harlequin's dismembered body (a dummy) falls from a second story window, is collected and hidden under a brown cloak, and later restored to life by La Bonne Fée certainly has roots in Saturnalia and earlier fertility rituals. But, just as the characters replace each other meticulously on stage, as if a certain equilibrium had to be maintained or the stage would fall in, so the fights and the violence and the chases seem almost orderly, nicely balanced, resolved even as they happen.

The dancing, however, is another thing altogether, very rich and round. The Scaramouches' wooing, which in terms of composition forms a background to Harlequin's dancing and mandolin-plucking serenade to Columbine, is like a quietly passionate underscoring of his unheard words. The drunken patrol of guards lurches about marvelously, all the funnier because of the men's determination to maintain—or at least return to—a vertical military stance. La Bonne Fée, coolly voluptuous, shows by her carefully assumed balances and steady footwork that she's a powerful goddess, no tulle-and-wings fairy. There are two marvelous pas de deux for Harlequin and Columbine. The one in the first act bridles a lot of impetuous dancing with decorous end poses. Innocent friendly bursts of kisses happen in chaste, even coy stances, after big, abandoned-looking lifts. The second-act duet dispenses with all that should-we-or-shouldn't-we stuff, and Harlequin and Columbine no longer look in the least like brightly-dressed dolls, but only like ardent, happy young lovers.

As with "Nutcracker," most of the plot of "Harlequinade" is resolved in the first act. The angry father, the rich suitor are not quite placated or sent packing, but we know it's only a matter of time. Otherwise why would the second act be one big party? The second act takes place in an enchanted forest and begins with an immense promenade by all the good guys of the first act, plus (this is new) hordes of children, ranging from very small to teenagers. These are dressed as Harlequins, as Pierrots and Pierrettes, as Scaramouches, as Polichinelles. There's a wonderful moment when these miniatures, dressed almost exactly like their adult counterparts, begin to join the march. You think for a second that you're seeing things, or that they must be adults—just farther away than you realized. Each group of children has a short variation in which a few attitudes or gestures characteristic of their adult counterparts become new choreographic material. The baby Harlequins pointing and tapping their magic wands, prancing with a mischievous wag of the head; the little Pierrots approaching their perky Pierrettes with despondent slouches and dragging sleeves—all serve to restate character traits in simpler language. You feel somewhat as you do when reading a story in a retold-for-children edition. It's a charming and curious device.

One of the strange things about this rather strange ballet is the lark motif. Harlequin sets his baby manifestations twirling a dazzling mirrored object, like a large top, to attract a flock of women dancers. He doesn't catch them; he just wants them around. And they flit—all straight quick legs and quivering arms—in and out through the grand pas de deux and between its sections as if to bestow a benison on the lovers. The effect is vivid and exciting, as if their fluttering represented the beating of hearts.

Edward Villella and Patricia McBride are wonderful as Harlequin and Columbine. His robust dancing style and mischievous, but deprecating carriage are splendid, and she is a marvel at showing a delicacy that never becomes brittle, but maintains a softly shifting flow of energy.

"Torna, Eurydice, al tuo consorte . . ."

The Village Voice, February 22, 1976

When you see George Balanchine's beautiful and enigmatic "Chaconne," it's useful to remember that Gluck's opera, "Orfeo," has a happy ending: Eurydice is regained. The ballet begins in a limitless space to music designated as the Dance of the Blessed Spirits from the Elysian Fields scene in the opera's second act—a scene in which Orpheus is united with Eurydice as in a dream. The extraordinary duet that Balanchine has made for Suzanne Farrell and Peter Martins also seems to be happening in a dream. They dance slowly and delicately, almost as if trying to remember how to dance together. Their energy is like that used by dancers when they mark quietly through a dance, humming to themselves, barely indicating some of the steps. They seem to hear or feel, more often than see, each other. The space is blue and softly lit; the dancers are in white, and her vaguely Grecian tunic floats in the wake of the movement. You're scarcely aware of choreography, only of tendrils of movement the dancers curl around each other. A couple of times, as I remember, he dips her down and slides her along on her toes, but instead of immediately swooping her up again, he pauses, leaving her almost horizontal to the ground for a second before helping her to twine around and rise. Moments like this, that you can almost read as awkward—or perhaps tentative—make the dance seem not only tender, but ineffably poignant.

Martins carries Farrell away, while she keeps unfolding her front leg over and over, climbing the air. Then, a shock of golden light and horns. The court arrives to celebrate—a corps de ballet of 19 garlanding the stage, soloists entering in groups. The men are all wearing white shirts and tights, the women plain white tunics, yet they suggest courtiers playing gods and goddesses in the guise of rococo shepherds and shepherdesses. The variations are all airy—a gracious trio for Renée Estopinal, Jay Jolley, and Wilhelmina Frankfurt, all in a line. While he dances, he mimes playing a lute, imparting a Watteauesque fragrance to the proceedings. The decorum, if not the actual steps, suggests 18th-century court dances. The same goes for what might almost be a sprightly galliard for Susan Hendl and Jean-Pierre Frohlich and a crisp quintet for Elise Flagg and four equally small, spry women who echo her steps.

Nothing really prepares you for the second duet of Farrell and Martins. Her hair is up, and they both look happy and thoroughly awake—the royal pair at the heart of this festive dance. But everything they do is more daring than anything that has come before, or the grand finale that closes the ballet. It is, of course, partly due to the two performers' marvelously supple phrasing and the generous scale of their dancing that they look twice as vivid as anyone else; but Balanchine has created some remarkable dancing for them. Martins's solo passages are full of smooth, dexterous footwork, and the way he keeps shifting his focus gives you the illusion of seeing many facets of the movement. Farrell's solos involve curious relevés on one toe, in which her gesture-leg flicks softly out in unpredictable directions while her arms or body curl into positions so extreme that you wonder how it is that she isn't pulled off balance. As in much rococo art, the skeletal structure is so slim it almost vanishes, and you simply see dancing unfurling in scrolls and tendrils and sprays. The dancing for the corps de ballet frames this, but cannot quite match the flexibility, the radiant vitality of the dancing for Farrell and Martins. It's as if triumphant love (and choreographic inspiration) had made this Orpheus and Eurydice more luminous than the rest of humanity.

Nobody in the New York City Ballet has ventured as boldly as Farrell into this sinuous, beyond-technique range of dancing. Young Nina Fedorova, cast as Sacred Love in Ashton's "Illuminations," in reaching for Farrell's almost offhand sort of poeticism, quite literally fell off balance one night. This may be fanciful—I frequently am—but I can see "Chaconne" as Balanchine's choreographic acknowledgement of Farrell's return to the company—first as a shadowy and tentative image, then, newly intrepid, gleaming at the center of a constellation of dancers. A truly happy ending.

Celebrating the Solstice with Candycanes

The Village Voice, December 27, 1973

The New York City Ballet has its own way of making the darkest part of the year less bleak. Balanchine's "Nutcracker" is all about warmth and light and sweetness. It's also, to everyone's delight, about a Christmas tree that quadruples in size, about a battle between toy soldiers and huge gray mice who wring their paws in panic and scuttle off with their fat wobbling, about a white bed that swirls its occupant away to a distant country where everything and everyone is edible, but no one important get eaten because everyone's too polite.

But despite the silent noisiness (shh, you'll spoil the Tchaikovsky) and high spirits of the first-act Christmas party, the ballet has a lot to do with considerate behavior, with people noticing each others' needs. The little party dances that Balanchine has made, keeping in mind the skill of the real-children-dancers involved, are full of this. At one point the littlest boy has no partner, so his mother—without making a fuss—slips into the dance beside him; young fathers promenade their daughters; the grandparents sweetly and stiffly join in the final dance; the nephew of the mysterious Drosselmaier is always attentive to little Marie's problems with her nutcracker doll and her rowdy brother—which may be why she dreams him her champion in the mouse battle, her guide to a grown-up land of sophisticated dancing, and the prince with whom she flies away in a magical boat.

I love it all. Even the awkward or forced moments entertain me—like the orderly jumps that the children execute in successive pairs when they first get a look at the Christmas tree; in a way, the whole first-act, except for the dances, has the quaint and cautious phrasing of an old storybook for children.

And then there's the snowflake scene Marie and her Cavalier pass through, with tons of fake snow falling from above and sixteen NYCB women in white leaping and swirling and rushing past each other. It's a wonderful dance—fairly simple in terms of steps (because of the slipperiness of the snow stuff), but turbulent in its patterns and sequence. Its speed and spaciousness make it an interesting passage from the enthusiastic, humanly flawed social behavior in the Stahlbaum parlor to the ideal manners at the court of the Sugar Plum Fairy, where every last candy cane knows his place and function and executes it beautifully.

The variations for all the limber comestibles are light and clever and brief enough to leave you with room for more. Who's to question why Tea is (has always been since Ivanov, I guess) a jolly Chinaman and two female companions who have this thing about pointing their fingers, while Coffee is a sexy harem girl on the loose (usually danced by Gloria Govrin with that light and marvelously unassuming voluptuousness that only she possesses).

The grandest dancing is reserved for the Sugar Plum Fairy, her Cavalier, and Dew Drop (I don't know how she got into the larder). On New York City Ballet's long-awaited opening night, Patricia McBride performed the Fairy's welcoming solo beautifully—suggesting in the easy, unaffected play of her head and shoulders, the soft clarity of her pointework, that decorum was liberating rather than confining, and something that made her intensely happy. In the pas de deux, she looked strained at times, as if we were seeing her from the wrong angle and she knew it. And d'Amboise stayed on the surface of the dancing—looking unsubstantial and oddly giddy. Gelsey Kirkland was the most ravishing Dew Drop I've seen. The clarity her small, thin body achieves in space, her demure head, the understated way in which she assaults difficult movements make you think you've seen her hang in the air—cool and sparkling—for seconds at a time. Audiences love the big, bounding dancers whose grinning assertiveness shows us how tough it is. (Like tenors, they take deep breaths before high notes.) But dancers like Kirkland provoke another kind of gasp—she achieves everything so effortlessly that we can't believe what we've just seen.

Maybe I like the Mouse King best because he looks so nonplussed—as if he's just woken up in time to be killed. Or maybe I like the tree growing, or the way Marie's mother doesn't mind her sneaking out of bed to sleep near the tree—just covers her up. Or maybe I like the snow. Or maybe . . .

Fireworks in Rome

The Village Voice, May 5, 1975

There ought to be something to which I could compare the Bolshoi Ballet's production of "Spartacus" just to clarify its effect. . . . Perhaps it reminds me of an orator who drops clusters of ripe, burnished phrases, the meaning of which I can never quite remember later? Or perhaps of a vehicle, draped in flower garlands and spouting fireworks, inching along in a parade? It would be a mistake simply to call "Spartacus" a pageant: you'd think I meant something statuesque and turgid without much dancing. The ballet is full of movement, but the dancing is conceived as a series of impassioned displays linked together by tableaux.

Aram Khatchaturian's prize-winning score is gestural, rather hollow—depending on flamboyant orchestration for its effects. The choreography, by the Bolshoi's artistic director, Yuri Grigorovich, while somehow sturdier than the music, is also flamboyant. There seems to be no limit to the amount of innovative leaping, jumping, whirling phrases Grigorovich can devise. And the plot oozes along, laden with grand gestures that are more like exhortations to action than action itself.

All of the principal characters (Spartacus, the leader of the slave revolt; Phrygia, his wife; Crassus, the scoundrelly Roman commander; his concubine, Aegina) perform "monologues"—solos in which they dance out their feelings. Interspersed between these passages and a few brief encounters between the principals are many huge unison dances that telegraph their messages in bold, heroic terms. Entire sequences are like metaphors for Oppression, Heroism, Corruption, etc. Few of them have the jaggedness of dramatic action. When a Roman soldier stage left mauls a slave, you can be sure that his stage-right counterpart is doing the same thing. The final battle consists of squadrons of Roman soldiers leaping across the stage and exiting, then slaves leaping across and exiting. The whole thing is cross-cut like a film, leaving the actual encounter to your imagination. The curtain falls on a great wedding cake of people: Spartacus's laid-out corpse held aloft by his comrades, surrounded by supporters, and topped by his grieving widow (invisible arms hoisting her up behind the group).

One of the few moments of genuine dance-drama occurs when Crassus, lusting to see a little blood spilled, orders a duel between two gladiators. The doomed fighters (one, of course, being Spartacus) blinded by huge helmets, circle the stage warily, thrusting their swords into the air. Khatchaturian has provided a suspenseful tremolo, in C. B. deMille epic style, and the whole thing is quite thrilling.

Perhaps one of the reasons "Spartacus" seems more like a pageant than a ballet is that it's psychologically static—a series of vivid, simple posters. Roman soldiers are strong, but effete; they goose-step like proto-Nazis. Roman women have curly golden wigs and dance pretty, stilted balletsteps. Slaves are handsome, vigorous, and confident, and the female slaves all wear becomingly tattered tunics, like Moonbeam McSwine. Watching the ballet, you're carried away by the bravura dancing, but because there seems to be so much *more* of it than necessary you're also aware of wheels spinning in place. It's a curious effect.

"Spartacus" is a ballet for men, and I never thought I'd succumb with so much pleasure to unending exhibitions of noble virility. But when twelve slaves and/or shepherds start hurling themselves across the stage, my pulse leaps wildly. Part of this is caused by Grigorovich's cleverly constructed phrases: often, movements fold in or double up, so that a subsequent leap looks like a real explosion. But most of the excitement is created by the dancers. If you take time to scan the men in the corps de ballet, you see that each one dances with the conviction and intelligence of a soloist. In "Spartacus," where vigor is the thing, they don't concentrate on "correct" positions at all—not even in transit. What they do is to show you the impetus of the dancing, how it can be curbed, unleashed, diverted. Often they control a gesture almost to its conclusion and then fling or flip it away, giving an illusion of freedom and daring. Although "Spartacus" is showy, the dancers don't play to the audience at all but treat the noble, hackneyed ideas with touching commitment. And, for all their virtuosity, the men don't have that sleek, deliberate, infatuation-with-own-muscles air that some male dancers do.

On the company's opening night at the Met, Spartacus was played by Vladimir Vasiliev and Crassus by Maris Liepa, both of whom won Lenin prizes in 1970 for their performances in these roles. Vasiliev is amazing—he looks a little the way Erik Bruhn might look if he'd been eating heartily and working out with weights. His dancing is huge in scale: I haven't seen a man encompass so much space with his gestures since José Limón. His leaps have a leonine ease and fearlessness. Liepa's Crassus is a carefully worked out portrait of a sneering, but militarily correct villain; every gesture, every leap becomes a jab or a thrust. Nina Timofeyeva, who created the role of Aegina at the premiere of "Spartacus" in 1968, is an admirably hardworking voluptary. Natalia Bessmertnova, a delicate, vulnerable dancer, makes Phrygia's every gesture beautifully elegaic. I'd heard so much about her that I was slightly disappointed by a trace of ballerina mannerisms—lifting shoulders and fancy, detached hands. Shamil Yagudin, as the defeated gladiator, and Vyacheslav Gordeyev, Vladimir Doshelev, and Victor Kozhadei, as three big-wig shepherds, stood out among all those outstanding men.

Grigorovich's blood-and-thunder "Spartacus" is the fourth version of the same tale that the Bolshoi has mounted in the past twenty years. I was taken aback by its unabashed romanticism: the hero, with the man-to-man geniality of a John Wayne, allows a dangerous captured enemy leader to saunter away, scotching the revolution and sealing his own fate.

The Visitors

The Village Voice, January 15, 1970

Who would have thought possible in this steely age a ballet not only set to Elgar's "Enigma Variations," but peopled by Sir Edward and his friends—patently undanceable types? Still, Sir Frederick Ashton has done it, and the Royal Ballet is doing it, and I am astonished at its power to move me. The key—or one of them—to the enigma of the ballet's beauty is the nostalgia inherent in certain things. Lorca once wrote that a flock of sheep bears nostalgia about with it; it need not matter whether one has longings at all relevant to a flock of sheep. I don't think that one needs to have known era, place, or people involved in Ashton's ballet to be beguiled.

The setting is Elgar's house in Worcestershire in the last years of Victoria's reign and of the 19th century. Everything about the ballet has an air of lateness: the composer's lateness in achieving recognition, the ripe late Romantic music, the autumn gardens, the amber of the sunlight. Julia Trevelyan Oman's set and costumes are carefully and poetically authentic. It's the kind of set that I loved as a child—so superreal that it's hard to believe that there actually is a backstage area and not just more lawns and paths. There is a brick entrance, a cut-away view of an interior stairway, hammocks, bicycles, trees from which occasional yellow leaves float. Those friends of Elgar's cryptically enshrined in the variations are conveniently brought together at one of those diffidently friendly house parties at which the guests need speak to each other only infrequently. They wander about the shrubbery—each emerging to do his (or their) variation and then strolling off. At the end, a telegram is brought announcing to Elgar that Hans Richter has agreed to conduct the first performance of the "Enigma Variations." Elgar's friends rejoice in his good fortune.

I see most clearly in this ballet what Ashtonophiles rave about. He is best at being quiet; his effects are modest, unflamboyant, but extremely sensitive to the nuances of character. One feels that he doesn't want his inventiveness to show. It's well-bred choreography, but in this instance without the dullness that the term might imply. Sometimes he creates character through rhythm and through subtle gestural grafts onto the ballet vocabulary. Other times (I like these less), he suggests eccentricities by requiring an eccentric manner of performing straightforward classical steps. He has a fine way with small understated lifts that seem to come with no preparation; the girl's feet make shy conversational steps barely off the ground. There are several of these in a bittersweet duet for Elgar and a very young girl (beautifully done by Derek Rencher and Antoinette Sibley), and in one with more promise of fulfillment between Matthew Arnold's son and Isobel Fitton (Robert Mead and Vyvyan Lorraine). I especially liked two delightfully brusque, erratic solos performed by Alexander Grant and Anthony Dowell; some affectionately conjugal passages between Elgar and his wife (Svetlana Beriosova); a dignified, almost comic, but very touching duet between Elgar and a friend (Desmond Doyle).

Ashton has one peculiarity that I do not like. In almost every ballet of his that I have seen, he contrived to get everyone from previous scenes "dancing" together in a finale. In the case of "Enigma Variations" it's a shame, because it almost results in breaking down the character differences that he has so carefully built up.

He does the same thing in "Jazz Calender," but then, "Jazz Calendar" is another story. There are hints that Ashton may have meant it to be funny. Surely so adept a choreographer would never have in seriousness chosen to depict Tuesday's Child (full of grace) as a flirty little piece in a shaggy bunny suit escorted by a couple of spinning-top partners, or have Wednesday's child mourning amid spotted green snakes, or have Friday's children stroke each other in mock-Vegas passion. Richard Rodney Bennett's music is fake Duke Ellington. Whatever the ballet is supposed to be, it didn't make me laugh—except in disbelief.

Button Up Your Human-Suit

The Village Voice, February 28, 1974

Maurice Béjart strikes me as a man who has forgotten what simplicity is, and just now, when he seems to want badly to deal with basics—man's private innermost center, the structures by which he guides his life, the stages he must inevitably pass through—he's hampered by the oratorical tone that has mysteriously and untraceably stolen away his own voice. Looking back over this sentence I've just written, I see that I've unconsciously encapsulated in it something of the Béjartian style: he can't make dances about men and women, because he wants to make dances about Man.

37

How ardently portentous his simplicity is in the new and relatively austere "Stimmung," set to the Stockhausen score of the same title. The singers (members of the excellent Collegium Vocale Cologne for whom the Stockhausen music was commissioned) walk one by one onto their little elevated platform and sit cross-legged around their red lamp: the dancers walk one by one onto the dim stage, striding in dancerly fashion, toes first, to neatly spaced-out stations on the stage. They sit, open their crotches carefully to the audience, and begin a slow pulsing breathing whose rigidly controlled exhalation takes them down to a lying position and back up again. Well, but "Stimmung" is supposed to be a ritual; the program says so. Ritual has become for Béjart a theatrical modus operandi, by which he can deal with human life without having to sacrifice the orderly formations and unison dancing which he obviously feels are an integral part of ballet.

So in this simple, sincere, but overwhelmingly unnatural theatre piece, the dancers work with great sobriety and intensity to depict for us what they already are. "NOW MANKIND PLAYS," their bodies say; "LOVES," they roar; "COMMUNES WITH NATURE," they sigh. And I don't mean the dancers are phony; they're splendid, just unflaggingly intense. They play—or one group of them does—by sitting on the floor in a spraddle-legged position, grabbing up imaginary jacks with gleeful zeal. They love by making complicated frozen-in-action lotuses out of prone men, split-legged women descending on them, and, occasionally, symmetrical groups of eggers-on. They commune with nature by picking imaginary flowers—looking like grandly skillful mimes bent on making every gesture important. God, but they're stately, these 11 attractive dancers in their flesh-colored practice clothes.

"Stimmung," the music, is also intensely serene. You hear a texture of wordless, nasal tones shifting harmonically. Buddhist chant, but more restless. You hear fragments of a German text, "magic names" of gods and goddesses from every known cosmology, occasional flat, spontaneous-sounding sentences. Stockhausen's plan is complex, with a carefully controlled indeterminacy which involves great sensitivity and rapport between the six singers.

The dancers also have certain options with regard to the number of times they repeat a phrase or the order in which they combine several possible motifs. At all times, only 10 of them are active; the 11th stands on a mirror looking down at himself (a metaphor for self-examination that seems appropriately dancerly, if shallow). Everyone gets a turn on the mirror. The dancing is slow, strong, and static; you get no sense of motion flowing through space, only of handsome bodies painstakingly doing things to themselves and each other—spacing themselves out evenly, and obligingly directing every design they make toward the audience. Some of the phrases involve a kind of muscular modern ballet style, but there's a minimum of virtuosity. Others involve ritualistic gestures or stylizations of natural ones. Because of the element of indeterminacy, the dancers often work in loose canon—each of them at a different point in the movement phrase, and this gives "Stimmung," despite its austerity, a freer and livelier look than many Béjart spectacles.

The work moves serenely along, and it ends in a mirror image of its beginning: we see the dancers' backs instead of their crotches as they breathe together. Two moments stand out in my mind as particularly interesting. In one, the dancers mime passing handfuls of some precious thing—hallowed earth or water, maybe—down the line. A simple idea, but it's one of the few times in the dance when Béjart creates a sense of directed flow through space or of communion between people. The other moment is almost comical. All of the dancers but one are immobile in carefully designed poses that imply copulation. The one (Niklas Ek in the performance I saw) crawls fluidly around the stage on his belly, his legs oddly motionless, peering closely into the still, hot faces and the hips stopped in mid-thrust. And that's the only time Béjart makes you sharply aware of an individual reaction; in the various solos that emerge from the group dancing from time to time, you notice the characteristics of a particular dancer, or a choreographic emphasis, or an underscoring of the text (when one of the musicians says that his soul is in his hand, Daniel Lommel stretches out his hand reverently).

At the second performance, one of the women singers broke up into giggles, trying to say a commonplace English sentence. A couple of the other musicians laughed too. What a shock. A real human response bubbling up out of all that Humanity.

You Can't Choreograph a Penis

The Village Voice, April 6, 1972

I'm not sure why I like the dancers of the Netherlands Dance Theatre so much. Perhaps this is the reason: they're frequently asked to perform flamboyant, melodramatic movement, and they do it with fervor, but without that sense of showing off for the audience that, say, Béjart's dancers have. They're glamorous, but not aggressive about it. They're also very fluid.

The company's image has changed since its last visit here. When Ben Harkarvy was associated with it, there were apt to be ballets—real period pieces—in the repertory. And in 1968, most of the dances were by Hans van Manen—heavy, expressionistic stuff full of interesting designs. Now the company has more dances by Glen Tetley, and his style and van Manen's have moved closer together.

I've seen two of the programs currently being offered at the Brooklyn Academy. Surprising, "Mutations," "Imaginary Film," "Squares," "Small Parades" all display a frosty chic and strongly linear space patterns and decor. The chromium and neon, the clean-lined white costumes, the total absence of color, the balanced designs in the choreography are like exhibits in some intergalactic industrial fair. Yet the movement itself is not dry; it's curved, elastic, dramatic—a mélange of ballet and classic modern dance. Aimless voluptuosity in an ice and steel prison.

Glen Tetley strikes me as a very brainy choreographer. Usually what I remember and cherish from his dances are moments in which his designs of bodies in space produce a quick, microcosmic symbol of his whole concept. I remember the women in "Mythical Hunters" carried in like goddesses in the frame of the white half circles they hold. I remember in the same dance the sudden rush of men that leaves a novice maiden curled on the floor. I remember the squat central figure of "Ziggurat" and a fish-like plunge of male dancers. I remember the magical entrances and T'ai Chi exercises in "Embrace Tiger and Return to Mountain." I remember Jaap Flier's bare, anguished torso set against the black-costumed Rembrandt men in "The Anatomy Lesson." I'm usually fascinated and frustrated by Tetley's work—fascinated because of his ideas or his images, frustrated because of the superabundance of weighty and complicated movement which shows no growth or change, and because he cannot seemingly let a dance be itself, but must always be angling it for you.

"Mutations" is not the first naked ballet I've seen, but it is the first in which nudity (and corresponding clothes fetishes) is the subject matter. Tetley works very skillfully at preparing the audience for the first live naked body, so skillfully that he almost achieves the reverse of what he intended. (Who knows what he intended? Typical shoddy critic-talk. . .) He teases you. Come on, Tetley, bring on the guys.

The pace of "Mutations" is slow and deliberate. The mood created is that of an erotic ritual. Many of the dancers enter down a ramp in the center aisle, emerging into a squared-off arena that is defined by its white floor and a fence of chromium tubing structures. (These look sort of like contemporary sofas without the seat.) The first male solo (Johan Meyer) and the group dance that later echoes him is muscular, deliberate, frontal, full of deep squats in second position. This is followed by a beautiful, slow motion film solo choreographed by Hans van Manen (he did most of the film parts and Tetley all the live ones). Gérard Lemaitre dances it naked. The action on stage alternates with filmed action until the end. Here are some of the things that happen on stage: two young men in flesh-colored jockstraps engage in a combat that has sexual overtones; four young men charge up the ramp, smear themselves with red paint, and engage in angry copulation—dancing with four women; three naked men dance with aggressive formality; a man and woman dance ceremoniously about the stage on tall platform shoes, he with a boxy padding around his genitals, she with a built-out plastic window that reveals her bare breasts—space age totem figures. The second film shows Lemaitre and Anya Licher in a dreamily intimate pas de deux on the floor. This time the camera is intimate too and roams over their bodies; he is naked, she wears what looks like a lavender polo shirt over trunks. The third film, slow motion, is of a clothed pas de trois. Finally, Lemaitre and Licher perform the short duet naked in front of all three films. The first film, by the way, is remarkable in a couple of ways. In the first place, Lemaitre has such a flawless sense of the line of his body that he is incapable of clumsiness, even in slow motion. In the second place, it is heartening, especially in this plethora of controlled dynamics, to see that the penis refuses to be choreographed.

Critics are pampered. We don't pay for our seats, which are generally choice ones. However, two angry letters pointed out to me that only those in orchestra seats could see the whole of "Mutations" in Brooklyn. The ramp extending into the audience was invisible from the mezzanine and the upper balconies. "To what degree," complained one letter writer, "do a choreographer and a dance company have a responsibility to the whole *audience?" It seems to me folly for a choreographer to use space innovatively without considering the kinds of theaters his work is going to be seen in.*

Impetuous Princes

The Village Voice, May 3, 1973

Rudolf Nureyev not only staged the version of "The Sleeping Beauty" which the National Ballet of Canada is showing at the Met; he not only provided "additional choreography after Marius Petipa," he *produced* the ballet. And God knows what that means anymore. From the way he was calling "lighting!" rather desperately out the side of his Prince-Charming mouth during the Naiad's dance on opening night, one could surmise that he felt personally responsible for the whole show.

His concept of "The Sleeping Beauty" gropes back toward the 1890 original in some ways (the Lilac Fairy's long heavy costume which precludes much—in this case, any—fancy dancing). In other ways, it picks up credibility from Stanislavski and purls on toward Freud, dropping choreography along the way.

It's the most sumptuous production imaginable. The rooms of King

41

Florestan's castle are all vast, gloomy, golden places; the light seems to be bouncing off acres of bronze. In every scene, pillars and domes soar to apparently limitless heights, grand staircases wind down from infinity. When the Princess pricks her finger and falls into her century-long sleep, one curtain of briars ascends in front of her while another descends behind her—creating a vista of immense thorny patterns. Nicholas Georgiadis (who rates a cartouche around his name in the program) designed the sets and the costumes. The latter are extravagant 17th century court clothes (or abbreviated versions of them). The last act, in particular, involves masses of curls, feathers, and brocade, with the princess's father looking like Le Roi Soleil himself.

Nureyev's "The Sleeping Beauty" is also extremely vivid in terms of the action. Some of his directorial touches uncover interesting tensions in the noble old plot without destroying that structure in which the ideals of courtesy and generosity are so delicately balanced that a single act of forgetfulness can unleash the forces of evil. The awakening scene is quite wonderful: Nureyev as the Prince racing down a sunny marble staircase into a gloom of sleeping statues, running from figure to figure—pushing this one, spinning that one—until finally he finds the Princess's bed. The Rose Adagio in the first act is also remarkable. The Princess's four suitors have become fops—calculating, indolent, and inclined to be huffy. They don't behave like props for Princess Aurora's cool feats of balance; these four princes seem to be weighing her worth, exchanging little glances of surprise or approval with each other. It's the first time I've ever thought of the scene as sexy, or been moved to tears by the little Princess's growing assurance and excitement. Nureyev also has the princes inadvertently slay each other while they are making sword thrusts into the thick fog which surrounds the wicked fairy Carabosse. A real and irrevocable tragedy to end the birthday festivities.

I'm no "Sleeping Beauty" expert, and I don't mind some of Nureyev's tampering. For instance, making the Lilac Fairy into a mime role again and having Carabosse played by a woman instead of a man in travesty creates a nicely courtly good-evil metaphor: two beautiful, imperious women making drastic gestures at each other. What I don't much care for is Nureyev's choreography. Where he has substituted his own stuff for Petipa's, the phrasing becomes suddenly abrupt with brainy, arbitrary looking changes of direction and emphasis. Often he seems to want to make a heroic gesture and freeze it at the expense of flow in the dancing. Even some of the jumps he gives himself preclude a resilient landing because of this need to display a grand end pose. Where Nureyev excels is in certain floor patterns for the group—beguiling ways of making, say, a foursome slip into three-plus-one and then into a pair-plus-two. And I must say that his devious style of movement works very well for a solo in which the Prince makes a journey over uncertain ground in order to follow the Lilac Fairy to the enchanted castle.

The dancers of National Ballet of Canada have a poised, well-bred style—no doubt modeled after that of Britain's Royal Ballet. There are no unbridled extensions to be seen; the dancers' limbs make neat, clear paths, seldom far enough away from the center of their bodies to suggest either flamboyance or rapture. Even Carabosse, as played by company director Celia Franca, seems more of a malevolent eccentric than an evil spirit, as she cuddles her troupe of monsters. Veronica Tennant's Princess Aurora is not a glamorous heroine: she's small and goodhearted with beautiful sturdy balances, and her way with rubato phrasing suggests both hesitancy and a melting trustfulness that is extremely touching. Nureyev plays Prince Charming with gallant warmth, although he is overforcing so much of his dancing that you seldom see the smooth ease he used to have.

The company has some excellent dancers, like Karen Kain; some gifted and promising ones, like Frank Augustyn; many very intelligent and expressive ones. There are also some with the frozen demeanor of nervous students. But I'm not in the business of rating and ranking. I even forgive Nureyev his brusque choreography because I so admired his ardent directing.

Sunday Pieces

Detective Story: Find the Work

The New York Times, August 20, 1972

Aestheticians know a lot of good guessing games. One of these concerns the performing arts, and it begins with the question, "What is The Work?" Properly, but confusingly, the answer might be that the work is the artist's creation as it is translated via musical score or play script into a performance which is received by an audience. To a scrupulous few, The Work may emerge dimly only through a concatenation of performances. To many, the printed text stands for the play, the musical score for the composition. This is convenient: nearly everyone can read, and many can read music. Therefore critics and interested spectators can examine a particular rendition of a work in terms of what they deduce from the printed page to be the author's intention.

If you ask, "What is The Work?", about a piece of choreography, things immediately become stickier. Sometimes you find that it no longer actually exists: it's no longer performed, was never filmed, can't be found among the Dance Notation Bureau's small but growing library of scores. All that remains of such a dance are photographs, reviews, choreographer's notes—if he or she took any—perhaps the musical score, costumes, sets. Small chunks of dancing or stage patterns may remain in the minds of those who once performed the dance or those who saw it—if they are still alive.

We who write about dance are so accustomed to grasping at straws that our precarious position scarcely bothers us any more. Clive Barnes, writing in this paper about the recent American Dance Festival revival of José Limón's "Emperor Jones" (1956), had to define the production's virtues and shortcomings in terms of an original-cast performance he had seen in 1957. For him, The Work is a 15-year-old memory. Would any music or theater critic care to take on a job with this kind of built-in handicap?

And are all first performances definitive? American Ballet Theatre has just mounted a sleek and passionate new production of Eliot Feld's "Intermezzo." Many of us who saw "Intermezzo" when Feld's own company first danced it have vivid memories of Olga Janke executing a particular movement in the ballet's only solo. While gradually sinking from arabesque on pointe to arabesque in plié, she traced several circles with one arm. You worried for her: she seemed to be using that windmilling arm to maintain a precarious balance, the way a tightrope walker

47

does. Now Cynthia Gregory, a far more accomplished dancer, makes that same gesture a barely noticeable rhapsodic embellishment to a kind of danced exhalation. Obviously, these are simply two differing interpretations (Feld presumably coached both women), but because they happen in a ballet and not in a play or a musical composition, these interpretations—one or both—are all we can use to define that particle of a minute in "Intermezzo."

It's just possible that nobody cares, either. Most people, consciously or unconsciously, accept each performance of a dance they're watching as The Work itself; if they see it again, they may adjust their mental picture. It's only in discussion or critical writing that you become aware of the ephemeral nature of even a frequently performed work. Alvin Ailey's classic "Revelations" is a bigger, splashier dance than it was 10 years ago, because of gradually accumulating changes, planned and unplanned. Members of the Royal Danish Ballet for years have boasted of their unbroken Bournonville tradition, yet there exists in Copenhagen a 1904 film which, compared with the Bournonville style of today, clearly demonstrates how much that style has altered as it has been passed down from dancer to dancer.

Some choreographers rejoice in dance's ephemerality. Natural Heracliteans, they understand that you can no more see the "same" dance twice than you can step into the "same" stream twice. Certain members of the dance vanguard don't even make it easy for you to *try* to see it twice. Twyla Tharp has said in a snappy "Ballet Review" interview that she's not interested in working on new pieces. Meredith Monk's "Vessel" (1971), "Juice" (1969), "Needlebrain Lloyd and the Systems Kid" (1970) have already become legends, partly because blocksized parking lots, entire museums and half a college campus aren't always readily available to perform in. However, Monk—like Yvonne Rainer, Rudy Perez, James Cunningham and others—often expands earlier work in later dances or embeds little pieces of the old in the new.

Still others—Merce Cunningham, for instance—keep dances fresh by changing for each performance the order in which the ingredients are added. Cunningham's "Canfield" is an example of this kind of indeterminate structure. Not only do Cunningham's dances involve perceptual processes different from those required of a 19th-century ballet audience, some of them ought also to impose differing modes of discussion and of written criticism. You can't chew the fat with someone about the third section of "Canfield" unless the two of you attended the same performance; your third section might have been his fifth one, or might not have been danced at all that night.

Part of dance's now-you-see-it-now-you-don't history is traceable to the lack of a dance script as convenient as music notation, even though scholars and the artists themselves have been experimenting with dance notation for centuries. Some systems remain most useful as shorthand reminders of something already known. Some, like Labanotation, are very thorough, but extremely difficult to learn to read or write quickly. Film is expensive as a recording device, and videotape, which seems more promising, still isn't being widely used. But both film and videotape, as currently utilized, have a built-in flaw: they show a single performance of the work in question—a performance during which mistakes may have been made or the leading dancer forced by intestinal flu to dance with a certain queasiness. In the past, the dance field has not had the money (will it ever?) to develop the equivalent of the music recording industry's A&R man, who can cull high notes from one performance and insert them into another. (Choreographers would probably reject this anyway as being inimical to the humanness of dance.)

Naturally, more people are excited about dancing and making dances than about chronicling or preserving them. This is particularly true in the field of American modern dance, wherein the deplorable lack of history may be the result of its own rallying cry: "Down with the old, up with the new!" Martha Graham's 1931 masterpiece, "Primitive Mysteries," was painfully reconstructed at Connecticut College in 1964 by a group of former cast members—their memories jogged by photographs, the musical score, and, presumably, a lot of amicable wrangling. The work now exists only in a plain-Jane record film of that reconstruction. Charles Weidman and former members of the Humphrey-Weidman company recently tried the same think-tank approach on the late Doris Humphrey's "New Dance" (1935), although because of the length and complexity of the work, the reconstruction may be more of a sensitive renovation. It's interesting to realize that to young people who saw the new "New Dance" and its 1936 companion piece, "With My Red Fires" (expertly reconstructed from Labanotation for the American Dance Festival earlier this summer), the 1972 performances *are* "New Dance" and "With My Red Fires." And in a few generations, perhaps only films made of these, if they are accessible, will remain to stand for the dances that a new audience may be curious to see.

In her later years, Doris Humphrey decided to strike a blow for history by allowing her new works and a few remounted old ones to be filmed and notated and the scores made available through the Dance Notation Bureau. Conceivably, a repertory company operating in 2072 could stage one of these dances. In doing this, Humphrey must have been aware that she was taking chances on feeble or time-warped interpretations.

Her contemporary and fellow rebel, Martha Graham, has apparently chosen the opposite course. She has hoarded her splendid dances until many of them have effectively ceased to exist. Only a few documentary films circulate; only a handful of her dances have been released to other companies; as far as I know, only one, "Diversion of Angels," has been notated. Many of her works (and, it is rumored, her private collection of record films) will die when she dies. It may be possible to present others only as long as those who danced in them still remember and attempt to preserve them with as little distoriton as possible. In a century, Humphrey's dances could be living history, while Graham's may be myth. Come to think of it, that's pretty much in keeping with what we know about the two women and their ideals of art.

Still, when I think of the several films, the notation score, the frequent performances of Doris Humphrey's "The Shakers" (1931), I think that our pride in dance's ephemeral nature may be a trifle defensive. Many young contemporary dancers have learned "Shakers" the way ballet students learn variations from "Swan Lake"; they can argue happily about the correct interpretation of the 9-count phrase. I can think of very few modern dances you can treat this way. When I speak of "Shakers" as The Work, I may even know what I mean.

This article aroused a storm of controversy, which delighted and puzzled the editors at the Times. *Most of the letters came from people connected with the Institute of Choreology, the headquarters for the Benesch System of notation. They were concerned that my not mentioning the Benesch system had in some way denied its existence as one of the major, widely used methods for preserving dances. They were* very *angry. My only defense was that I wasn't really writing an article about dance notation, and the article I* was *writing had been generated by the Doris Humphrey revivals that summer at Connecticut, and Doris Humphrey utilized Labanotation.*

Get Out There and Dance like a Man!

The New York Times, August 25, 1974

The late José Limón, in an article he contributed to Selma Jeanne Cohen's book "The Modern Dance: Seven Statements of Belief," wrote that he had always thought that dancing was something for girls to do until he saw Harald Kreutzberg perform. He then realized that "a man could, with dignity and a towering majesty, dance."

Limón, like many male dancers in America during the first half of this century, started his training late; in those days, for social and economic reasons, people didn't encourage their sons to aim for a career in dance (many still don't). Such men brought to dance—particularly to the so-called modern dance—bodies that were springy and strong, but without much finesse. A limited limberness coupled with mature back muscles would have kept many of them from, say, lifting their legs high in arabesque, even if they had wanted to. Most didn't. They looked— and tried to look—like men dancing rather than like dancers who happened to be male.

I remember Limón's company of the fifties. A lot of the men were built like runners. Supporting Limón in his various versions of the tragic-hero role, they emphasized qualities most Americans think of as masculine: strength, directness, a kind of brusqueness that doesn't preclude tenderness. Limón himself, with his huge gestures, stabbing footwork, often seemed to plunge into dancing—shoulders first—like a magnificent bull.

Times have changed. This summer, Connecticut College's American Dance Festival, where Limón was for many years cock-of-the-walk, proved to be—among other things—a small anthology of male dance styles. Watching Daniel Nagrin perform some of his famous solos from the forties and fifties, I was struck by how different most male dancers of the seventies are from this tough and charming man with his gallery of recognizable male archetypes. Nagrin's characters have less grandeur than Limón's did: he's adept at portraying the suave heel, the gambler, the frustrated city dweller, the gangster. (Imagine Humphrey Bogart dancing.) Nagrin's style turns on a dime, shoots straight, and doesn't mess around.

It's difficult to pinpoint exactly how, when, and why dancers and choreographers began to modify this rugged ideal of male dancing. Certainly in the fifties, men like Donald McKayle and Talley Beatty, who adapted modern dance forms to black subject matter and dealt with their heritage—African, Caribbean, or American—as they understood it, showed without any fuss that a man could ripple his body, roll his head around, move his hips and rib-cage in independent circles and not tarnish his image.

When, also during the fifties, Alwin Nikolais began to develop his theater of light-magic, sensuous colors and shifting forms, one of his avowed intentions was to get away from the story-telling aspects of dance. Unlike most directors of modern dance companies, he was not his own star performer, and he neither wanted nor needed to create heroes whose griefs an audience could identify with. In Nikolais' works, the dancers are only part of his fantastic environments. Together they may suggest a complicated organism or pulses of energy or a kaleidoscope of bright patterns. Sex plays little part in Nikolais' dances, and his movement style doesn't emphasize differences in gender. Nikolais dancers tend to have highly articulate bodies; they can execute many intricate gestures simultaneously. Men and women are equally light, fluid, and subtle. (That some of the dancers—Gladys Bailin or Phyllis Lamhut, for instance—have been sexy is a piquant point, but not a vital one.)

A few weeks after the Nikolais company appeared at the American Dance Festival, a young going-places-fast company called Pilobolus took over the stage. And although Pilobolus was formed by four athletes who began studying dance while at Dartmouth, the dancers make few overt demonstrations of manliness. They're awesomely strong, but they soft-pedal their way into complex designs made out of several bodies. Linking onto each other, standing on each other, the dancers can form a fluid succession of pyramids, inkblots, many-linked creatures. Their choreography makes the individual disappear and reappear in the same way Nikolais' does. The two women now in the company are used, for the most part, simply as valuably light-weight bodies.

Not all unisex choreography is sexless, however. In the Louis Falco Dance Company, the dancers are vibrant, highpowered, beautiful to look at. In cheerful dances, they celebrate their own prowess with almost voluptuous satisfaction; in tragic ones, they hurl their bodies around as if abusing or exhausting them were an appropriate metaphor for spiritual torment. Their sexual contacts are acrobatic and casual.

When Falco danced with Limón several years ago, he looked like a strong and beautiful baroque angel—part male, part female—swirling in the orbit of an aging king. He is a splendid example of the breed of male dancers that developed as society's definition of sex roles began to stretch and slacken. Many of these dancers were able to begin their training at an early age. They can arch their backs and raise their legs high; yet supple as they are, they still emphasize strength. They can toss women around and at the same time compete with them in flexibility. They suggest not adult men, but idealized images of youth.

Their virtuosity endears them to many choreographers. During the sixties, even Martha Graham, who had once cast men as stiffly strutting phallic figures or sturdy lovers, began to make dances full of a muscular, almost ornate eroticism—dances in which both men and women seemed as turned on by the motions of their own bodies as by the sight of anyone else on stage. And, although in classical ballet male and female roles are carefully delineated in terms of movement, many contemporary choreographers working in ballet have also exploited the possibilities of the limber male body. Some of these choreographers, Jerome Robbins for instance, deliberately play around with traditional roles, letting men support men, or women support men; others, like Gerald Arpino, capitalize on the excitement an audience feels at seeing a dancer's limbs stretched to capacity.

However, the new generation of experimental choreographers, those who avoid role-playing altogether, might consider the aggressively glowing muscularity of the dancers in Falco's company just another kind of sterotyped role. (Even a rapscallion of an old avant-gardist like Merce Cunningham lightly acknowledges a difference between men and women in his dances. His dancers' bodies, their genders, are part of their individuality, important for the subtle variations they impart to his movement style.) Some men who choreograph now, who build a style on their own bodies, appear to be uninterested in implying how they as men *ought* to dance. They don't limit what they do, but neither are they flamboyant with their bodies. Take, for instance, Ted Rotante, who with his partner and co-choreographer Nora Guthrie, closed this summer's festival. Rotante has trained in a variety of styles, but I don't know whether it's his eclectic background or his sensitivity to movement that gives his dancing an unusual amount of nuance and variety. He can power gestures from deep inside his body like an African dancer; he can look as light and dry as Fred Astaire or as nimble-jointed as Murray Louis (once Alwin Nikolais' leading dancer, now director of his own company), or as strong-man as he chooses. But whatever his role of the moment, he is undeniably himself dancing, apparently unworried whether or not he is creating an indelible masculine image.

When I watch him and other men developing along similar lines, I think that maybe male lib is finally hitting the dance world. It's nice that men can dance like kings or tough guys or the boy acrobats of antiquity, but why should anyone have to play those roles all the time? Especially in dances that purport to reflect the changing rhythms and patterns of contemporary America, it seems unnecessary to harp on the differences between men and women—and equally absurd to deny that such differences exist.

It Takes Space . . .

The New York Times, August 12, 1973

Dancing does not simply inhabit space, but carves and molds it—creating and erasing bridges, islands, continents of air. Yet the place where dance occurs is important too, since it imposes boundaries both on the dancing and on how we look at it. (Do we expect anything relating to the stage action to happen in the aisles of one of those velvet-swathed opera houses? No. And if it did we'd shush it and glare at it and tell it to mind its manners.)

The rectangular proscenium stage is terrific for slice-of-life histories or mannerly and extravagant displays. Everyone and everything is seen from its best angle. (The "fourth wall" that has been removed is seldom the bathroom wall.) For the most part, we Americans and Europeans have kept our theatricals as cleanly separated from us as our religious rites. Celebrated in the round, the Mass loses a lot of power.

On our traditional picture-box stage, everything looks flat; the depth is hard to perceive unless you can see the stage floor. Classical ballet is at home there. Those ardently elongated body lines have a two-dimensional clarity, and from time to time the flow of the dancing congeals in poses that the eye and mind of the spectator grasp and remember.

The balanced and orderly patterns of Marius Petipa works like "The Sleeping Beauty" or Balanchine's neo-classic ballets seem to affirm rectangularity. Not only does the dancing stitch back and forth across the stage, but you often see rows of identically dressed people lined up from the front of the stage to the back—as if the choreographer were trying to indicate a vista of depth by presenting a parade of flat surfaces. In cheap imitations or bad examples of this genre the corps de ballet tends to look like vigorous wallpaper.

The late stage designer Arch Lauterer wrote that Martha Graham ought to get off the proscenium stage: her movements were too 3-D to be seen properly from row H. But she never has. Her dances show the circular patterns of early ritual theater and the jagged thrust of modernism, but she wants to enforce a point of view, not change a way of life.

A lot of other important contemporary choreographers have stuck with the proscenium stage. For one thing, it makes touring easier. But some use the conventional stage space unconventionally. Merce Cunningham scrambles his designs in space and time so that what you see on stage seems like a part of something that's also going on in the wings, the dressing rooms and the streets outside. Dancers pass through, each intent on some private business, each doing something different from the others, while your eyes rove over the space, taking in what interests you. Robert Wilson, in his "The Life and Times of Sigmund Freud" (1970), organized the stage space into several horizontal corridors, each of which had its own snail's-pace parade of discrete and mysterious activities.

Some choreographers can present their work almost anywhere. Twyla Tharp and new choreographers like Wendy Perron and Rosalind Newman spill their dancing inelegantly onto the performing area, seemingly caring more about molding the space between the lightly jostling bodies than about connecting with the boxy walls of some auditorium. Rudy Perez makes his own rectangles, lines and boxes out of squadrons of dancers, but he can adjust his works to fit a gym, studio, stage, lawn, or parking lot.

During this spring's outdoor festival in New York, Trisha Brown performed one of her small-scale fluid "accumulations" (she executes one movement, repeats that and adds a second, repeats those two and adds a third, and so on) in the sunken plaza of the McGraw-Hill building. To accommodate her dance to the huge space and the unruly drop-in lunchtime crowd, she simply had four women do the movements instead of one, and instructed two men to enter at one point and move the women from place to place, while the women doggedly but gently kept on with their phrase, which by then consisted of over 30 separate moves. The dance ended stunningly when the women were forced by the demands of the phrase to roll down a flight of stone steps where the men had finally placed them.

But if some choreographers make works so unframed and so casual that they can be seen anywhere, others are very specific in regard to space—and sometimes so elaborate that their works can't easily be repeated after the initial series of performances is over. Once Elizabeth Keen created a dance which utilized the drainpipes, ladders, arches, and vents of a particular city roof, and this spring each of Trisha Brown's dancers occupied a roof over a distance of several blocks and relayed the movements from dancer to dancer, from roof to roof, in one beautifully deteriorating sequence.

Meredith Monk, who once used the entire Guggenheim Museum in a dance, situated the third part of her opera-epic, "Vessel" (1972) in a city parking lot. Armies fought, children played, motorcycles roared through, pioneers camped by firelight—among the hundred other elements embedded in the elaborate and meticulously executed mosaic. Last summer at Connecticut College, Don Redlich's "She Often Goes for a Walk Just After Sunset" began with a serene lady in an old-fashioned white dress and hat walking out of one of the campus's old stone buildings. A tiny, solitary, gracious figure raising her parasol and strolling toward us over miles of clipped lawn. And it *was* twilight, and a storm was coming, and the summer wind meddled with her hair and her parasol, and the audience was transfixed.

Sometimes when dances are presented in unusual places, you can't always be sure of the boundaries. Perhaps the old man gesticulating on the sidewalk is in the dance. Are the cramped halls or icy streets you wait in to see Meredith Monk's works a kind of prologue? Is your own discomfort *in* the dance? When you go to see one of William Dunas's scrupulously made, parsimonious solodances, you walk past the crumbling, decaying empty buildings in lower Manhattan where everything appears both threatened and threatening. The painfulness and mysterious danger that hangs over his numbed dancing is appropriate. Will any of us be able to get home when it's over?

These choreographers and others have made me so aware of space that I can even postulate ideal theaters for more conventional work. Balanchine is a big space man. At the New York City Ballet's summer home in Saratoga, you can leave the amphitheater, walk up the lawn, and, looking back, still understand what's going on, so great is the dancing's clarity in space and time. Certain fast, theatrical, high-intensity styles (take that of Lar Lubovitch, for instance) look phony close up, dionysiac at some distance. José Limón was a middle-sized-theater man. When American Ballet Theatre performs his "The Moor's Pavane" at the New York State Theater, you see vividly the symmetrical dance patterns torn by the tensions of four characters, but you can't quite see the nuances and fleeting ambivalences in the way those four relate to each other.

The little dances—pieces being made today for lofts and galleries—lure the spectator into casual ways of looking. You can't take in the whole "stage picture" at once: you're too close to it. So you focus on details—a single dancer, a single gesture, an area of wall, the run in someone's tights. Even though you're hemmed in and sitting still, the experience is more like browsing through a store: you look at what catches your attention. The dancers can use a very low degree of intensity and very tiny motions and still interest you immensely. But often if these dances are transferred to a stage, they disappear, because they weren't constructed with an eye to vivid linear patterns, or can't be performed with the kind of attentiveness to vast space on the part of the dancers which can pull the audience's attention across the chasm of the orchestra pit.

There's been talk recently about finding a theater for dance in Manhattan. That'd be nice. But I'm not sure any more that one theater could serve all dance. It would have to be capable of being both round and square and odd-shaped, large and small, formal and informal. Myself, I wish that a lot of interesting theaters and other public and private buildings could be persuaded to make space available for dance at certain times (and at reasonable rates). Some churches and office buildings have already begun, in a small way, to do this. We have too many kinds of dances to insist on one kind of dancing-place and then to consider all works that can't be performed there as "experimental," "far out," "nonprofessional," no matter how intricate the work or how skilled its maker.

What Are They Up To?

The New York Times, October 28, 1971

Once everyone—artists and audiences both—understood clearly the functions of narrative in ballet. Narrative was those little bits that glued the dancing together and sometimes even influenced it. The hero would perhaps perform some hapless and charming dumb show for the heroine; she would then rise up onto her pointes and tear off a solo that would be a kind of emotional gloss on the resultant changes in her situation—or plight, as it was more likely to be. The format is similar to that of opera with its alternation of recitative and aria. Whatever the story of the ballet might be, it had to offer good opportunities for dancing, and, come to think of it, this may be one of the reasons why so many of the early ballet libretti involved royalty: they could always give a ball.

The 20th-century ballet choreographers and pioneer modern dancers began to have different ideas about narrative or "content." Some worked from a basis of human gestures and actions—amplifying them and stretching them into dance until whatever story there was could be carried along by appropriately expressive movement, instead of by pantomime or acting. Antony Tudor's "Romeo and Juliet," recently revived by American Ballet Theatre is a brilliant example of this kind of drama in ballet.

Others, starting with modern dancers Isadora Duncan and Mary Wigman, saw the symbolic or metaphoric possibilities inherent in the gestural approach to dance. They and their followers experimented with dance forms that involved a mood, an ambience, a role, or perhaps one simple dance task—a slave breaking his bonds and standing erect, sea waves rolling up to the shore, a primitive race growing into knowledge. During the Freud-conscious fifties, the spectacle of a solo dancer tying himself into improbable knots was certain to suggest an inner bout with his psyche.

Martha Graham made some drastic innovations in dramatic dance. Influenced possibly by film techniques, by Oriental theater, by Jung, by Einstein, and goaded by her own genius, she fractured the orderly progress of time perceived as a series of causally related events. Her dances, the Greek myth ones in particular, show a linear logic within small sections, but she has rearranged the order of these sections or stacked them up on stage so that they coexist in space while occupying different corridors of time. Her flashbacks permit you to see the past in the midst of the present.

Until quite recently, whatever the narrative or dramatic content of a dance, audiences understood most of what was going on. Since ambiguity wasn't considered interesting, copious program notes often let them in on the choreographer's intentions. It was usually pretty clear, too, when a dance was simply "about" dancing. The choreographers arranged their dancers in formal patterns and bounced them in and out of phase with the music, and the dancers smiled happily over the edge of the stage—proud to be showing off the splendid bodies that their hours of work and gallons of sweat had produced.

But there was something interesting and dangerous lurking all along under these tidy distinctions between dramatic and nondramatic dance. Some people were clever enough to see it; others became aware of it only when it was forced on them, and then they were puzzled and annoyed. In the middle of a nondramatic dance of the sixties, or even earlier, spectators might suddenly have found themselves looking at the dancers and wondering, "Who are these people, and what are they up to?"

Not surprising. After all, one of the essential ingredients of dance is dancers, and dancers look and act like people—improbable ones at times but still people. Their bodies are not impersonal elements like musical notes; they never completely disappear into the fabric of a dance. One can make polyphonic structures with them, but seldom homophonic ones. When singers hold a unison note, you hear a blend; when dancers strike a unison pose, you see the pose multiplied by the number of dancers. Each component is still isolable. It is the human quality of those bodies that makes dance what it is, and even when a dance appears to be only about speed, impetus, shapes in space and time, even then the human gestures and implicit human relationships surface with or without the choreographer's consent.

This hidden drama in dance has become more evident during the past 15 years or so because dance forms have become more irregular, more lifelike, even random. The neat patterns, steady predictable rhythms, unison virtuosity of traditional dance tend to militate against this kind of vision. Except from children. I remember once watching a flashy classical pas de trois, and the applause woke a little girl dozing on my lap, who explained that she had fallen asleep when "that lady started taking so long to make up her mind which of those two men she liked best."

Some choreographers have made deliberate use of this sort of drama. They employ collisions of bodies, eruptions into recognizable human gesture like words that never add up to a sentence, sentences that don't quite make a paragraph. An extremely obvious example occurs in Balanchine's "Scotch Symphony" when, out of a snatch of clever dancing, a group suddenly poses. A girl is surrounded by men who fence her in with their arms while staring threateningly toward another group of men. "Don't touch our sister," says one rival clan to the other. It's a charming joke, later repeated but never pursued.

Today's avant-garde choreographers assert their right to incorporate anything they wish into their dances—speech, song, gesture, you name it—and they are aware of the connotations and relish them. Suddenly in a dance, someone barks out a very good and serious dog imitation. (Yvonne Rainer did this once.) It's like gluing a piece of newspaper onto a collage. The resultant picture isn't "about" newspapers any more than the dance is "about" dogs. In a solo once, Judith Dunn did a slow turn, paused in plié, and raised a pointed index finger. By using such a natural gesture surrounded by more impersonal dance movement, she seemed in one sense to be insisting on its right to exist as pure movement, yet in another sense she momentarily urged us to be on guard—perhaps against her.

The more outrageous a choreographer, the easier it is for audiences to accept these slices of life, even if they don't like the work. When Meredith Monk in her lawn dance "Needlebrain Lloyd and the Systems Kid," had a group of people tear through on horseback, no one asked what it meant, but marveled at the speed, beauty, unexpectedness of the act. Although some did ask whether it was dance. When Robert Wilson in his "Deafman Glance" asked some men to construct a wooden bin on stage and billed them as "Bin-Builders," no one thought to ask what the bin was to be used for.

It seems to be the flash of characteristic human behavior—or what, because of the way the dancer accentuates it, looks like human behavior —in contemporary ballet or in plotless works of choreographers like Merce Cunningham that confuses some people. Here is a prominent drama critic's view of Cunningham's "Rainforest": "The story seems to be about one man seducing another's girl then another man stealing the man and so on for a while, There is little structure or build to it and it concluded in the middle of nowhere."

The critic in question is not simply insensitive or ill-educated. Merce Cunningham in making a work may think only of movement; however, sound, costumes, lights—added later—inflict an atmosphere. Also his rhythms are irregular, his groupings unusual, and something about the relaxed way his dancers perform, coupled with the strangeness of what they are doing, often reminds us of something we know, something we have perhaps seen on the street.

When two men stand and look down at a girl lying at their feet, there is a fugitive human drama to the moment. But it is fatal to begin wondering actively whether she has been hit by a car or whether the two men are planning to leave her and go off together. If the spectator seizes on this event too tightly, he is bound to be disappointed; it won't be developed, but will sink back down into the current of the dance. It's like a chance form—a spot of mold on a wall that looks, from a certain angle, like a dog. A nice thought to play with, but one to be held lightly, so that it can give a richness of texture, but no irrevocable associations that would inhibit all other possibilities.

It may be pointless to speculate on what audiences will or won't accept with ease and pleasure, because one is so often proven wrong. The mysterious sense of community that the dancers show in Jerome Robbins's "Dances at a Gathering" seems to have caused nothing but delight. The dancers are private with each other, specific with the space. They appear to be assuming and discarding a variety of roles. In Robbins's new "The Goldberg Variations," there is less of this behavior. The large, hierarchically arranged groups are dancing very beautifully for you, the audience. They begin simply, become more daring and elaborate. They look pleased and concentrated, as if the Bach music were a dolphin they were riding. I find both dances wonderful in their separate ways; many prefer "Dances at a Gathering," and I think it is the subliminal meanings that move them.

This is an astonishingly rich period in American dance. All forms and styles from the past coexist with the newest experiments. And our own ways of seeing are changing and widening. I find it endlessly fascinating to be able to watch a dance, wondering fleetingly, "Who are these people and what are they doing?" and to expect or need no answers.

I think I was wrong about "The Goldberg Variations." After seeing it again, I noticed quite a few ambiguously dramatic events within it. I now think that the reason "Dances at a Gathering" suggests a community while "The Goldberg Variations" does not is that there are fewer dancers in the former. Since we get more opportunity to watch them dancing with different partners in different ways, we may feel we know them better than we do the many dancers who appear—and disappear—in "The Goldberg Variations."

The New Improved Razzle-Dazzle

The New York Times, November 23, 1975

There is a new breed of musicals on Broadway these days—musicals that are built on a dance impetus instead of conventional plots. In shows such as "A Chorus Line," "Grease," "Chicago," "Pippin," "The Wiz" and "Candide," choreography is the lubricant that oils the wheels and maintains the momentum of the productions, some of them like roller coasters designed to thrill you within an inch of your life and deposit you intact with a smile frozen on your face.

The musicals of 10 years ago (pre-"Hair," anyway) were musical *plays*—stories in which some clever people had poked holes and planted songs and dances. During the post-"Oklahoma!" years, choreographers and directors battled this format in an effort to integrate the musical numbers into the show. Games, fights, parties, dreams were all good pretexts for dancing. Sometimes the dancers pretended to be objects: two facing each other with lifted arms could be a doorway; three kneeling side by side could become a sofa. Paving the way for long, juicy musical numbers without sacrificing the forward momentum of the plot became a crucial problem for directors. Remember those moments when a character would arrive home and the audience waited to see what would catch his eye and trigger a song or a dance?

The directors and choreographers of the new musicals have returned to a pre-"Oklahoma!" practice: they often make no attempt to pretend that a "number" is anything but what it is. By working with the same techniques of fragmentation and incongruous juxtaposition employed by the experimental theater and dance people, today's musical-makers don't even need the elaborate pretext of the Backstage Musical. They have created a new convention which contemporary audiences accept. Pianos rise out of the floor; microphones are handed around; actors step out of their roles to introduce each other or chat with the audience.

Roles—though a necessary convention—needn't be taken too seriously anyway. For instance, in "The Wiz" (directed by choreographer Geoffrey Holder and choreographed by George Faison), one sees the familiar Oz characters—Scarecrow, Tin Woodman, Cowardly Lion—principally as charming and expert song-and-dance men come together to team up with Dorothy (Stephanie Mills), a hot new vocalist. The nimble young Scarecrow (Hinton Battle) does his ragdoll splits; the Woodman (Tiger Haynes) does stiff, spry tapsteps; the Lion (Ted Ross's role is currently being played by James Wigfall), mincing and strutting, is a smart-mouthed, stand-up comedian. And the Yellow Brick Road turns out to be those four spiffy guys in canary-colored suits and red wigs, noodling around in the background with canes. "The Wiz" isn't just a hip update of a sentimental fantasy; it's a fast-moving anthology of black theatrical styles from Bojangles to Aretha Franklin and Bill Cosby. The big cyclone routine features the dancers neither as distraught Kansans nor as personifications of wind, but as a crowd, nattily dressed in black, dancing in Faison's sharp, fast variant of Alvin Ailey's style—wrapping what remains of Dorothy's house in black streamers while Miss Eye of the Storm (tall Evelyn Thomas) bestrides the roof and lashes her elegant torso around.

Like "The Wiz," the Bob Fosse musicals, "Chicago" and "Pippin," operate on two levels. It's hard to believe in the bedrooms, jail cells and courtrooms of "Chicago," everything is an act in a twenties nightclub, with chief murderesses Roxie Hart and Velma Kelly (Gwen Verdon and Chita Rivera) as the toughest of hoofers. "Pippin," despite its flimsy historical pretext, is a carnival show with the devil as barker and star magician.

In the Fosse shows, it is the chorus dancers—along with magic-show lighting and highly active sets—who seam the whole thing together. As well as functioning in the "numbers," they provide prowling or prancing transitions from one to the next. These dancers, almost constantly active, wear clownish combinations of tatters and finery (top hats, frock coats, garters, armor) that outline or bare lengths of thigh, morsels of breast and buttock. They look gleeful and sinister, oozing along, suddenly freezing into out-of-kilter poses. Their pelvises are hyperactive; their feet jab into the floor. The men tend to hunch their shoulders and make elaborate, flippant hand gestures; the women, stridently voluptuous, snake their arms. Everyone moves as if perpetually horny, yet meticulously obedient to some unseen puppeteer. Fosse has ranged himself with such prophets of decline and fall as Petronius and Berthold Brecht—although where their tone is rancidly ebullient, his is precise and icy—and the dancing in "Pippin" and "Chicago" is as glossily cynical, violent, and depraved as everything else about them

Here's a paradox. When choreography provides the basic texture of a musical and helps generate the high-intensity, driving energy that everyone seems to agree are Broadway sine qua nons, it must not call attention to itself as Dance, or the pace will stall. It certainly can't be inappropriate or idealized (no farm girls with superb techniques on pointe), and sometimes, for the sake of appropriateness, it must be tacky, inexpert, self-mocking, or even invisible.

This last is true of the choreography Patricia Birch provided for "Grease" (directed by Tom Moore) and "Candide" (directed by Harold Prince). In both shows, "Candide" particularly, there is an immense amount of motion, but nothing that the eye is supposed to light on as "choreography"—no people who stand out as trained dancers. The kids in "Grease" are raucously virtuosic singers: the fifties high school they're supposed to be attending is littered with microphones—since any emotional crisis of adolescence can best be expressed by an Elvis Presley. But rock-singing of the fifties was a highly developed style with its own elaborate conventions, while rock-*dancing* was defiantly do-your-own-thing. Consequently, aside from wild and clumsy carryings-on in the prom scene, the "dancing" in "Grease" consists of the jaunty struts, the restless jerks from immobility into action, the shrugging shoulders, and the twitching pelvises that signal turned-on teen-age libidos.

If Birch's contribution to "Grease" was to imbue the actors with suitable personal, and historical, movement styles, for "Candide" she must have functioned as an adroit and adventurous traffic cop. As if the failure of "Candide" in the fifties had convinced everyone that having a distinguished score and a distinguished book was no way to succeed in show biz, Prince and Birch have made the action move so fast that you can hardly take it in. They've staged Candide's travels rather like a frantic board game along the perilous ramps that festoon the Broadway Theater: a throw of dice by invisible and capricious hands may send an actor scooting five scenes ahead or immobilize him, while two scenes back someone dear to him is being raped. There may not be any fancy steps, but Charles Kimbrough, galloping brilliantly in and out of three major roles, performs what amounts to a marathon solo dance.

There's a lot of genuine dancing in "A Chorus Line." It's all about dancing—a "real" backstage musical. Yet even here the choreography doesn't draw attention to itself as Choreography. In fact, one of the greatest triumphs of choreographer Michael Bennett (who also directed the show and thought it up) is that he has refrained from making the dance element too distinguished. The audition material doled out by the show-within-a-show's director, Zach (Robert LuPone), is the usual unremarkable stuff: a little ballet, a little tap, a little jazz. The big number for Cassie (Donna McKechnie)—the soloist trying out for a chorus job in order simply to keep dancing—is a skillfully built pastiche of everything that a splendid and glamorous dancer like Cassie/Mc-Kechnie may have been asked to do in a musical comedy. Here are the whizzing pirouettes in a hugged-in ice-skater position, the big strides, the flung back head, the pauses for come-hitherish undulations of hips and arms. "A Chorus Line" isn't a hymn to the beauty of dance, but to the hard work, bravery, and persistence of dancers. The people in the show are the kind who know they can do anything if they just push a little harder.

Yet, although perhaps any skillful craftsman could have choreographed "A Chorus Line," only a fine choreographic sensibility could have structured it as Bennett did. The dancers line up along the front of the stage for Zach and for us. Their reminiscences can make that line soften, send out tangents, disappear; but *they always return to it.* This superb device whispers clearly and insistently the same irony that the finale shouts: why do the dancers have to submit to this unusually painful audition, baring their individual souls, when this director needs them only to be components of a flashy anonymous border?

The dance format of these new and expertly crafted musicals has enabled them to avoid the old pitfalls. One can certainly lament a dearth of dancing that is beautiful and rich in its own right, but the reason for this is obvious: dance is being used to boost the illusions of speed, danger, aggressive energy we seem to crave. If these musicals, being popular entertainment, are accurate barometers of public taste, the implication is that not only do we not want to think, we want to be perpetually stunned. When a critic can enthusiastically compare the dancers in "Pippin" to tracer bullets, when even "A Chorus Line" has to fight for its integrity against metallic overmiking and performances screwed up to a desperate pitch of intensity, I begin to worry that this business of momentum and propulsive force can easily get out of hand—like a sleek car that tempts its owner to recklessness and provides neither a means to a destination nor a vivid view of the landscape, but only noise and speed and shiny surfaces.

I have, with considerable glee, restored my original title and the word "horny," which the Times *editors objected to. I remember screaming into a pay phone that "perpetually sexually aroused" (their alternative) was an abomination—in terms of euphemy as well as rhythm.*

The Hybrid: Very Showy, Will Root in any Soil

Dance Calendar, May 1975, Vol. 1, No. 5

A while back—I think it was during the late fifties—people started talking about an eventual "marriage" of ballet and modern dance (the kind that used to be written with a capital "m" and a capital "d"). I forget just why it was supposed to be a good idea.

It never happened. At least, it never happened in the way we envisioned it. Balletmakers like George Balanchine or Frederick Ashton or Jerome Robbins have kept right on making ballets—concentrating on pushing deeper into the possibilities inherent in the classical vocabulary and making their concessions to contemporary life through an increase in speed and drive and complexity or by subtly altering the ways dancers on stage treat each other. And what is commonly called "modern dance" has continued to produce rebels who shake things up—producing works that look no more like modern dance in the great Graham-Humphrey-Limón tradition than they do like ballets.

But a cross-pollination did occur, and it produced a hybrid style that, typically, is showy, bright-colored, and intricately convoluted. It's my theory that the development of this style—modern ballet? balleto-modern dance?—has been abetted by studio-hopping dancers. These days, many dancers train in all styles; they're ready for anything and committed to nothing. Their high extensions and lithe, powerful bodies have inspired ballet choreographers like Gerald Arpino to create "modern" works and choreographers with backgrounds in modern dance (as venerated as Alvin Ailey, as up-and-coming as Kathryn Posin) to experiment with the kind of virtuosic display that modern dance has traditionally shunned. And today, there are quite a few choreographers whose works seem at home in the repertories of either ballet companies or contemporary dance companies: Lar Lubovitch, John Butler, Glen Tetley. Tetley, one of the most gifted and influential of balleto-modern choreographers, is now the artistic director of the Stuttgart Ballet (due to visit New York at the end of May), and, incidentally, he may have been one of the first of the new breed of versatile dancers. During the fifties he performed with the companies of Martha Graham, John Butler, *and* Robert Joffrey. (I remember the shock of his beautifully arched feet in the days when male modern dancers tended to have that rough-hewn, "I-am-a-man-who-happened-to-learn-to-dance" look.)

The dances created by those choreographers who blend ballet and modern dance techniques don't, of course, look all the same; but the hybrids do have a lot in common. Most of them contain generous saltings of ballet steps like pirouettes and arabesques, but don't project the long-lined clarity, the precision, the essential lightness of ballet. In fact, almost all of them tend to emphasize strength (not simply as a necessary concommitant of the dancers' technique, but as a carefully fostered illusion). This strength isn't the vigorous, direct, spare strength of early modern dance, but a kind of voluptuous forcefulness, a pressurized, high-protein muscularity. Deep weighted pliés, rippling arms, contracting and expanding torsos, frequent falls to the floor: these are just some of the modern dance "discoveries"—so suitable for dealing with 20th century angst—which have been helpful in beefing up the repertories of ballet companies here and abroad.

Modern ballet appears to have appropriated the gloomy, soul-searching subject matter that was once considered the exclusive province of modern dance. And the guilt. I'm constantly being surprised by the conservative attitude with which many balleto-modern choreographers approach the matter of sex. Which they approach often, and closely. They're not inhibited about the use of graphic positions, but the grim tone of the exquisitely sculpted couplings, the guilt and anguish that so often precede and follow them might be the products of a remorselessly puritanical consciousness. In John Butler's ballets, sex is often a stylized combat; with deadly accuracy, the woman wraps her legs around her partner, and the two of them fall to the floor and roll over and over. The pace is brisk and the tone almost gruff. The savage rite that Brian Mac-Donald concocted in "Time Out of Mind" is a nasty business for the participants—none of your Gleeful Primitive stuff. The baleful stares that Béjart dancers sometimes project toward each other pre- and post-coitum link sex to a painful operation.

There's undoubtedly something cathartic about stages full of beautiful, limber, contorted bodies dancing out our (?) guilts, but I think the catharsis arises more from the movement style than from the somber subject matter. The choreographers deal so drastically with the dancers' bodies—stretching them to their limits, but never allowing them to snap or flip away; twining them around each other in astonishing postures; making them press and thrust and push slowly through dancing, as if the atmosphere on this planet were getting thick from all our misdeeds. Yet the ugliness is seldom really ugly. Bad guys are sexy and menacing; they melt into handsome positions whatever their moral persuasion. They don't look weak or twisted or truly demented like, say, the Eldress in Doris Humphrey's "With My Red Fires" or Medea in Martha Graham's "Cave of the Heart." And good men and women move like Olympic gymnasts. Happiness doesn't make them dance in a carefree way; it only makes them more athletic.

The style shows to best advantage in pieces like Tetley's "Mythical Hunters" or "Embrace Tiger and Return to Mountain," which seem to depict a world of alienated and priestly acrobats. The worst examples of the genre usually occur when portentous drama confronts ballet's traditionally easy-going approach to virtuosity: a girl who's just been raped and is about to be stabbed executes a masterful—if pleading—triple pirouette before succumbing. The problem, I think, is that balleto-modern— however lofty the ideas, however distinguished many of the choreoographers creating in this vein—is potentially an art of spectacle. Because it's so bold and squashy and vigorous and melodramatic, it can easily grab a popular audience in the gut. It can also, inadvertently perhaps, pander to an audience's response to stunts and to surface beauty ("What an extension!" "Did you see that jump?" "Does he have anything on?" "How can she stay up there?"), and in so doing draw attention to the materials of dance, rather than to dance itself.

Modern Dance: Pioneers and the Second Generation

Visionaries and Visions

The Village Voice, November 30, 1972

Alvin Ailey has decided to do his bit for history: he's trying to have certain important works from the recent past mounted for his company. This "Roots of the American Dance" program has begun with a staging of Ted Shawn's "Kinetic Molpai." What a dance. It's grandiose, smugly chauvinistic, and at the same time strong, plain, and cleanly made. As my husband said, it makes you want to bravo and boo at the same time.

Shawn made "Kinetic Molpai" at Jacob's Pillow in 1935 for his famous men's company. It racked up 500 performances on the road, although in this Ailey restaging (by Barton Mumaw) the work is getting its first New York performance. I saw it in the early '60s when Shawn revived it at the Pillow with a hastily assembled, but all-star cast (Norman Walker did Shawn's role).

According to the program, the themes of the dance are Strife, Oppositions, Solvent, Dynamic Contrasts, Resilience, Successions, Folding and Unfolding, Dirge, Limbo, Surge, and Apotheosis. A neat blend of manly emotions and dance problems. "Kinetic Molpai" as a whole is a pictorialization of masculine energy. The nine bare-chested dancers thrust their heels forward into big purposeful strides; they clench their fists, assume heroic, broadbased stances. Everything they do is immensely emphatic and deliberately-paced. The space patterns—circles, squares, parallel lines, diagonals—reinforce the feeling of joy in a Spartan, well-regulated life. In more negative moments, the dancers sag utterly —dumping their weight on the earth, bowing their backs under mighty burdens. In one important moment, they create a vast canonic wave of falls and rises. You leave "Kinetic Molpai" remembering the plumb line of the erect body, a few romantic curvings away from that line, and the hasty, resolute way the men return to upright postures after their moments of near-prone despair.

Shawn was a great haver-and-eater-of-cake. For most of "Kinetic Molpai," he wanted to show what he thought a real American man dancing ought to look like: strong, assertive, brave, forward-looking, kinda plain, able to flourish under discipline. The sort of guy who obeys orders unquestioningly when he must, but who shows initiative and daring when given a chance. And then, somehow, Shawn could not resist adding: and we American Modern Dancers, we Real Men Dancing, can beat you ballet boys at your own game any time we want to. So in the

Apotheosis, the clenched fists flutter open, and the men take off into some basic, aerial ballet combinations in waltz-time. The leader whips off a string of fouettés stage center. Even though a few of the men solo in big, forceful leaping passages, the feeling is still—compared with the preceding parts of "Molpai"—radiantly effete. Having proved their virility by a lot of somber posturing, the men can now show the audience that dancing is not for sissies. It was a fine and necessary message during the '30s.

And the dance is very enjoyable. The Ailey dancers (Dudley Williams, Kelvin Rotardier, Hector Mercado, Clover Mathis, Kenneth Pearl, Michihiko Oka, Masasumi Chaya, Dennis Plunkett, with John Parks as the leader) are not yet quite tidy enough doing it, but they look splendid, and they are, so far, resisting the temptation to pander to those in the audience who see the dance mostly as Camp.

What makes you want to laugh is not so much the choreography or the ideas behind the dance, but the relationship of the movement to its accompaniment. Jess Meeker's piano score (played by the composer and Mary Campbell) was designed to support and underline not only every mood but every gesture. It reminds you of the kind of clueing-in that piano music for silent movies was supposed to do. This use of music was part of the aesthetic of early Modern Dance, and you have to appreciate that fact even though you laugh at the kitsch of a downward-plunging scale to accompany a fall and a heroic major triad that jerks the faller to his feet again.

Monumental Martha

The New York Times, April 29, 1973

As a choreographer, Martha Graham is also a brilliant archeologist. Or is it psychologist? At any rate, during her long career, she has been adept at exposing famous old scars of the Western world and making them bleed significantly.

Paradoxically, although we consider her one of the creators of "American Modern Dance," she has made comparatively few dances with specifically American subject matter or themes; and her extraordinary movement vocabulary developed, it seems to me, not only from her own motor impulses, but from shrewd borrowings from the dance styles of other, more ancient cultures. Her work provides an object lesson in the uses of the past, for her style has never looked eclectic, has never looked anything but authentic and wildly original.

This isn't the serious article that ought to be written on the evolution of Graham's style. I think I'm in the business of throwing out teasers. Martha Graham began to work with Ruth St. Denis and Ted Shawn in 1916 and stayed with the Denishawn Company until 1923. (In 1919 she got her first big part—as the fierce heroine of Shawn's Aztec ballet, "Xochitl.") Seven years of Denishawn. The influence had to be profound; Graham utilized it profoundly.

St. Denis and Shawn were interested in exotic genre pieces—evocations of various oriental, archaic and primitive styles, or what they imagined these styles to be. (In spite of their earnest research, I suspect that they viewed even the American Indian exotically or, at any rate, romantically.) Many of Graham's own early dances—which she has since denounced in print—seem to have been little antique studies. But as early as the late twenties, she began her important process of exploration, assimilation and transformation.

For one series of works, among which is the 1931 masterpiece, "Primitive Mysteries," she created a "primitive" style based in part on the straight, narrow look of American Indian dancing. This early Graham style had the purity of an earth-sky rite, with its rooted look, pounding feet, stiffly vertical posture, arms that branched occasionally into angular gestures. Austere, hopeful, unambiguous dancing that reflected her ruthless asceticism and her desire to purge dance of all trivialities of movement. Graham has returned occasionally to elements of this style—especially for male figures like the Christ in "El Penitente," the Creature of Fear in "Errand into the Maze," the Revivalist in "Appalachian Spring." Among other things, it conveniently turns men into living phallic pillars.

Graham also utilized—beginning I'm not sure when—features of the so-called "archaic" style derived from Egyptian friezes. Perhaps she liked this style originally for the simple strength of its designs. But, as performed by a living human body, the artificial stance—feet walking in one direction while the upper body twists open against that base—can easily become, and eventually did for Graham, a metaphor for a kind of ardent ambivalence. She kept the twist, increased it, bent the body in several places, tipped it slightly off center, until in her famous fall sequences, she arrived at a position in which the arms opened in one direction, while the knees remained pressed together, hips averted from the focus of the reaching arms. An agonized and somehow reticent posture and one ideally suited for the dire predicaments of those Greek heroines she dealt with from the late forties on, when she began to become the unhappy high priestess of our collective unconscious.

Elements of various Far Eastern styles have also enriched Graham's vocabulary, but these, too, she restructured. Frantic, beating arm gestures or a bowed head made decorative Cambodian knee-walks look anything but decorative. She added a twist to a flex-footed attitude (also

Cambodian or Siamese), so that her head could look backward—away from where her feet were going. A position reminiscent of Lord Shiva drawing his bow (Indian Bharata Natyam) looks entirely different when the dancer's spine pulls away from the direction of the gesture. Tiny, smooth Japanese steps; arm gestures like oppositely curving half moons; hands bent stiffly at the knuckle: Graham pressed all these oriental movements and poses into violence and ended up with something startlingly expressive of all of our illustrious Western dilemmas, like the polarity of spirit and flesh.

Just as some Eastern styles do, Graham made us aware of the shape of the dancing body in still positions, but she linked those poses together not with flowing transitional steps, but with tense little runs, or by a process which involved unmaking the pose for a second and then abruptly reforming it one step further on in space. Although the long, breathing stillnesses that punctuate Graham dancing are very Eastern, little else about the dynamics of her style relates to the controlled fluidity of much oriental dancing. Graham, until very recently anyhow, wanted her movement performed with tremendous tension. One set of muscles inhibited or restricted another. In many of her important works of the forties and fifties, you felt the dancing shuddering along in huge jerks, propelled by the violently contracting and expanding bodies. When I first saw Graham in 1955, I was stunned by the whiplash of her spine; by the way, as Medea in "Cave of the Heart," she writhed sideways on her knees—simultaneously devouring and vomiting a length of red yarn; by the elegantly neurotic quivers that went through her Emily Brontë in "Deaths and Entrances." What she did wasn't like any dancing that I knew; it was more like a body language consisting solely of epithets.

Conventions of Eastern theater have merged with gleanings from Jung, Einstein and cinema in Graham's art. In the course of one dance sequence, characters can jump back and forth in time—acting, meditating on the results of that action, expressing their feelings in relation to it. They can be both narrators and protagonists. Two people can portray one or one portray two. Everyone can be her own grandma. In "Seraphic Dialogue," three aspects of Joan of Arc wait, immobile as decor, for an agonized fourth Joan-who-remembers to call them to life. Symbolic props not only create devastating images—think of the vast red cloak in "Clytemnestra" which spreads like blood over everything—but also free Graham from the anathema (to her) of impressionism. In "Dark Meadow," for example, a little branch pops out from a pillar, and we know it's spring and don't need anyone being a flower, or even smelling the air. The dancers can get on with the business of peopling that spring.

Recent Graham works have often approached a kind of exoticism, almost as if the style were reflecting a morbid nostalgia for Graham's own lost dance-power, or else as if the physical weakness that comes with age had imparted a flabbiness to her dances that she was too overwrought to notice. I don't know how else to explain the voluptuous profusion of movement, the beautiful, limber, half-naked dancers sinking into the movement phrases as into a warm bath, the absence of the old percussive force. Sometimes things looked pretty, dreamlike, absentminded; sometimes wilfully decadent. And she herself remained on stage at the heart of many of her compositions, portraying any number of unhappy ladies remembering their flaming pasts. The works had to be shaped around this almost immobile central figure, whose brave attitudes had no muscle power behind them, who seemed driven by a blaze of nerves.

Now in her 70's, Martha Graham has finally retired as a dancer. She will not dance in her two-week season which starts Tuesday at the Alvin. But other dancers have taken her roles successfully before and will again. (Mary Hinkson and Pearl Lang will alternate in the title role in the revival of "Clytemnestra.") Let's hope, selfishly, that she reconstructs some of her great works for us. Perhaps too, through the act of retiring as a dancer, of reaffirming herself as a choreographer, she can again make works for the company that will have the vitality of "Diversion of Angels" or "Canticle for Innocent Comedians."

I hope she outlasts her imitators.

Goodbye Martha. And welcome back.

This article is really style analysis disguised as a pre-season public-prodder. I had wanted to call it "Martha Graham and the Mysterious East."

Two Journeys from Darkness

The Village Voice, November 7, 1968

New York's first large-scale, wide-angle lens modern dance festival has begun at the Brooklyn Academy. It began, quite properly, with Martha Graham. For the occasion, Miss Graham revived "Errand into the Maze" (1947) and "Dark Meadow" (1946).

In both dances, Graham's use of myth and mysteries seem more deliberately metaphorical than in works like "Cave of the Heart" and "Night Journey," which were created around the same time. There is something potently non-specific about both "Errand" and "Dark Meadow," especially the latter. They are drenched in meaning of an almost prelogical sort; the spectator can shift contexts and landscapes as he likes. In both dances, a female protagonist seeks identity, an artist explores the dark sources of creativity. In "Errand," she is more her own mistress; in "Dark Meadow," the cyclic ritual unwinds her on its inexorable cord.

"Errand into the Maze" has some of the trappings of the minotaur legend, but it's best not to get too involved with thinking about Theseus and Ariadne. A woman possessed by nameless terror prepares to confront it. She follows a snaking rope path, passes through a horned portal, lashes herself inside. Until she has harrowed her particular hell, she will not allow herself to come out. The bull-monster that lies in wait for her is a strange adversary. For one thing, his arms are bent up over a stick laid across his shoulders; he is strong, but he must move his whole torso in order to reach anything with his hands. He is compelling—sternly erotic—and dominates her easily. Perhaps this, in the end, is what is not to be borne. She kills him, unlashes the doorway and leans against it—half in, half out, but looking outward again.

It is interesting to observe the shape that performances give to a dance. A long time ago at Jacob's Pillow, I saw Helen McGehee have her first go at the woman in "Errand" (originally, of course, done by Graham herself). McGehee was very pure in it, as I remember, very much the chosen maiden on a sacred mission. Her fear was taut as a bow-string. She performed it this season also, with Clive Thompson as a partner, and I'm sorry I missed it. Instead, I saw Matt Turney and Dan Wagoner, and I'm also glad I didn't miss that. Turney is a soft, remote, but extremely feminine dancer. The mission seemed almost beyond her; her fear the sort that turns one's insides to jelly. She emphasized the desperation, the increasing exhaustion. Dan Wagoner makes a good bull—a lumbering, groping creature nuzzling at the woman—almost as blind as she in the darkness. Wagoner is also an oddly lovable monster, recalling Jean Marais in Cocteau's "Beauty and the Beast" or the minotaur that the Incredible String Band sing of, who bellows that he "can't sleep well because of his horns." One fancies that the woman regrets slightly having to kill so appealing a spectre. I suppose one's own fears are attractive in a way.

"Dark Meadow" is a great difficult desert of a dance. The protagonist is called "One Who Seeks," and her search is arduous and eternal. The other principal figures are "He Who Summons" and "She of the Ground." Five men and four women are "They Who Dance Together." The set, by Isamu Noguchi, suggests the herms of fertility ritual. There are other fertility trappings too—mostly handled by Matt Turney as the Earth Mother figure. It is she who turns the herms to reveal a more brightly colored side, she who brings in flowering branches to plant at the summit of one of them or makes leaves pop from the side of another, she who whips briefly through with a bowl of some red stuff (blood? pomegranate seeds?). It is also she who at the end of the dance spins in a green cloak, spreading out a vernal joy and affirmation, while the seeker continues her seeking, perpetually hungry, already at the verge of new winters. This driven woman experiences love and loss, spring and winter, life and death as if she were being dragged through them on a leash.

Again, the performances are interesting and important in terms of what they do to a dance. I found the most beautiful sections of "Dark Meadow" those that were performed by the "chorus." In the first place, into the absorbed stamping of the girls and the cleansing sensuality of the male-female parts, Graham has put some of her most beautiful and powerful choreography. It is the dancing of "They Who Dance Together" that creates the ritual and acts as its fulfillment. Matt Turney's "She of the Ground" was warm and gracious, slightly abstracted as she performed pre-ordained tasks. Beautiful Mary Hinkson (she alternates with Linda Hodes) danced the "One Who Seeks" with a hard, rapt drive. Bertram Ross as "He Who Summons" gave his part the weighty dignity of a high priest.

Basically, a dance work becomes for a spectator the particular performance that he sees. It is difficult and, for the most part, pointless to speculate about the work separated from the performance of it. In the case of "Dark Meadow," however, I have the strangest feeling that something was missing somewhere in the performance of the three principals. It was as if there was some important direction that was never given them, some vibrations between them that were never set up. Patches of puzzling aridity kept cropping up in what was a beautiful and important work. Is it my imagination? What was "Dark Meadow" in 1946? I know one thing: I've seen a picture of Martha Graham in the role of the seeker. She's not wearing a long dress, but a sort of pajama affair with one arm covered by a great sleeve. Her arms and legs are flailing, and she looks possessed. I know pictures are deceptive, but I can't help wondering . . .

Paring Down to the Quick

The Village Voice, May 9, 1974

The most astonishing thing about the wholly astonishing season of Martha Graham's company is that the vibrant and intelligent dancing makes us understand Graham's greatness all over again. In recent years, we had to try to peer into the essence of her work through a fog: most of the great dances out of the repertory; a few splendid performers miscast, undirected, and, in some cases, out of shape; Graham herself defeated by age, savagely determined to go on holding down the center of the arena.

Now, she has done what I imagine for her must be a very brave thing: she has directed the power of her ego away from her own dancing body toward the body of her work and toward the young dancers who perform them. She has finally become vain again about her choreography. Robert Powell is her new associate artistic director, but I doubt that anyone but Graham herself could have clarified the motives behind the action or the shapes of the movement and made the dances as lucid as they now appear.

For instance, we watch Janet Eilber as the Chorus in "Cave of the Heart" and see that she is often shrieking, sobbing, attempting to stop the murderous course of Medea's jealousy. Was all that always there in the dance? Remember Matt Turney—who was lovely, but vague—drifting around looking upset? When Ross Parkes plays Oedipus in "Night Journey," he emphasizes the childish arrogance that Graham planted in the role. When he knots an ingeniously designed cape about his body in a variety of ways, but is always able to thrust his fist through some hole you didn't know was there, the force of his gestures is relentlessly phallic as well as kingly. You can understand why Jocasta sits there transfixed with fear and desire, and you say to yourself—and anyone else who'll listen—so *that's* what that scene was about. In "Seraphic Dialogue," David Hatch Walker, as St. Michael, is a strong, fervent force that shapes the action. When "Deaths and Entrances" was revived briefly five years ago, without Graham's aid, Mary Hinkson gave an extraordinary performance in the central role of Emily Brontë; the other sisters seemed barely visible. But now Janet Eilber as the older sister (Charlotte, I guess —Graham doesn't want the Brontë analogy carried too far) and Diane Gray as the younger make you notice that they, too, are desperately ambitious and frustrated women. Eilber does a phrase across the back of the stage—spinning, curling her body in, and then slashing it out into a violent horizontal plane (leg kicking out in front of her, body pulled back); and Gray turns ceaselessly back and forth, wrapping her arms around her body, averting her head from everything.

Traditionally, Graham dancers have learned new roles from those who once performed them or from work films. (For this Mark Hellinger season, former company members Ethel Winter, Patricia Birch, Linda Hodes, and Carol Fried helped remember and teach.) I often thought that this was the reason for the lack of communication between performers: their minds were trapped inside their own bodies trying to reproduce the correct positions. They looked to be dancing in a passionate trance. Even as recently as last season—at the "new" company's debut—William Carter was one of the few who appeared to be interested in the other characters on stage with him. This season, however, all the dancers look more intelligently focused; this makes the intensity of Graham's style terrifying or beautiful, rather than self-indulgent.

Takako Asakawa made Medea in "Cave of the Heart" both terrifying *and* beautiful. The rapid, minute quivering of her rigid body when she first becomes envenomed by her own jealousy is almost unbearable in its unabashed violence. Yet, the core of this production is more than virtuosic dancing by Asakawa. It is the way she watches the lovely little princess and her own braggart husband, Jason (when Graham's women are nastiest, the men often look as if they deserve what they get), and the way they watch each other. Yuriko Kimura, splendid this season in slightly softer, more questioning roles in the repertory, danced "Errand into the Maze" as if she never stopped sensing the dark, clumsy brute of a Minotaur behind her. Ross Parkes, whose performing has often struck me as slightly self-absorbed, has acquired a fine new liveliness by directing his attention toward the other dancers. So has the indisputably beautiful Pearl Lang, who often disappoints me by scattering her concentration onto slipped shoulder straps, loose boards, and God knows what. Lang's Jocasta in "Night Journey" is pale, ripe, foredoomed and very moving, although she occasionally stalls the flow of the movement at worrisome transitions. But in one particular performance of "Letter to the World," she danced with deeper radiance than I've ever seen her give. The role of Emily Dickinson suits her: no one can produce so vividly the illusion of maidenly charm, of virtue with a trace of impudence.

Another interesting thing about this season is that it offered works from several different periods of Graham's choreographic career—from "El Penitente" and "Letter to the World" (both made in 1940) to the just completed "Holy Jungle." In Graham works of the '40s, when she was a dancer of power, the movement is amazing—full of odd tensions and stresses, rich in dynamic shading. The dancing that goes with the leading roles—especially those which she herself used to perform—is mysteriously, compellingly private; it seems dragged from the characters by the pressure of events and other characters. A dancer could study at the Martha Graham School for years, I'll bet, and never be taught certain of the gestures from "Deaths and Entrances" or "Letter to the World." The phrasing of these middle period dances, even in the ceremonious scenes, seem quicker and more intense than that of later dances like, say, "Clytemnestra" (1958). The passions in "Clytemnestra" are there, all right, but they're contained by ritual; they parade before you, they don't burst out and scald you the way they do in "Cave of the Heart." In her wittily divagating speech on the opening night program (a cleverly designed lecture demonstration and sampling of Great Graham Moments), Graham remarked that too much had been said and written about her theory of contraction and release; it was, she said, a simple matter of exhaling and inhaling. All I can say is, you could kill yourself breathing like that. In both "Cave of the Heart" and "Errand into the Maze," the heroines stand there, contracting and releasing their rib cages so fiercely and so rapidly that you think their bodies have been taken over by a shuddering convulsive enough to be a fit.

The dances Graham made during the '60s tend to be slower and rounder. The male characters lose most of their phallic stiffness; their percussiveness turns into a strong, slow stretching and flexing. Curves blossom where there were once only angles. All the dancers indulge themselves in the movement; it looks as if it feels good. "Circe" (1963) offers a perfect theme on which to hang this kind of dancing, and the best thing about the piece is the sinuously evil movements of the men Circe has turned into animals (Mario Delamo, Dan Maloney, David Chase, and Eric Newton do these parts wonderfully; Maloney's performance is the best I've ever seen him give). The piece is unsatisfying because Ulysses and his Helmsman are almost as sinuous as the men-animals and the Enchantress. At times it's hard to tell when the two heroes who are trying so hard to row home are caught by Circe's spells and when they're not. And Circe herself, a role Graham created for Mary Hinkson, not for herself, is not very powerful, just a bewitching and lusty little creature, flashing her hips around and caressing everything in sight. The dance seems made to have a powerful figure at its center, but no one is there. Graham was obviously unwilling to abdicate in 1963.

Much of the movement in Graham's later dances has a patented look. Perhaps because she was unable to draw new movement from her own body, she used a vocabulary that she had built up. Whatever the other dancers may have contributed, it deferred to established "Graham technique" (the animals in "Circe" are an exception). Her dances of the late '50s and early '60s have an impersonal look—although they can thrill you with their impressive ritual drama. But her earlier pieces can make you cry because, although you've never in your life seen movement like that, you feel that something in your blood and your bones performs at times inside you with the same reckless force.

The very latest Graham dances are soft, opulent parades of dream images. Everything is diffuse; even when the stage seethes with motion, nothing appears very active or focused. The movement unwinds as evenly as thread from a spool; it's hard to find any sharp edges. "Chronique" (the new version of last year's "Mendicants of Evening") and "Holy Jungle" remind me of the last paintings of Renoir and Degas, in which everything disappears in a blaze of color. The meditative "Chronique," with its celebrations of farewells and new beginnings, its impersonal parades of "humanity" and personal encounters of lovers, has been strengthened, although not really clarified, by structural changes and a new score by Carlos Surinach with a lot of quiet guitar sounds. But "Holy Jungle" is cluttered with ornate symbolic props (by Dani Karavan) that range from a huge flame (or fish or banana leaf) made out of silver wire to an absurd little umbrella of what look like ping-pong balls (decidedly tacky as forbidden fruit). Graham says she was inspired by some of Hieronymous Bosch's fantasies of visions and temptations, but in this great tangle of dancers, it's hard to tell who's tempting whom. Peter Sparling plays the seeker, the pilgrim, and he's taunted by Diane Gray (mysteriously billed as Follower), a sex kitten in black harem pants. There's a Lady of the Labyrinth (Janet Eilber) and men who enjoy her favors. Sparling pursues a dream bride (Judith Hogan) back to Eden. Lucifer is there in red (William Carter), and so is a heroic angel (David Hatch Walker). The most interesting character is called the Hell Eve, and she's a huge woman (Armgard Von Bardeleben) with a mirthless laugh and a big skirt from under which pop mean little demons of women to add to the perils of pilgrimages. The stage seems full of people most of the time, but you seldom see clear intentions or know when an action has been completed. Nothing, and no one, rests. In a way, the stage *is* like a big Bosch painting, alive and wiggling, but not in a purposeful way.

Another fine thing about this Graham season was all the multiple casting of roles. I wanted to go every night; some people did. Even those dancers not quite ready for the roles they played revealed some new angle of the choreography you hadn't noticed before. I didn't get to see enough of David Hatch Walker or Diane Gray or Mario Delamo or Peggy Lyman. (What puzzles me is, with all these performers working so beautifully to make these dances communicate, why does Graham still cast the same man as Paris-Hades-dead Agamemnon in "Clytemnestra"? As if role were the important thing and not who played it?) Some of the dancers force things a bit; many of them have developed a mouth mannerism that makes them look as they were angrily snapping up flies out of the air. Never mind; what they and Graham have accomplished could be likened to what a restorer does to a painting. The dust has gone, and the shapes and colors glow again.

Two Who Fought a Good Fight

The New York Times, June 11, 1972

"Wow," said a young choreographer drifting back into the Juilliard Theater, "she really knew her stuff!" "She" was the late Doris Humphrey; we were watching Juilliard students perform revivals of four Humphrey works, "The Shakers" (1931), "Day on Earth" (1947), "Lament for Ignacio Sanchez Mejías" (1946), and "Passacaglia and Fugue in C Minor" (1938). Also within the past few weeks, the company of Humphrey's former partner, Charles Weidman, has presented part of her masterwork, "New Dance," as well as some of his own important dances. This summer, the American Dance Festival at New London, Connecticut, will offer more Humphrey-Weidman revivals.

Choreographers of the new generation are picking their way through another dance rebellion—collecting those shards of past conventions which they consider still useful, throwing out everything else with the requisite blithe arrogance of revolutionaries. Their tousled choreography would probably appall Humphrey, but it's easy to understand why some of them admire her work—specifically that done during the thirties and earlier.

The same crowd of youngish artists had also flipped over the 1965 revival of Martha Graham's "Primitive Mysteries" (1931), and it was a crowd one seldom saw lining up to buy tickets for her latest dances. Humphrey's "Water Study" (1928), with its obstinate simplicity, natural unaccompanied rhythms, and flowing movement based on the cresting and breaking of ocean waves, seems more contemporary than the more complicated works that she made later for José Limón's company and Juilliard Dance Theatre.

The content of some of these early dances is not as exciting now as it must have been when the dances were first performed. During the thirties, Humphrey and Weidman, like many other artists, developed huge social consciences. Humphrey was often didactic, even priggish, about what was good for mankind, but her stylishness, her theatricality got her message across with sweet strength to what was in those days a message-hungry audience. Through its many stylistic transformations, her theme remained the perfectability of mankind through the pursuit of noble ambitions. She and Weidman also pointed accusing or mocking fingers at bigotry, prejudice, and the pursuit of such unworthy goals as money, power, position. I'm thinking of her "With My Red Fires," "Theatre Piece," "Life of the Bee"; his "Atavisms," "Traditions." Over and over: down with the old and corrupt, up with the new and idealistic. It was a stirring and appropriate exhortation.

In the new Humphrey-Weidman dance tradition, movement reflected character and theme in a very graphic way, e.g., bigoted people were given rigid repeating patterns and often used their limbs stiffly. The heroic principal couple in "New Dance" lead the group in flying wedges and flowing processions toward the bright future. Today, we can look at "New Dance" as a serene and powerful suite of dances for men and women—as many members of the audience at the time may have, too. But if we read Margaret Lloyd's analysis of it in the "Borzoi Book of Modern Dance," we learn that its formal patterns represented two leaders demonstrating the way to a Utopian society, gradually drawing the group with them, and then retreating into the democracy they had spawned, in order to show that they didn't aim to be dictators.

But it's not the heavy ideas that make me admire these early dances of Humphrey and Weidman. It's not even the impressive craft or the theatrical impact, it's the wonderfully uncompromising nature of their "new" movement vocabulary. I marvel at how anyone could have contrived to make whole dances in which *nothing* looked anything like ballet. Sometimes deliberate avoidance was necessary. When the dancers curved their arms overhead, they took care to face the palms of their hands frontward or to clasp their fingers so that no one looking at them would think they were executing ballet's 5th port de bras. When they held their arms out to the side, they spread their fingers as if to grab the brave new world. They pointed the arches of their feet, but let the toes relax and flip upward. When they kicked their legs to the front, they leaned their bodies back as a counterweight, and vice versa.

Unlike ballet dancers, they were interested in making effort a visible and dramatic element, in yielding to the tug of gravity. Following Humphrey's famous "fall and recovery" theory of motion, dancers could perform almost any movement in a precarious state of balance. I've never seen anything quite like this constantly leaning, suspending, falling style. The performers seem to be grasping for balance with an indrawing breath, even as their bodies are arching toward the floor. And in lyrical dances like "Passacaglia," the thrusting, softly dangerous dancing is contained by the stately architectural patterns proper to an orderly society. Humphrey must have known everything that could be done in—and expressed by—a line, a circle, a triangle, a square of dancers; and by using a set of large platforms, she was able to extend these patterns into vertical space.

Edwin Denby has written that the modern dancers of the thirties made dances that were like "a series of outcries." Every gesture had an emphatic thrust to it. Perhaps this was because, in the fierceness of their creation, they wanted no movement that wasn't vital to the composition. Later, they, and especially their followers, conceded somewhat to ballet and achieved a more fluid phrase shape by the addition of those unimportant-looking linking steps that enable ballet dancers to swoop pleasingly to the next big effect. They lost their infatuation with the ground and even began to work with lifts, which hitherto had been used sparingly—all but unthinkable in a society in which man and woman were to be equal partners. (Graham's art was sexier than Humphrey's right from the start.)

The pioneering work of Humphrey and Weidman exerted strong influence and later blended into that hectically acrobatic balletomodern style in which spectacle and weighty ideas fight for preeminence, in which a just raped woman can whip off a beautifully centered triple pirouette (albeit with a worried expression), or a newly born human being has everything to learn about life, but nothing to learn about high kicks. And so, today dance is into an interesting, often wrong-headed new revolution, in the midst of which some of the early dances of Doris Humphrey and Charles Weidman have a desirable aura of integrity. Noble strangers who fought a good fight.

To Charles: Farewell

The Village Voice, August 18, 1975

Looking back through the crazy-quilt dance calendars I make for myself, I see scribbled on the margins of most of them: "Charles: every Sunday, 7:30." In my hand I have a flyer announcing performances by Charles Weidman and his Theatre Dance Company on July 20 and July 27. But Charles, who had always liked surprises in dance, surprised us one more time, by dying—the day after his performance on July 14, Sunday evening, at 7:30.

Charles loved to make people laugh. I felt apologetic about the tears. But I suspect that many of us who wept for him did so, in a sense, because we had taken it for granted that he would always be around—gabbling his charming and almost unintelligible spoken program notes to audiences sweating in his tiny (seating maybe 20?) Expression of Two Arts Theatre; performing his wonderful kinetic pantomimes; occasionally dancing, his 73-year-old feet in black ballet slippers, looking light and small and stiff—as if they had regressed to some touching second childhood of footdom.

Sometimes he would telephone me. "Hello," he would say, in a cheerful, newsy voice, "This is Charles." (And, of course, no modern dance person would need to answer, "Charles who?") And he would tell me what he and his loyal young company were going to do next—a revival of one of his important dances, or maybe a new work. And we'd chat for a while, my ear straining to extract historical import from what always sounded like a string of non sequiturs, but was undoubtedly a genuine stream of consciousness: "And Doris (Humphrey) always said she thought it was my best work . . . but that was before the Lewisohn Stadium thing . . . and Katy (Manning? Litz? Don't try to stop him now.) I remember, tripped over her, uh, dress, you know those jersey dresses had to be just the right length, or else. . . . Miss Ruth really knew how to manage drapery. Kids these days don't take the time to figure out that kind of thing. Anyway . . . my kids are dancing beautifully, I think, and I hope you'll come because I think you'd be interested. Everything all right with you?"

Actually, I've been crying—as inconspicuously as possible—for

82

Charles ever since I first saw him. I missed the heyday of the Humphrey-Weidman company when Charles was young and noble-looking, his supposedly lean and incisive style a splendid foil to Doris's lyrical one. When I met him in the mid-'50s, he was embattled and not admitting it. A little earlier, he had hit bottom financially, artistically, and spiritually. During the late '40s, Doris's crippling arthritis finally put an end to her career, and she began to function as artistic director of the José Limón Company. Without her to point out the straight-and-narrow of art, Charles gradually skidded downhill—helped by bad friends, unwise decisions, and a very large thirst for alcohol. But by 1955 or 1956, he had successfully passed through AA and was trying in the most humble way possible to keep on working in dance. On weekends in Viola Essen's studio in Carnegie Hall we performed a lecture-demonstration, his "The War Between Men and Women," some of his wonderful Thurber fables, "Flickers" (in which, as a fiercely intent Valentino in a flapping sheik headdress, he tangoed his partner right up the wall). The company, as I remember, consisted of a few old pros, some sardonic young men who had stayed loyal but weren't happy, several sweet-tempered, soft-muscled older women, and a couple of very young girls. Once Doris Humphrey came to see a performance, and he introduced her to the tiny audience (even, I think, remembering to add her last name), asked her if she would sit by the wall so she could man the one little switch that controlled all our lighting, and then took some time trying, as clearly as he could, to tell her when to turn it on and off. Someone must have been sick that night. Someone was always sick.

During the past few years, Charles patiently and unobtrusively resurrected his career, but he seemed always to be taking care to keep it small and manageable. He attracted a company of young, attractive, loyal dancers; he got out-of-town dates; his work received respectful reviews in Toronto and raves in Bergen, Norway. But in New York, the company continued to perform principally in the horribly cramped studio theatre on 29th Street. I think Charles liked it—maybe the coziness reminded him of the good old pioneering days, maybe he never wanted to be in debt again. I wept then for the pathos and dignity of his performing, for his simple perseverence, and for the good-hearted dancers who also switched the lights and the tape recorder on and off, sewed the costumes, and tried not to wince when they crashed into each other while endeavoring to sail around the small room.

Charles made such a muddle of his career that it's hard to say how he'll be remembered. Certainly as an innovative dance comedian, Margaret Lloyd wrote of him in the late '40s, "As dancer and choreographer he was always more limited than Doris. But what he did do he did without waste, with clear-cut, pointed immediacy. He delighted in incongruities, in fragmentary, mercurial movement, ringing abrupt changes of tempo, rhythm, and dynamics in the broken pieces he let the spectator put together as he would. He jested in stroke and curlicue, lampooning right and left with his pencil-slim body, making jokes with his fingers and witty observations with his bare toes." He could tell a story well in dance, but he also found ways to sever pantomime from its usual story-telling function and present literal gestures for their immediate impact. In the lovely, simply patterned, spinning and falling "Brahms Waltzes" that he choreographed during the '60s in honor of Doris Humphrey ("made out of the kind of movement she loved to do and did so beautifully"), there is one section in which the dancers walk around and peer at the ground, at each other, into the distance. Has one of them lost a contact lens? Have they lost their place in the music? Their angst? Who knows, but the strangeness, the humor, the jarringness of the moment is typical of Weidman.

Charles was a very good choreographer, as far as I can tell. I wish I'd seen his autobiographical dances, "Daddy Was a Fireman" and "On My Mother's Side;" I wish I'd seen some of the Broadway shows that he so enjoyed choreographing (to Doris's horror). And I think that a lot more of Charles went into so-called Humphrey-Weidman technique and into some of Doris's dances than we realize. They often collaborated on works. He composed the men's section in "New Dance, " the movement themes for some of his solos in other dances of hers. It was on his body that many of the vigorous, angular positions, the thrusting gestures we associate with American modern dance of the '30s were built. Together Humphrey and Weidman did things that perhaps neither could have accomplished alone.

I think Doris ran on brilliant brain-power, Charles on intuition. And by hard work. If he hadn't been a good worker, his gentle, humble, charming, rather foolish nature might have gotten him into even more hot water than it did. On stage, he could be profound without even trying. You had the feeling that all he had to do was think about tonight's dinner to make you see King Lear, Priam, Abe Lincoln. His face—big mobile mouth, long upper lip, cavernous cheeks, bristling eyebrows— could look magnificently proud or forlorn as easily as it could look harried or gleeful.

I'm glad that at the end of his life Charles became intrigued with his own historicity and reconstructed old works, also mounting what seems to be a creditable version of Humphrey's "New Dance." I wish he could have written a book; even his gags could teach you a lot about dance history. And I'm grateful that he died so quickly, between one performance and the next. We may be stunned, but it seems entirely appropriate that death should have come to Charles Weidman as a non sequitur.

More New London Revivals

The Village Voice, August 3, 1972

The first thing you see in José Limón's powerful dance-drama, "Emperor Jones" (1956), is a throne that looks as if it has been hacked out of a thornbush, and sitting on it, slumped forward, a figure wearing a plumed tricorne and an ancient and elaborate military jacket with gold braid and epaulets. Dark men crouch around him pointing and whispering, then slide away into the shadows. When the man on the throne raises his head, hoists himself up, you notice that he is mad. As he stalks his little domain his body leans back, away from his striding legs, with an arrogance that is also fearful. Even the ground might betray him. For Jones is a tyrant, has set himself up as the ruler of a group of credulous islanders. He splays his fingers, rakes in air, as if his craving for power had become a habit instead of an appetite.

Enter the White Man—any white man, or all of them. He's seedy even in his clean white suit and hat. Shambling, slinking behind the crazed Jones, he has no straightness about him anywhere. Even his joints are deceitful; his arms, legs, head flip out in different directions like ribbons. He looks boneless, spineless, infinitely corrupt. Jones still has some dignity, but you can see that it was white men like this one who gave him the idea that the only thing worthwhile is to control others.

The ghosts that haunt him merge with the natives who, egged on by the White Man, are hunting him down. Bare chested black men lean and spring from behind three bushy totems. Limbs, heads appear and disappear; the movement at each totem is exactly like that at the other two. Are you (and Jones) seeing six men or three incredibly agile ones? Or the same two tripled by the shadowy light? The men become the writhing cargo of a slave ship, are sold at auction by the White Man, are chain gang victims feeling his lash. Jones is among them, young and defiant.

Limón makes these scenes from the past seethe up briefly from circles of leaping, rolling bodies, and then sink back into the darkness. The men, now almost naked, form a symmetrical moving totem figure. In the red light, they look like some huge and deadly Venus flytrap, opening and closing its petals. What might be part of an ancient African initiation rite is also the murder of Jones. While the craven White Man watches insolently, Jones's body is hastily decked in jacket and hat, hoisted up, throne and all. A figure of mockery, yet seeming in death the god he had pretended to be.

Until this New London revival, the roles of Jones and the White Man had been played, and played superbly, only by Jóse Limón and Lucas

Hoving. The American Dance Festival Repertory Company has cast Clay Taliaferro and Edward DeSoto in the parts, and they are fine in a different way. Taliaferro with his tall, strong body and gentle face makes Jones very much the noble savage turned demented by a corrupt civilization. He is as arrogant, but not as insane as Limón. DeSoto projects a wonderfully sleazy, cowardly evil as the White Man; Hoving was able also to suggest a depraved elegance—a con man imitating a wealthy planter who had drunk too much rum for too long.

The revival of Doris Humphrey's "With My Red Fires" (1936) also takes up the theme of power that corrupts. The dance was conceived as the middle section of the trilogy that concluded with "New Dance." It's a mysterious and stunning work. The first part is a fertility ritual, almost phallic in the way small phalanxes of women recurrently thrust their way into the space and then retreat, and also in the driving rhythms of the movement, the near-absence of curves, and the rigidly leaning bodies. The group seems to be searching for a couple whose actual mating will express something, maybe achieve something for the community. One couple is tested briefly in the ring of watchers, but nothing comes of it. Finally two other young people are found, pushed together, and, after a fiercely joyful dance-hymn, left alone. Yet from the way their bodies curve around each other, lean together, you can tell that they are fulfilling a more private ritual of love.

Without a break, the second section, subtitled "Drama," begins. From behind a pillar the Matriarch emerges, peering into the shadows, beckoning with a lash of her long, long skirt. She's not, as you might have been led to expect, the goddess-ruler of some pre-Hellenic tribe; she's turn-of-the-century Boston and furious that *her* daughter has run off with an unsuitable man. A little window curtain flips out of the side of the pillar as if to reassure us of the domestic nature of the whole drama. She gets the girl in, weeps enough to make her cry too. How odd! The stylized way her mouth opens and her fingers cup just beneath her eyes makes her look like a Greek mask of Tragedy. She thinks it's all settled and leads the girl to lie down with her, but the young man steals in and elopes with his betrothed.

When the Matriarch awakens, notices the girl is gone, she pushes the curtain away again and strides from her pillars. This signals a curious change. Not only does the subsequent action return to being public, large-scale, outdoors, but we seem to have left Boston entirely. The Matriarch is more than an irate mother; she is the vindictive and potent ruler of a society that wouldn't dream of questioning her authority. She stalks the stage, whipping her skirt out of the way, twisting her head from side to side like a predatory bird. The harsh tango rhythm in this section of the Wallingford Riegger music makes her dancing even more macabre. She climbs the pillar and summons the mob with furious

gestures and rough, almost lewd grindings of her hips. The idea of anyone thwarting her will is driving her mad. At one point she marshals the
group into a circle, with lines of two or three or four people spoking
out from the center where she now stands. They run and crouch like
bloodhounds in brief sprints and long freezes. Her exhorting gestures
start and stop too; so does the music. It's a terrifying effect, as if of
some great force being wound up by stages. The crowd brings in the
runaway lovers, but she doesn't stay to see what happens to them.
(How can you believe she's still no more than a mother whose daughter
has done the wrong thing?) Her rage has made her come completely
apart in a fit of rigid frenzy, of mindless shaking, of primitive fury no
longer directed toward an object. She disappears, but she's given the
command. The crowd rips into the two lovers; a squad of men efficiently
tosses their limp bodies into the air, drags them to the foot of the long
steps that cross the stage horizontally, and leaves. The lovers painfully
rise and, holding each other, arch their faces and breasts hopefully up to
the sky and the morning.

Although a gradually intensifying narrative and dramatic thread
runs through "With My Red Fires," Humphrey evokes many aspects of
dictatorship, public and private, and several kinds of ritualized societies.
It is the curious, almost imperceptible way in which these layers dissolve
in and out of the texture of the work which gives it the ambiguity that
is so fascinating. And the movement and the ordering of it are marvelous. In the opening choral hymn, three and four groups of men and
women often work contrapuntally, yet everything is made clear and
strong, so that you get a sense not of disorder but of accumulating
force. The movement is full of angles—flexed feet, bodies bent at the
hips, sharp turns at wrist and elbow and knee. Executed in steadily
pulsing or pounding rhythms, it looks elemental and extraordinary at
the same time. The spareness of individual gestures is wonderful: the
Matriarch lifts a leg only twice, and it becomes an extension of her
pointing, accusatory fingers.

For "With My Red Fires," the Repertory Company was augmented
by Connecticut College dance students in order to make up the ensemble of 20. They all danced quite splendidly. Indeed, the company
is performing so well together now that it is a pity it must disband when
the summer is over. Dalienne Majors, looking at moments uncannily
like photographs of Doris Humphrey, projected a great deal of demented
strength into the Matriarch's rigid twistings and writhings. Nina Watt
with her soft fragility, her pallor, her slight and touching awkwardness
made the girl into a sacrificial lamb, and Raymond Johnson was warm
and ardent as the young man. Marc Stevens as the Herald did some
splendid leaps. Now and then, other figures emerged from the group,
too—Pamela Knisel and Ryland Jordan stretching toward each other in

the little duet, Randall Faxon jumping ecstatically at the center of a jubilant trio.

We owe the reconstruction of this Humphrey masterpiece, not only to the dancers, the college, the festival directors, and numerous granting organizations, but to the Labanotation bureau, to Christine Clark who staged it, and to Ruth Currier who acted as artistic adviser. Thank God they thought of doing it and managed to do it so well.

Allies of the Ground, Eye on the Sky

The Village Voice, November 15, 1973

I'm terribly pleased that so many important ballet companies are mounting works by some of the dead geniuses of modern dance, but my pleasure has made me all the more edgy and critical. I see that care and expense have gone into the staging; I see the dancers trying hard to capture the style; but what's missing in most cases is the specific dynamics of the dance style.

Dancers tend to think a lot about the shapes their bodies are making, probably because of the strain and skill involved. Dancers these days are very versatile about shape-making, but, in concentrating on *what* gets done, they don't always remember to think about *how* it gets done.

The reason I'm shooting my mouth off now is that I've just seen the City Center Joffrey perform José Limón's "The Moor's Pavane" and Washington's National Ballet perform Doris Humphrey's "Water Study." "The Moor's Pavane" is already in the repertory of several ballet companies; dancers who performed the four principal roles (Othello, Desdemona, Iago, Emilia) in the Limón company have been responsible for teaching and rehearsing it. This makes me wonder if, having always been *in* the dance, they understand what it's supposed to look like from the outside. Maybe they just fall into that proud-of-their-pupils attitude that excuses so much.

"The Moor's Pavane" is one of those dances that almost always comes off. If every moment of the dancing doesn't stir you, you can still be carried away by the fierce theatricality and wait for the next impressive moment. But, since all the drama of Shakespeare's "Othello" was compressed by Limón to ride on top of and weave through and eventually tear apart a formal court dance, it matters a great deal how the dancing looks.

The Joffrey's second cast consisted of Paul Sutherland as the Moor, Pamela Nearhoof as his Wife, Robert Estner as the Moor's Friend, and Starr Danias as the Friend's Wife. So, okay, Estner was sharp, thin, and conniving; and Starr Danias, proudly sensual and clever as a little fox, makes a fine Emilia, may be wonderful any moment. Pamela Nearhoof's Desdemona seemed innocent to the point of foolishness, and she looked more as if she'd been told she couldn't go to the college of her choice than that she was about to die. Paul Sutherland relied more on his face and hands to convey jealous rage and offended love than on the twist and lunge of his body, but he was burdened by a luridly red robe (and tights to match) that was short-waisted and diminished rather than accentuated the powerful-shoulder look, which was part of Limón's personal style.

On the opening night for this cast, the orchestra, conducted by Seymour Lipkin, played the Purcell music as if it were all dirge, and, of course, that must have troubled the dancers. But I think the real problem is that they're unaccustomed to giving in to the weight of their bodies as much as Limón's style requires. I remember Limón drawing himself up from a wide-legged plié into a balance on one straight leg, as if the ground held him back, or the air were thick to move through. That kind of awareness of the pull of gravity made him—and his dances—look powerful: the struggle of muscles became a metaphor for the struggle of souls. The Joffrey dancers, trained as they are to emphasize lightness and to use low positions primarily as a preparation for flying upward, have the air of treading on the surface of the movement and the music. They look intense, but insubstantial. At this point, they are also adhering slavishly to the beat of the music for dramatic gestures, rather than giving the gestures their own impetus and fitting them into the musical sequence. When Emilia gets the handkerchief away from Desdemona, she tosses it into the air and catches it several times, smoothly and right on the beat, which seems untrue to the impetuous triumph of the moment. In another sequence, Othello lunges away from Desdemona—doesn't want to see her, and Iago forces him to lunge toward her; they do this several times. Sutherland and Estner lose the harsh struggle of this, so that you can't tell exactly what the moment is all about: you see them sway forcefully from side to side with fierce expressions.

The National's "Water Study" is also on the right track, but also—maddeningly—just misses being excellent. This very early work of Doris Humphrey's (1928) is exquisitely simple. It's a brilliant and stirring lesson about dance structure and movement quality, as well as being an impressionistic study of water—the shapes it makes, and its changing energy. When the curtain goes up, 14 women, crouched in profile, fill the stage. In the silence, they breathe and heave almost imperceptibly. Then the women on one side of the stage rise to their knees, arch their bodies, and fling their arms forward. Before it is finished, their action has set the women in front of them to rising and arching too, and this motion travels across the stage. But each set of women arches lower than the previous set, and the last dancers plunge over onto their stomachs. So each body is making a wave, and all the bodies together are making a single huge wave rise up and crash over and spill onto the ground. That's just the beginning. Smoothly, always in silence, the women make patterns suggesting whirlpools, waterfalls, spouts, small rivers. The movement is sustained, giving its rhythm by the ebb and flow of the dancers' breath. The dancers of the National breathe for all they're worth, but, like the dancers of the Joffrey, they can't quite bear to be heavy, to give in to gravity and then rebound up with the intake of breath. Where they should be simply heavy, they are strong, forcing their weight to the floor so emphatically that no natural rebound is possible. They have the most trouble with running—say, from a kneeling position, across the stage, and into a lunge. The Humphrey-trained dancer, I think, would have shown you a single, long crescendo, as if the original position were a magnet whose pull gradually decreased the farther the dancer was able to get from it. (If you had to sing the equivalent of that run, you'd ascend the scale and get louder.) The dancers of the National get from place to place with chains of pattering little steps that have nothing to do with where they've been or where they're going. "Water Study" looks pretty and fluid, but its surge has been tamed. It was directed and reconstructed from Labanotation by Virginia Freeman and Barbara Katz.

Limón Pursues His Visions

The New York Times, October 8, 1972

I can remember when José Limón was the King, and we, his fervent subjects, tried to dance and to think about dance the way we thought he would have wanted us to. Not that he cared: he was occupied with his private vision of art and tired out from the hard work necessary to articulate it. When he talked to you, his eyes—solid black pits in the marvelous Indian skull—seemed fixed on a point either deep inside himself or miles behind you.

He was in those days—undoubtedly still is—crazy about Shakespeare, Bach, El Greco, Michelangelo, about art that was powerful and heavy and complex. Art that shook you up. He made his own works accordingly. In the chapter he wrote for "The Modern Dance: Seven Statements of Belief," he said, "I try to compose works that are involved with man's basic tragedy and the grandeur of his spirit."

In many of Limón's dances, he cast himself as towering, but tormented figures: Judas Iscariot, Othello, Julian the Apostate, Adam,

Emperor Jones. He plowed his way from innocence through acceptance of guilt to redemption and, quite often, death in a virile, yet brooding dance style. I remember a way he had of keeping his head lowered and slightly averted from his presumed focus; the gesture looked fastidious but at the same time suggested a bull goaded from all directions and wondering which way to charge.

I remember the Spanish line of his pulled-back arms, the bent-legged bourrée that he used so much. I remember especially the huge, slow paths his arms blazed through space; he seemed to be gathering in chunks of air or lifting himself up by pressing down against tremendous invisible resistance. Although his face and hands sometimes reached upward in the supplicating gestures suitable to the Judaeo-Christian hero, he seemed eternally locked into his own body. Every muscle strained against another. When you watched him, your eye traveled around and around the curving, circling designs he thrust himself into. It was like looking at the Michaelangelo figures Limón so admired: like them, he was massive, tense, yet appeared almost incapable of acting decisively.

I seldom remember him *doing* anything in these dramatic dances. Much of the time, he danced about how tragically impossible it was for him to follow any course of action. The dancing was turbid, magnificently thwarted, self-preoccupied.

The upper echelon of Limón's kingdom has always, of course, consisted of his company. During the mid-fifties, when I was an ardent disciple, the composition of the company influenced—and was influenced by—the kind of works he wanted to do. There was Lucas Hoving, whose light, spidery style made him an ideal antagonist for Limón: he could play saint to Limón's villain, villain to his saint with equal ease. There was Pauline Koner—vivid, tiny but powerful, fast on her feet. There was a small core of women—interesting, defiantly unglamorous, chosen perhaps for a kind of lyrical delicacy. Two of the most prominent of these, Betty Jones and Ruth Currier, for all their technical strength, retained a charming gaucheness. They always looked vulnerable—maybe because they so frequently played victims of a male lust for power. (Only Koner looked ready to fight back.)

Then there was a fairly large group of men, say six, who usually functioned as a unit in the dramatic dances, portraying disciples, soldiers, slaves, visions. There was Limón's wife, the late Pauline Lawrence, who designed the costumes and kept the books and generally held things together. Most important, there was, until her death in 1958, Doris Humphrey, who—no longer dancing herself—made works for Limón's company and acted as its artistic adviser.

Limón had started his dance life with the Humphrey-Weidman crowd. He had learned the craft of choreography from Humphrey. Invaluable lessons, because Limón at his best reveals dramatic content through structure, rather than through emoting. I feel in many Limón works a searching for equilibrium and sanity in a world—inner or outer—that is unbalanced and shifting, and the forms of many of his major works express this. (This loss of proportion is another quality that allies him with the Mannerist art of El Greco, Michelangelo, late Shakespeare.)

The small courtly world of his Othello piece, "The Moor's Pavane," is under constant threat: if one of the four dancers engaged in the carefully balanced quadrille pulls away, the whole structure may topple. Each time they separate into two couples—Iago to rouse Othello's suspicions, Emilia to cozen Desdemona—you sense the impending peril which will indeed lead to first one character, then two, falling away from the dance and from life. Because of the tight, sociable patterns, a long diagonal that the tormented Othello makes with Iago clinging crab-like to his back is alarming. You feel that they may just keep on going and never come back.

The heroine of "La Malinche," by changing allegiance from her white conquistador lover to the embattled Indian Everyman, makes the scales of power dip and rise. The struggle is between the two men, but it is her weight added to first one and then the other that structures the dance. "There Is a Time," based on the well-known catalogue of mutually exclusive opposites from "Ecclesiastes," is an idealistic hymn to balance and proportion ("A time to plant and a time to pluck up that which is planted," etc.).

Some of Limón's works stress odd viewpoints, disturbing angles. In "The Traitor," we, the audience, often see Christ through Judas's eyes, become, like Judas, an outsider wanting to get closer to the divine presence. In this dance, we're shown a world of Renaissance perspective crumbling away. The disciples hold a white tablecloth, and Christ takes his accustomed place along the side of the Last Supper table. They spin the cloth, tilt it toward us; now he's at the head of the table, and we're looking down on the scene from a balcony.

Limón has had a number of failures. He can be light in a dry, strong way, as he proved in his 1955, all-male "Scherzo," but he's not a successful funny man. He's produced some heavy-handed, botched comedies that have a naive, almost schoolboyish coarseness about them. (I'm thinking of "Comedy" or "I, Odysseus"). On occasion, he can be literal almost to the point of banality, or remorselessly didactic, as in "Legend."

Over-literalness is perhaps one of the pitfalls inherent in Limón's essentially gestural approach to choreography. Even in many of his non-dramatic dances, the movement expresses exuberance or despair or searching—not just by the way it is performed, but by the way it is designed; and all this meaningful movement can cramp into turgidity or stall the flow of dancing when it is attached to a complicated idea, as it was, for example, in his defunct "Blue Roses," based on Tennessee Williams's play, "The Glass Menagerie."

It was in 1958, when he made "Missa Brevis," that Limón began to display an intoxication with numbers. Augmenting his company with members of Juilliard Dance Theatre, he created some massive group patterns, a kind of liquid architecture in which the center is constantly dissolving and reforming—an apt formal metaphor for the elusive healing power of faith. "A Choreographic Offering," made in 1964 in memory of Doris Humphrey, is even more opulent—a baroque symphony of dance steps, more serene and balanced than earlier Limón works, in which Humphrey's breathing rhythms and tilting, arching phrases are set into huge wheeling circles, parades, spirals, criss-crossing flights.

By 1966, Limón was beginning to phase himself out of dancing, and he was also working with a new kind of company—younger dancers, many of them student of his from Juilliard. Louis Falco, Sally Stack-house, Jennifer Muller, Carla Maxwell, Laura Glenn, Daniel Lewis, Clyde Morgan, Jennifer Scanlon—people like that. For them, he made an im-mense suite, "The Winged," and it seemed a new and different kind of Limón work. Its solos, duets, trios, group sections are only loosely linked to real and imaginary types of feathered life. Freed of all plot, of all necessity to unify, Limón produced a rich, soaring flood of dancing. Only occasionally did he become tricky, or make the audience overly aware of his compositional expertise.

Two of his most recent pieces, "The Unsung" and "Dances for Isadora," continue this ripe, almost serene lyric vein. More austere than "The Winged," they are suites of solo dances—the former for men, the latter for women. The Indian chieftains in "The Unsung" dance in si-lence. We know they are victims, but they are not playing the victims for us, as they might have in earlier Limón works. They are dancing about speed or strength or watchfulness or anger. The dance doesn't show us the doom of the Indians, but rather the vitality and beauty of a group of young men dancing. And this restraint, curiously, produces a more powerful and haunting intimation of death.

The solos in "Dances for Isadora" beautifully evoke the art of Isa-dora Duncan, and the work is only slightly marred by a bit of simplified biography that comes last—as if Limón had been attempting to contrast the purity of Duncan's artistic impulse with her tragic and ramshackle life.

José Limón is in his sixties, and he doesn't dance any more. But he keeps making dances: he's made two new ones for the City Center American Dance Marathon and his company is dancing in them through Wednesday. Choreographers working today tend to be cooler and lighter than Limón. They go in for less grandeur and far less optimism. They're not too concerned with expressing goals or resolving destinies—whether formal or metaphorical. Untouched by fashions in art, Limón continues to develop along his own lines. Within the dance he now seems like a king in exile from a foreign country. But a king, nonetheless.

When I wrote this, José Limón was dying. Everyone knew it, but no one could bear to think about it. Sometimes it's good to be able to write a eulogy when the person you're writing about is still around to read it.

Calligraphy

The Village Voice, November 23, 1968

If any choreographer could be called an apostle of darkness, it is Anna Sokolow. She holds a merciless light over man's terrors, subjecting them to a kind of artistic third degree. They talk, all right. This she does without consistent identification of a dancer with one character. Her characters are Anyman and Anywoman swept from one peak of emotion to the next. Governed by her particular genius for group design, the result is a kind of calligraphy of feeling.

The program that her company performed in the current Brooklyn Academy festival included a scaled-down version of "Odes" (originally choreographed for the Juilliard Dance Ensemble, which at that time had a huge group of dancers); "Memories", a supposedly new dance with distinct links to another that Miss Sokolow created for the Juilliard group; "Steps of Silence," new to New York; and "Tribute."

"Tribute" is just that—a dance epitaph for Martin Luther King. Brief, stark, elegaic. It has the same feeling as a verse composed by a fine writer for a friend's tombstone: not that writer's best work, but certainly heartfelt and as funerary verse goes, a damn good poem.

"Steps of Silence," performed against music by Anatol Vieru, opens in darkness. The voices of the eight dancers emerge one by one, reciting fragments of poetry, prose. Spotlights come on and isolate each dancer in a circle of light. From then on, the grouping and separating and regrouping of dancers proceeds at a fierce pace. Scurrying solos into scrabbling duets into flights into wary groups. Men and women shake and wrench at each others' arms. A man works his way between two who seem about to fight to the death; it is he the mediator who falls. Finally an invisible wind releases a storm of torn newspapers into the bleak stage. The dancers, resisting fruitlessly, are blown into a limp pile in the center of the stage.

"Odes" and "Memories" are similarly despairing, although the former has one fluttering lyrical duet. I like "Odes" very much and find "Memories" less satisfying. Still, there is one strange, decadently beautiful section in "Memories" in which veiled men and groups of girls extravagantly garlanded with flowers twine around three individuals— smothering them in a sinister parody of growth.

Sokolow has her own approach to dance movement. She uses highly trained dancers and demands difficult things of them. But you sense that she wishes to keep her performers looking very human and natural at all times. This is especially evident in the way she choreographs arm movements. The dancers' arms rarely move for the sake of design. Mostly they hang down or are simply held out to the side. Sokolow saves them, in a sense, to function in dramatic gestures—to reach, pray, claw, clutch the head—to fall into positions that express emotions in an immediately recognizable way.

After these four Sokolow dances, the audience slumped exhausted from the theatre. There's no catharsis in her art because positive action either doesn't exist in it or is obviously doomed to failure from the start. Her dancers are victims, pounded through the dances, beaten down when they raise their heads. They stare offstage at invisible forces out to get them—offstage and out at you the audience. Sokolow has put you in the bad guy's seat doing this to her people, and she will not let you off the hook.

Parts Can Blur the Whole

The Village Voice, January 20, 1975

I've become obsessed with trying to understand the paradoxes seemingly inherent in dramatic dances—why parts that ought to work don't and why some brief, unostentatious moments often express the ideas behind huge chunks of plot. Take some "successful" dramatic ballets: Limón's "The Moor's Pavane," Tudor's "Lilac Garden," Robbins's "Fancy Free," and . . . How odd, I snatched these at random out of my storeroom, and only now realize what they have in common. First, of course, the choreographers developed action through movements that are gestural in origin—from small, naturalistic gestures like the sailors' cocky handshakes in "Fancy Free" to immensely metaphorical ones (the moment in "Moor's Pavane" when Iago attaches himself to Othello's back like a leech and rides him across the stage.)

But there's something else. All three of these ballets take place in situations where "dancing" is one of the things that's going on, and so you don't feel that dance passages interrupt the plot, but rather that they carry it along. Limón chose to contain the action of Othello within the framework of a pavane; every change of partners, every unison passage prods the tragedy along, and the constant return to the formal "dance" measure also becomes a metaphor for the meticulous, hierarchical social structure that is about to become unstable and fall apart. In "Fancy

Free," the sailors coolly get up and dance for each other and the girls they're trying to impress. Solo dances might not be appropriate in the real-life equivalent of this situation, but something with a similarly show-off structure would: a card trick, a risqué joke. And "Lilac Garden" takes place at an Edwardian party. (There may even be dancing going on in the house.) The encounters and exchanges dictated by decorum or motivated by passion belong to some vast dance-like structure (approach, dance closely with someone, separate, change partners). The form of the dance and its content (thwarted love, mismated couples) are structurally identical.

But in doing a dramatic ballet, many choreographers adhere to the operatic patterns of recitative and aria. They stop the plot so that characters can elaborate on how they feel about what they're doing. And, unless the dances are extraordinary or reveal something I didn't know about the character, I become impatient for the story to continue.

All this musing was generated by Pearl Lang's "The Possessed," an expansion of her earlier short piece, "Legend." Lang, attracted to the dance-like characteristics of Ansky's play, "The Dybbuk," has tried to create a three-act drama without words by means of a series of inter-locking danced episodes. Unlike Jerome Robbins with his "Dybbuk Variations," she has stayed close to the play's structure, even using pan-tomime when necessary.

Sometimes, the ideas in the play bloom vividly. The score by Meyer Kupferman and Joel Spiegelman provides a sound environment that in-cludes music, muttering, shushing voices, wind, bells—it intensifies seen actions and evokes unseen ones. Lang is adroit in her use of stiffly ex-uberant Hasidic dances steps; and the way the men clutch themselves, hunch forward, and twist their torsos from side to side in short jerks eloquently expresses the doggedness, the blinders-on view of life, the frustrations of the Talmudic scholars. Lang's own rippling, sweetly sinuous style makes a poignant contrast.

There is a wonderful scene in which Leye (Lang) comes to the synagogue—to mend the cover of the Torah scrolls, I think. We see the young men sitting around a table, bent over their books, swaying. We hear their mutter, almost like a humming of bees. Channon (William Carter) stands by a lectern watching Lang. No one "dances." And suddenly we see Lang—very beautiful and gravely devout in her white dress—through his eyes, see that she is a spring in this dry desert. Lang gives you time to feel his thirst. In this one scene, the events of the whole play become explicable; no further justification is needed for their love, her dutifulness to her father, Channon's fever and death and his subsequent possession of her spirit, her acquiescence to the terrible exorcism rite.

Some of the dances work beautifully without stopping the action:

the first duet of Leye and Channon (a second draws attention to itself as a virtuosic "love duet"), a fierce dance of scholars, parts of the exorcism, a dance of crippled beggars. This last is one of those fortuitous dances within a dance; the bride is expected to dance with all comers and not look too exhausted or revolted. The moment of possession is suggested with eerie succinctness: still photographs of Carter fly, frameless, across a dark sky (projections by Virginia Hochbert) while Lang stands motionless.

One key scene that didn't work for me is the dance that expresses Leye's possession. In the first place it's a solo; and we don't see anyone seeing it. Lang, doesn't show a body being molded by an alien will, she just shows us a distraught woman; the fingers that she flutters near her mouth—to indicate Channon's voice, I suppose—seem unconvincing as an expression of this climactic moment. Perhaps she didn't clearly differentiate in choreographic terms between Channon's way of her moving and her own; you can see his themes take over her body, but they neither seem alien to her, nor deformed by the macabreness of the situation.

The cast, Lang, Carter, Bertram Ross as the Rabbi, Alexander Mintz as Leye's father, and a large number of other skillful and sensitive performers, dance and act wonderfully.

Calm Sky: No Squalls Ahead

The Village Voice, November 6, 1969

I'm always astounded by the controversy that the work of Erick Hawkins generates. Usually, before I even get to a concert of his, I've already been bombarded with the impressions of others: disciples, associates, ardent supporters cannot help raving; others call me on the phone with tirades against Hawkins. How to keep an open mind? Is there, indeed, such a thing? It's the same at the end of the actual concert: scattered booing competes with the storm of bravos. And there I sit in the middle —happy, applauding—feeling that both boos and bravos are antithetical to the carefully wrought, non-showy dances that Erick Hawkins makes.

Trying to write criticism involves stepping into all sorts of shoes. I can understand why some people can't swing with Hawkins. The first time you see him can be a little like your first visit to a fine Japanese restaurant; all those small elegant dishes—a slice of white radish and a watercress frond floating in a bowl of clear soup—make some people think longingly of a hunk of steak. On the other hand, I can also understand why people intrigued and delighted by the exquisite understatement of his best works can become cultish about him.

As an audience, we have been conditioned, I think, by 19th century theories about the sublime and the beautiful. The sublime is supposed to be large, stormy, a bit ragged or wanton with form. The beautiful is decidedly a minor category. At one time, aestheticians tossed works into one classification or the other with rigorous zeal. Perhaps those who scream for Hawkins are trying to say that peaceful beauty, imaginative elegance can be sublime, that an artist needn't be tempestuous to be major.

Hopefully cultivating objectivity all the way from the Village to 125th Street, I went to see Erick Hawkins's new "Black Lake"—one of a series of dances offered during a week season at Riverside Church, which was sponsored by PLAY, a group of Columbia students and faculty members. If you like "Eight Clear Places"—as I do—you'll like "Black Lake," because it's eight clear places in the sky. The black lake is the night sky, and the dancers are those beings that briefly populate it: the setting sun, a star, night birds, the moon, a comet, thunder and lightning, the Great and Little Bears, The Milky Way. These sections are small ceremonies that emerge and disappear into darkness. One lovely idea that shapes the whole dance: Hawkins and three other people, half-masked and dressed in black, are like fragments of sky that can conceal the astral bodies so that they can appear to gleam fugitively, as if from behind clouds. 'Black Lake" is like a mysterious ritual from the first moment when Hawkins ties a mask on Beverly Brown (as the sun setting) until the last when all the dancers slowly untie their own masks.

"Black Lake" is excellent Hawkins, a quietly magic experience. It is ceremonious; it is oriental in several other ways too. Although the dancers make curving paths through space, they always seem to take their own space with them; this gives a curious privacy to their movements. Also the various changes of direction on the body resolve or come to rest (like dissonance into consonance) when the dancer is facing the audience; this imparts a cut-out clarity to the design. There is sly humor in "Black Lake," in the sequence for the two bears. There are also some subtly stirring dynamics.

"Black Lake," as a matter of fact, has sections that are dynamically more interesting than anything by Hawkins that I've seen. Beverly Brown's solo as the setting sun has a kind of imperious rage, a controlled sputtering; her zig-zag lightning paths around Hawkins, as the ponderous summer thunder, have the same unexpectedness. Her performing had a beautiful clarity. But in "Black Lake," I think Hawkins has used his company in a very full way; each dancer is given a chance to shine— Hawkins himself no more than the others, and they respond by giving their best. Nancy Meehan danced the moon and the first star with her customary translucence. (I had noticed, too, that in "Early Floating," hers was the only face that had that lovely quality of relaxed attentiveness: Robert Yohn's was too closed-off, Hawkins's too tense—telegraphing the stress of the movement to come.) Yohn and Kay Gilbert have made great strides as performers, and their duet as the bears had a clever shambling charm about it. I am pleased when a choreographer who is a strong dancer feels that his company can execute his ideas well enough for him to merge into the texture of a dance with them. Some are never willing to relinquish that stellar position even for a moment.

As usual, Hawkins had the collaborative support of Ralph Dorazio and Lucia Dlugoszewski. Dorazio's straight simple robes and squared-off, slit-eyed masks enhanced the mystery and the ceremoniousness. Dlugoszewski's music was performed by an ensemble (violin, clarinet, percussion, piano) conducted by Gerard Schwarz. The composer managed the piano and a score of other things with her usual sensitivity, but the texture of this whole work seems denser than some of her music. The score has a kind of tempestuousness, as if it were creating a mass of scudding clouds for the dance to float on.

Brooklyn Scramble

The Village Voice, December 7, 1967

One of the things that makes seeing a concert of dances by Merce Cunningham such a great experience is his air of absolute assurance as a creator. You feel that he knows exactly what he is and what he is doing. And, of course, he does it brilliantly. For me, going to see his work—as I did last Saturday at the Brooklyn Academy of Music—is a celebration.

His creations are classically contained, but never static. In fact, they're almost constantly shifting. It's as if his main purpose is to distill in dance the forms of growth and change in living things. For the most part, each dancer moves in a pattern different from any of the others. When their paths converge or their bodies impinge on each other it can be by chance, or by deliberate choice, or the result of an inevitable path. Dancers roll into others and set them off in motion. It's like Hume's billiard balls: you actually see only the activity, but you infer cause and effect. As a matter of fact, you infer many things from a Cunningham dance, based on your own conditioning or your mood of the moment. Cunningham creates a place where people move beautifully; he shows you forms and relationships; he may also set a predominant atmosphere through the movement he chooses, light, sound, and decor. The specific emotional colors are added by you, the audience, if you choose. You can notice certain things more than others. You can watch any or all of his fine dancers, each one invidivual in appearance and character and approach. He himself, with his taut, alert air, can seem one of the gang, a gentle manipulator, or the victim of his own creation (as he does in "Place").

"Scramble" was Toshi Ichiyanagi's score—sounds like ripping and static, And Frank Stella has created a marvelous environment for it—narrow colored pieces of canvas, each stretched between two supports. They look a little like the backs of giant directors' chairs. The lowest is the longest and vice versa. They are moved about, added, or eliminated to change the shape of the dancing area. The performers can disappear behind the lowest as if sinking under a wave. At moments the dance has an aura of discovery, at moments one of ritual. The dancers appear easy, relaxed—like friends engaging in some pleasurable activity together. Sometimes they wait for a leader's signal to begin something. Certain ones leave; as if a vacuum has been set up, others flow in. The movement is sometimes balletic, sometimes derived from modern dance, sometimes pure Merce with crazy little steps that shoot limbs in all directions at incredible speeds. The only thing I didn't love about "Scramble" was Toshi Ichiyanagi's score sounds like ripping and static so loud that they gripped my head in a vise. This element was an odd contrast to the gentleness of the dancers and almost made the dance appear to be taking place on the brink of disaster. Wouldn't it be nice if we had earlids?

Gordon Mumma's better, but equally cruel, score works perfectly for "Place"—one of the best dances I've ever seen. The whole mood is ominous. Part of this is due to the atmosphere that Beverly Emmons has created with rectangles of lattice and newspapers hanging at the back of the stage, also with two Japanese-style lanterns that Cunningham carefully trains on the dancers at one point. The shadows these lanterns cast are somehow menacing, although beautiful, like Miss Emmons's use of the stage lighting and the plastic dresses she has designed for the girls, which glitter harshly as if wet. Ominous, too, the way Cunningham stalks warily about, the sudden outbursts of violently fast movement, the odd positions couples find themselves in, the way the dancers in a certain section must move only one at a time to get where they are going. The end is really frightening with Cunningham thrashing along the floor, his lower body in a long plastic bag. Is he trying to get in or out? Finally he rolls upstage and disappears. Either he has left the "place" or been absorbed into it.

The program ended happily with "How to Pass, Kick, Fall, and Run." While John Cage, lubricated with champagne, read some of the hilarious little entries in his memoirs, the dancers bounded and sprinted with only occasional moments of calm. They seemed surprised and delighted to find each other on the stage. It was the exuberant momentum of the dance and not the grimy IRT at all that swept us laughing from Brooklyn to Manhattan.

Cedar Shrine, Doe Stands C.

The Village Voice, January 15, 1970

I'd much rather watch Merce Cunningham's dances than write about them. They already get more exegesis than they need, because people like to talk about dances afterward in order to prolong their (the dances') ephemeral existence. Anyway, you have to have something to do on the subway ride from the Brooklyn Academy to Manhattan.

Perhaps my best course would be to spit a bunch of grapefruit seeds onto a piece of land I call mine and dedicate the resultant grove, or barren patch, or maybe just the ceremony of spitting, to Merce. As soon as the ground gets softer . . .

But in the meantime, I'd better add my arid analyses to the heap. (The first question I was asked after I had lectured—I thought quite cleverly—to students at Ohio State was "Why bother with criticism at all?") To me, Cunningham's most innovative work in recent years has been in his tamperings with stage space. His dancers dart and streak over the area in a way that makes space elastic, able to bend and change from second to second. The sudden collisions and intersecting paths set up knots of tension that then release the energy in new directions. Also fairly recently, the various people who do Cunningham's decor have abetted this process of breaking up the conventional proscenium while staying within it.

For "Tread," Bruce Nauman has planted a glittering beanrow of tall electric fans across the front of the stage; they all spin their blades, but some revolve and some do not. The dance is breezy, and the audience in the front part of the orchestra feels this as well as sees it. Cunningham and his nine collaborators streak about the remaining space with a thoughtful impudence. The men wear woolly pants and shirts, the girls have legwarmers and skimpy gym suits that reveal a fair amount of their buttocks. In parts of the dance, people skid into ornate positions with each other and are then carefully rearranged or separated by others. Usually, some are sitting watching those who are temporatily more active. You get a sense of people imprinting themselves or part of themselves on each other, on the floor, on the air.

Cunningham's other new dance, "Second Hand," turned out to be most surprising. It begins with a long solo for Cunningham himself. He stands—in one spot—making the movement ebb and flow very slowly within this small compass of space. Carolyn Brown enters, and the two perform a sober, balanced duet. The unstudied, unforced perfection of her dancing never ceases to delight me. Then the whole group enters, in leotards that shade delicately into each other as the stripes of a rainbow do. Suddenly, strangely, "Second Hand" begins to look slightly like parts

101

of other Cunningham dances (certainly typical recent Cunningham movement) done in slow motion. The company strides, darts, turns at an almost somnolent pace. The music (this is unusual too) reinforces the serene rhythm of the dance: John Cage doodles sweetly and sparsely on a piano something that he calls "Cheap Imitation." It is, apparently, an imitation of Satie's "Socrate," performance rights for which were denied at the last minute. Toward the end, bands of dancers keep breaking into brief unison passages; then they quietly detach themselves from this temporary alliance and return to their own soft fragmentations. Finally, they are forming into changing couples and trios, sliding and bending against each other. At first, I couldn't get with the dance, but near the finish, the accumulation of beauty finally became too heavy and dropped over me, and I succumbed.

This Brooklyn Academy season also featured a revival of Cunningham's "Crises" (1960). Chance procedures were employed in its creation to determine things like the predominant modes of movement in each section, the number of participants in each section, some factors to do with isolation of a particular part of the body, etc. Chance also determined the methods of using circles of wide elastic, by means of which the dancers can become temporarily attached to each other. The music (some of Conlon Nancarrow's "Rhythm Studies for Player Piano") was added later. The dance was to be "about" the joinings and separatings of four people (one man and three women); by slipping a hand under an elastic band worn around someone else's waist or wrist, a dancer could be joined to another and yet free. Seeing "Crises" now, one is tempted to say that Cunningham was concerned more just then with radical use of movement than radical use of space. Viola Farber has rejoined the company as a guest artist to recreate her original role in "Crises," and the movement for her is truly astonishing. Her body, elegant yet earthy, is capable of an infinite number of little isolated shifts within a longer line. As Merce says about her in one of his perceptive scribbles (at least I think it's about her): " . . . her body often had the look of one part being in balance, and the rest extremely off."

It's interesting how dancers can change the look of a dance. Carolyn Brown, of course, was in "Crises" when it was composed, but Marilyn Wood and Judith Dunn have been replaced by Sandra Neels and Susana Hayman-Chaffey. I didn't see "Crises" with its original cast, but I can imagine the difference. Neels and Hayman-Chaffey both happen to have wise, supple legs that appear to reach all the way up to little-girl faces. Often paired in "Crises," they look like members of one sleek, beautiful species. Dunn and Wood could hardly be more dissimilar: the former possessing a fluid kind of weightedness and an uncompromising gaze, the latter long legged in a slightly brittle, heron-like way. "Crises" must have been quite another dance. In the same way, "Rainforest" now has a slightly different quality because Meg Harper has replaced Barbara Lloyd, and Chase Robinson has replaced Albert Reid. Harper (now delicately foxy looking, probably owing to a diet so stringent that I don't even want to think about it) brings more than a trace of eroticism to the opening duet with Cunningham, and Robinson begins his dancing with a tautness that seems directed toward them. "Rainforest" opens with a very human tension that I don't remember being in the dance when it was first done. Strange, by what subtle and intimate means a piece of art unfolds its possible meanings.

As usual, Cunningham and all his dancers and musicians performed with absorption and beauty. Andy Warhol's mylar pillows for "RainForest" were the only element that tended to deflate.

My comments on "Second Hand" typify the dilemma of the critic who isn't sure what he/she has seen, but writes about it anyhow. The pseudonymous Michael Snell in Volume 3, number 6 of Ballet Review *and Carolyn Brown in the brilliant article she wrote for the book* Merce Cunningham *(edited by James Klosty) have both pointed out the close formal connections between "Second Hand," Satie's "Socrate," and Plato's "Phaedon"—the dialogue which recounts the death of Socrates. Perhaps Cunningham would not want us to know this; he has been almost belligerantly reticent about imposing "meanings" on his dances. However, it is impossible to watch him perform and not know that his movements have significance for him. Even forgetting "Socrate," it seems to me that I didn't* see *"Second Hand" clearly or deeply.*

The title of this article was my attempt to make an anagram out of "Tread" and "Second Hand".

Spirits

The Village Voice, April 23, 1970

I don't know where the dancers in Alvin Ailey's American Dance Theater get their energy. No matter how tired or dispirited or under par they may be, they always burst onto the stage like a pride of lean lions that haven't been thrown a Christian in God knows how long. They run with the movement—fierce, but with the ease that comes from sureness of one's own power. They rarely just execute choreography; they deliver it to the audience gift-wrapped.

They're all in fine form over at the Brooklyn Academy right now. Judith Jamison, Consuelo Atlas, Michele Murray, Linda Kent, Renée Rose, Sylvia Waters, Dudley Williams. Kelvin Rotardier—the ones we know and love—are there. The batch of newcomers includes John Parks, whose long, almost fragile, arms and legs and angular face help make him a fine Daedalus in Lucas Hoving's "Icarus." Best of all, Miguel Godreau has rejoined the company. He's one hell of a dancer—small and strong, but not at all stocky the way some short dancers are. He often projects a slightly sinister mischievousness. As Icarus, the set of his head and other small emphases subtly flaw the character's innocence with a touch of greed. Interesting, I thought.

The company's repertory includes works by quite a few different choreographers. Now Ailey himself has made a new work called "Streams," and I think it's one of the best he's done recently. The music, by Miloslav Kabelac, a 20th century Polish composer, sounds a little like some of Hovhaness's Orient-influenced fantasies. Ailey picks up this quality in a series of quiet deliberate processionals, skating steps with the other leg raised behind in attitudes reminiscent of Cambodian or Thai dancing. Interspersed solos and duets are built around contrasting moods or dynamics. A very formal sort of piece.

Ailey has always been an extremely stylish choreographer. Two of his most prominent characteristics interest me, because they are a source of great pleasure, but also of annoyance. One is his heavy reliance on unison dancing, and unison dancing set evently and symmetrically into the stage space. It is one of the secrets of the beauty of "Revelations"; in that dance, the clean-edged patterns have the stylish charm of primitive paintings. And unison work, of course, gives a phrase of movement tremendous power and emphasis; the dancers temporarily surrender their individual feelings to project an image of dancing beyond what any one of them could express. Too much unison seems boring and even bothersome to me these days, however, and it can easily look crass as well as hokey. For me, therefore, the finale of "Streams" leaves an unpleasant taste—a sock-it-to-'em Broadway chorus that shamelessly wraps up the dance and bats it across the pit to make the crowd howl.

The other thing Ailey does that can be good or bad depending on context has to do with rhythm. He seizes on the pulse of the music and drives it along in rich, spacious movement. It keeps you on the edge of your seat. But every now and then, you wish he'd use a little stillness for contrast, or be a little more strange with rhythm.

"Streams" has some other lovely sections in addition to the expansive opening procession. There's a wonderful solo for Consuelo Atlas; it's meditative, but with some surprising angles and twists to it. There's also a beautiful slow twining and touching section for pairs of dancers (no unison either) that fills the stage with a soft, unhasty sensuality.

Some sections may have been less exciting from a choreographic point of view. But even when Ailey isn't doing his best choreography, he always creates dancing—that is, he makes something that the dancers can tear away with, delighting you by their spirit and beauty.

The Only Thing He Doesn't Do is Dance

The New York Times, February 3, 1974

What kind of dancing is this? All you can see are green hands vibrating, while behind them on the dark stage, a huge luminous painting of brown and gold shapes seems to be coming apart and reforming. Occasionally the dancers reveal themselves wholly—pale and eerie, pulsing with life.

Choreographer Alwin Nikolais, whose first Broadway season begins Tuesday at the Lyceum, is a magician in every sense that I can think of. A proscenium stage attacked by his visions becomes an elastic world in which opulent colored forms swim into sight, change, and vanish, in which dancers' bodies are printed with light, and the motion of those bodies creates living charts of mysterious domains. Nikolais' awesome sleight-of-hand, the luminosity of his palette, and his antic humor restore to us the vividness of a child's vision: a door or a piece of rope become powerful beings capable of growing or shrinking or taking over our lives. And best of all, ladies and gentlemen, it's all happening right before your very eyes. Oh, there may be places to conceal things, but nothing can be magicked in some studio cutting room.

Nickolais, however, is more than a facile showman who mixes lights, slides, props, costumes, electronic sound, and human bodies into a mind-blowing optical party. Often he presides over a potent theatricalized ritual. Most attempts at this sort of thing have been biographies of passionate gods with towering, unapologetic egos who can suffer, die, and be resurrected for us every evening at 8:30, but Nickolais' dances suggest earlier rites which existed before gods had names and personalities, when men assumed the shape and motion of rain or corn or fire in order to feel that they were part of a terrifying universe. Nikolais has written that he preferred to think of man as a "fellow traveler within the total universal mechanism rather than the god from which all things flowed."

Practically speaking, however, this philosopher of humility controls almost every aspect of his dances. He is the choreographer, the lighting designer, the one who paints the slides and figures out how tricky costumes and props must be constructed. Since 1957, he has also created the electronic scores that accompany his dances. The only thing he doesn't do is dance. In the old days when his company was in residence at the Henry Street Playhouse, you could see him during performances through the glass front of the light booth, flicking switches and twiddling knobs. Odd that a benevolent despot, so precise and so technologically adept, should want to create perilous kingdoms in which man is not the boss, but part of a larger pattern.

Some of Nikolais' dances, such as "Runic Canto," "Totem," or

105

"Sanctum," have suggested primeval rites, but he is in no way a throw-back. He brings a medicine man's sensibilities to the bogies of modern life, or to natural phenomena as contemporary science views them. In one early dance, "Prism," each of the dancers represented a color of the spectrum; the spectacularly vigorous finale had them running up the bare back wall of the stage in a fury of refraction.

One group of the peculiar denizens of "Imago" might be single-minded ants as they skitter smoothly back and forth on horizontal paths, occasionally colliding or doing rapid about-faces, but Nikolais has titled the section "Boulevard" and costumed the dancers in bright, bulbous robes, and so we come to think of them as crazed drivers. The jabbering, speeded-up crowd in the comical "Tower" does build a veritable Tower of Babel, but the style and their problems are pure Levittown.

But although Nikolais is psychologically in tune with the child and with primitive man, his works don't have that kind of awkward vigor. Expertise is evident in everything. The colors and shapes and energies he plays with can be beautiful and profound, or funny, or simply pretty, but they're not often violent or crude. Nik is an optimist: you sense that he's driven to create orderly patterns or bring existing ones to our attention.

I suspect that works like "Grotto" or "Foreplay" or "Scenario" seem less deep than "Somniloquy" or "Tent" because in them he uses human emotions and attitudes as choreographic motifs. His impulse appears to be to tidy up those emotions and set them in patterns that can be stopped and started at will. These particular dances make you feel as if he's looking at us from uncomfortably far away, the way we look at the tracking of ants. Nikolais the puppet-master, instead of the Nikolais who can make mysterious forces visible.

When people refer to Nik's work as "dehumanized" (he may even have given up gritting his teeth about it), they mean, I think, that not only does he not aggrandize man's role, but he doesn't keep his dancers downstage and brightly lit. However, without the dancers Nikolais' theater wouldn't be what it is. True, sometimes ingenious costuming alters their shapes into something non-human: the men in "Mantis" (part of "Imago") wear jersey sleeves stretched over a series of disks, which give them absurd long appendages tipped with suction cups where their arms ought to be. In "Noumenon" (from "Masks, Props, and Mobiles"), three women completely encased in red jersey make them-selves into faceless deities or slabs of wax being squeezed and molded by giant invisible hands.

Sometimes the dancers create illusions from their own bodies, help-ing each other to sprout extra pairs of arms and legs. Sometimes they fuse with the environment, perhaps disappearing into the texture of a slide projection. Sometimes they function as invisible prop men, folding and opening big sheets of paper to catch the light patterns, or sidling around in blackness making a dance of flashlights. In the early struggling days of the Nikolais company, a lot of dazzling effects were achieved by dancer-power.

And sometimes Nikolais dancers simply dance, with great sensitivity to the nuances of dynamics and shape. The style didn't spring from impassioned psychological sources—as did the styles of many other modern dancers. The ideal Nikolais dancer doesn't stalk about on a strong pair of legs gesturing heroically at the universe. His body is capable of many small articulations: a jerk of the knee sets off a quiver in the arms, a twist of the head, a shift in the hips, and an expansion in the upper-right rib cage. You see joints where you know none exist. The fluid body, the light responsiveness, the spatial clarity, the famous ball-bearing walk make the Nikolais dancer ideal for the flexible role he's been assigned.

Murray Louis, for years Nikolais' leading dancer and one of those on whose bodies the style evolved, now choreographs for his own company (the two companies are sharing the Lyceum season), and he employs a variant of the style with great skill to show purely human encounters—deploying the current of energy flowing through space from one alert body to another in order to make complicated kinetic jokes or erotic statements, or whatever he wishes.

Nikolais' dances, seldom having heroes and heroines, have no story lines. Each is made of discrete segments thematically linked. In some of the lightest and brightest of them, Nikolais' delight in sensuous display tends to make you greedy for the next part. In his deepest works, however, the effect is cumulative. And sometimes the end is a holocaust: the environment swallows the dancers.

In the beautiful and disturbing "Tent," the immense multi-purpose white fabric billows down over the dancers and gently presses them to the ground. In "Structures," the dancers build a little town out of the three-paneled screens they've been playing so many witty games with; flickering red lights set their structure on fire while lifesized dummies hurtle out from behind it. "Echo" ends with the dancers vanishing into the dark floor while the projected patterns, which have been wrapping their bodies, gather together and reign from the backdrop.

Come to think of it, in "Echo" Nikolais probes deeply into the scary puzzle which appears here and there through all his works—one that concerns all proper magicians and children: Is an echo any less real than what it repeats? Are we any realer than our shadows?

107

Rebel Turned Classicist

The New York Times, March 10, 1974

I still look back with awe and pleasure on the spectacle of Paul Taylor playing Paul Taylor in a ballet by George Balanchine. Actually, "Episodes," when it was given its premiere in 1959, was an unlikely two-part collaboration between Balanchine and Martha Graham. And in the middle of Balanchine's half of the ballet, Paul Taylor, then a member of the Graham company, walked onto the stage—dwarfing the exiting ballet dancers—and began, with great composure and the winsome deadpan he often affects, to bend his body into some astonishing knots.

Then, as now, he looked like an aberration of an Olympics Decathlon contender, velvet-gloving his strength for us. Balanchine seemed to have ferreted out all of Taylor's most individual movements and strung them together with a speed and fervor habitual to Balanchine, but unusual for Taylor.

No one in the New York City Ballet could perform that solo; it was dropped after the first season (as was the entire Graham half of "Episodes"—a stylish, skeletal version of the tragedy of Mary of Scotland). Now that Taylor, acclaimed here and abroad for his own choreography, is about to offer New York his first full-evening work, "American Genesis"—on Thursday through Sunday, this week and next, at the Brooklyn Academy of Music—I think back to that solo, because Taylor, having started out in modern dance as a rebel, is now in his own way almost as much a classicist as Balanchine.

Taylor was, by all accounts, the most impeccable and studious of rebels. Shortly after his late start in dance—he had almost finished college—he fell in with vanguardists like Robert Rauschenberg, Merce Cunningham and John Cage. He was, as far as I know, the first choreographer to make a dance equivalent to Cage's rigorous essay in silence, $4'33''$, in which the pianist sits at the keyboard, but plays not a single note. In "Duet" (1957), Taylor stood and his partner, Toby Glanternik, sat for three minutes, the duration of the dance.

This experiment obviously proved to Taylor that he preferred moving to standing still. During the next few years, he produced a series of brilliant, skewed works like "Fibers," "Meridian," "Three Episodes," "Insects and Heroes," "Junction"—works that were more ambiguous than modern dance at that time was supposed to be.

"Belligerently unintelligible," critic John Martin called Taylor. Many of us loved those dances, loved, for instance, the way the mysterious insect in "Insects and Heroes," a black creature with inefficient, but decorative spines, fumbled grandly around the other dancers—looking sometimes like an eager, untrained pet, instead of the expected menace.

108

Some of Taylor's dances presented, still do present, a dire vision of humanity; this caused Louis Horst, the cantankerous guardian of modern dance morality, to rebuke Taylor in his magazine, Dance Observer, saying that he'd never get anywhere if he insisted on being so pessimistic.

In 1962, Taylor choreographed "Aureole," and that should have mollified those who found him unintelligible and those who thought him pessimistic. "Aureole" is a blithe dance about people dancing to Handel music. With this work, Taylor's idiosyncrasies, his light, loose handling of Martha Graham's dance technique, seemed to have blossomed into a definite style, with a vocabulary of movements which he could employ—with necessary permutations and additions—to express a variety of themes.

Today, "Aureole" can almost be viewed as a primer of Taylor dancing: in it you can see the chains of ground-skimming leaps; the parallel feet (as opposed to the turned-out ones of ballet); the archaic Graham poses with jutting hips which give the dancers the look of frolicking satyrs; the flyaway hands; the swinging, twin-armed gestures; the fluent knots.

And, above all, the buoyancy. Taylor is a big man, but his style has a light, smooth, spongy quality, which all of his dancers acquire. However difficult the steps, however perverse the choreographic non sequiturs, the easy, almost tactful way the dancers exert their strength minimizes all effort and imparts a fluidity to whatever they do. With shifts of emphasis, the style can appear carefree, as in "Aureole"; pacific, as in "Lento"; neurotic and violent ("Scudorama"); mincingly elegant ("Piece Period"); hypocritical ("Churchyard"); or erotic ("Private Domain").

But no matter what the mood of a particular work, the dancers perform with a sort of warm aloofness, surveying the dance and their roles in it from a certain emotional distance—with interest, but no alarm. Taylor himself often performs as if he were having sardonic second thoughts about art and life. The coolness tends to make funny dances funnier and lewd ones even more depraved.

So, by taking his idiosyncratic movement style and treating it as if it were neutral, by performing it dispassionately, by patterning it with grace and ingenuity, Taylor has arrived at his extremely odd brand of classicism. The dances that he's made since 1966 might also be considered as classical art in that they're neatly balanced, formal equations in which his inescapable quirks of thought are framed or resolved in images that have theatrical vividness and comprehensibility. (I'm not sure whether this sanely proportioned clarity is a product of Taylor's ripening as an artist or the exigencies of the company's increased performing schedule. Both maybe.)

Some recent works seem to have been made principally to display a gracious equilibrium, like "Lento" (1967) or "Foreign Exchange"

(1970) or "Orbs" (1967), a heavy work so stately, and heavy with cosmic correspondences, that it all but stifled Taylor's supple wit. However, Taylor's quirky classicism also derives strength from his apparent view of evil as an active force—guiltlessly relished by those who perpetrate it. He's a master of stylish lewdness.

In "Agathe's Tale" (1967), for instance, a raunchy Satan, disguised as a monk, battles St. Raphael to a draw for a maiden's favors, while she cleverly escapes with a third party. "Churchyard" (1969) formally opposes false virtue (priggishly genuflecting nuns and clerics) to gleeful vice (lascivious creatures deformed by outrageous carbuncles); the dance themes of the first part are literally turned widdershins in the second part, to conform to the structure of a Black Mass.

In "Big Bertha" (1971), one of Taylor's most recent and bitter excursions into the heartland of America, a grim, coin-gulping automaton on an old nickelodeon works a sinister spell on a typical "nice" American family, so that father rapes daughter, while uncaring mother strips down for the audience. Father (Taylor) ends up on the nickelodeon—presumably destined to be Big Bertha's accomplice in the next chilling encounter with wholesome vacationers.

Paul Taylor's dances don't alarm or perplex people as much as they did. "Aureole" is in the repertory of the Royal Danish Ballet, and in 1971 Rudolph Nureyev appeared with Taylor's company in London and in Mexico City—dancing Taylor's own roles in "Aureole" and "Book of Beasts"—and performed an altered version of "Big Bertha" on television. Perhaps Taylor's choreography strikes some of the ballet world, too, as an unconservative but comprehensible form of classicism—ballet in a foreign language.

Make no mistake, though, Taylor's still an eccentric, and those of us who still occasionally mourn his lost intransigence are perhaps really lamenting the inevitable passing of our own astonishment that anyone could do such wickedly beautiful things to the art of dancing.

When I was writing the final draft of this article, I couldn't find the review by Louis Horst which I had unearthed some weeks earlier and intended to quote. I took a deep breath and paraphrased it anyway. Months later, I found the review: it was not by Louis Horst, but by Nik Krevitsky (a contributor to Horst's Dance Observer), *and the gist of it was that Paul Taylor was eschewing the "nihilism" that afflicted many of his contemporaries. There's a moral here that I'm sure I needn't explain.*

110

The Third Generation:
Mostly Rebels

Far-Out Ladies

The Village Voice, February 13, 1969

Talk about biting off more than you can chew! Last week I saw dances by—let's see—Don Meredith, Monk Hay, Yvonne Hoving, Rainer Tharp, and . . . you see what I mean? Groggy. O. K. let's start out with the ladies of the avant-garde and their concerts at the Billy Rose. Twyla Tharp, Meredith Monk, Yvonne Rainer, and Deborah Hay (represented by one piece on Rainer's program) all have considerable intellects—although Monk enjoys letting her id run rampant over hers. They have constructed new and very influential theories about making dances; indeed, I find their works often more exciting as illustrations of theories than for their own sakes. That is, I watch with interest how the thing is done, wonder what material will appear next. It's like being a spectator at a pleasant, small, not very competitive game: "How's she going to get out of this one?"

Although the four women work very differently, it might be worth noting the few things that they appear to have in common, and in common with quite a few other contemporary artists. One is a concern with process, with incorporating the creative process into the resultant work. Who said "the subject of art is art"? Thus Tharp's "Excess, Idle, Surplus—a Reconstruction" is performed to tapes of a rehearsal; the dancers count from time to time; Tharp herself claps a beat or occasionally stops perplexed in the middle of a movement. The difficulty of remembering and reconstructing the original dance becomes an integral part of the new version. Monk uses process for her particular brand of irony: at one point in "16 millimeter earrings," her taped voice describes the movement that she thinks the section calls for (it sounds terrific), but Monk herself is doing some deliberate, heavy stuff—her feet stubbed into fuzzy, encumbering slippers.

They're concerned with the relation between actual clock time and artistic time, even sometimes to the point of trying to deny the latter. Tharp prints the length of minutes for each dance on the program. Monk tells you that she is going to hold a pose for two minutes and does so. All of them—willing to be thought boring—let a thing go on until it has exhausted most of its possibilities. Images and energies borrowed from sports appear all the time: Rainer's complicated, but relaxed jogging-rhythm patterns; the way all of them use a plain, easy walk to get from one peak section to another; a lot of "go," "and," "one" verbal signals

113

between dancers. Needless to say, in none of these dances does anyone pretend to be someone he is not or act out anything contrary to the flow of the proceedings.

Twyla Tharp has changed a lot since I last saw her work in 1966. She has purged her dances of almost every element but movement. Two out of three at the Billy Rose were performed in almost total silence; I counted only one deliberately illusory use of lighting effects and one prop—a small red chair. Her all-female company is stylishly costumed by Robert Huot—uniform for each dance, varying from dance to dance. Tharp's mathematical space ratios, the chaste atomism with which she sprinkles her dancers all over the stage, their rarely colliding orbits, the purity of their attention on the movement give her dances an almost Spartan feel—a super-cool college of vestal virgins. And this despite the beauty and richness of her movement. She has been able to do what I thought might be impossible; she has transferred her own incredible style to her company. This style—speaking very superficially—involves acquiring a strong classical technique and then learning to fling it around without ever really losing control. The dancing is difficult, quirky, beautiful, stylish. She varies the amounts of it though. "Disperse," for example, in two of its sections uses only walks and variations on one turn. The new work "After 'Suite' " has a softer fuller style, half-created I think by the lovely afterflow of sleeves and pantlegs on Huot's beige jumpsuits. I thought "After 'Suite' " a fine dance; I liked the way brief duets and trios floated out of the mass of independent particles and then floated back in. Tharp has some marvelous dancers—she'd pretty well have to have. I was especially pleased by Sara Rudner's pure line; the impudent, almost biting way with which Theresa Dickinson attacks things; little Sheila Raj's generally winsome style. But this isn't fair . . . they were all good.

Meredith Monk isn't pure or Spartan at all—except perhaps in her carefully limited style of moving. She fills her theatre pieces with objects and sounds and films. Most of these have a super-personal emblematic value. Her stage becomes a kind of macro-microcosm of her own person —small areas within her externalized, blown up, and projected on the stage. She herself moves, speaks, and sings through this private and fantastic playroom. You almost feel that it would collapse if she left the stage. She rarely does, and often when she does Phoebe Neville—identically costumed and billed as a stand in—takes over. Once, a woman walked across the stage, stopped center, said to us, "I'm Meredith's mother," and walked away. I like Monk's humor, her outrageous justapositions, her confiding vulnerability. I also admit to being bored, irritated, dismayed some of the time.

"16 millimeter earrings" is a particularly thorough and inventive foray into Monk's world; it's the piece in which she puts a paper lantern thing over her head, and a film of her face is projected onto it. "Earrings" also has a great ending. Monk, wearing a ruby-red wig, sits for a moment on a white box with ruby-red streamers blowing up out of it. She then gets in a trunk and closes the lid while a colored film is shown of a doll standing and then toppling over in a burning enclosure. Monk raises the trunk lid and stands dimly naked—silhouetted against the last flames.

Recently Meredith Monk has been experimenting in different kinds of spaces. The Billy Rose didn't give her much leeway, but she did manage some "lobby exhibits" in the form of people reading by flashlight inside corrugated cardboard "houses." During each intermission, a few emerged until at the end of the evening they were all out and lying on the debris of their huts.

With Yvonne Rainer, I've discovered that once I fit my body rhythms into her easy lope, she makes me feel good. Her dances are big, clever, nicely silly games, and her dancers are adults unselfconsciously at play. Most of Rainer's pieces are in the form of a string of little sections, each built around a kind of motif. I'm happiest when she keeps the changes coming at a fairly good clip. She called her Billy Rose evening "Rose Fractions." A few of the things in part one I'd seen before or seen in different form. I love the two trios—one male, one female—who, arms around each others' waists, perform given movements in a given direction, but in an order they decide on. They back-somersault, run or walk in several different ways, crumple sideways to the floor, crawl over and under each other, and so on. The night I went, the film of Arnold and Paxton playing with the white balloon (already seen on the DTW program at Riverside Church) was shown simultaneously with a pretty ugly sex film shot by a hard-core camera. All of a sudden the two in the original film seemed terribly innocent in their nakedness, and also civilized to the point of being jaded on their chic white couch. I suspect this is another of Rainer's uses of pornography to clear the decks, or to point up the actual innocence of much that is called dirty. I also thought it wry of her to have Becky Arnold wallow erotically in a pile of unread books or Barbara Lloyd cuddle down on a "horse" that was later used for nice vaults and balances. The patterns Rainer makes with some of her simplest movements are deceptively complex. The evening ended with Trio A from "The Mind is a Muscle"—that longest dance phrase in living memory. It was first performed by relative non-dancers in silence, then (pepped up by the Chambers Brothers) by four dancers, then by everyone (still to music), including the unscheduled Valda Setterfield who performed the tour de force of learning it as she went along. It was fascinating and exciting, and I could kick myself for not learning Trio A too.

While I've still got breath: Deborah Hay contributed 26 variations of eight activities for 13 people plus beginning and ending. That's a title as well as a description. The people were 13 attractive young women in street attire. The activities involved walking forward to stage left, running backward to stage right (in various overlapping patterns), walking up three ramps, posing, walking back down, or jumping off. As in all Hay's pieces that I've seen: simplicity, severity, easy-going movement tension, yet subtly drill-like patterns. Interesting that the girls were seen in profile almost throughout the thing—leaving a curious, inscrutable impression.

Some people were outraged or bored by the avant-garde performances, which is—I think—as it should be. These dancers are venturing in a new direction; if their work is delightful to a mass audience, then it is not de facto avant-garde. It's the business of the avant-garde to be astringent and uncompromising to keep us from getting too comfortable with the old forms. The rest of us may never reject all our ideas about dance, but we'll sure as hell re-examine them. We may even follow wholeheartedly in the new direction; then after 10 years or so, the new avant-garde will revolt against us.

Country Dance

The Village Voice, April 8, 1971

Trisha Brown announced that she was going to do "Another Fearless Dance Concert." Boy, was it. Her "Falling Duet I" (1968) is the most gorgeously fearless thing I've ever seen. People's gasps for Nureyev or Villella always seem quite formal to me—an anticipated and planned response, but we at the Whitney were gasping and squeaking and laughing with Brown and Barbara Lloyd, and afterward I wanted to cry just to release all the excitement.

The idea that triggered such a big response is not complicated. The two women walk out and stand on a big tumbling mat. One falls; the other must catch her; they take turns. Their trust in each other is phenomenal, and neither faller tries to make it easy. Often the catcher decides to run all the way around to get underneath the falling body and fall with it. Laughing and breathing hard, they pile up on the ground, take a second's rest, and get up to challenge each other's speed and coordination again. Once Lloyd chooses to fall straight backward away from Brown while Brown is still clambering up from the previous fall. This time, Brown cries out too, but she makes it. It's beautiful: one woman very still, trying to feel which way her body wants to fall; the other eyeing her warily, maybe edging around her; then the slow, treelike leaning that gathers speed (or the sudden plunge); the rapid move of the catcher; the slow tumble to the mat in a tangle; the pause to renew strength and breath; the rise to begin again.

Brown's other falling duet (1971) with Steve Paxton is interesting too, but less friendly, almost painful. This one involves lifts and carries in which the lifter then deliberately tosses or tumbles both people to the floor. More manipulating is necessary in this one—more calculating too.

Playing with gravity and weight is Brown's game these days. In her new "Leaning Duets," several couples adjust themselves in communal loops of rope with small backboards for better support. The two step into the circle, place their toes together, and then gradually lean back away from each other. By moving carefully, or by instructing each other to "take" or "give," they can move in different directions or turn their own bodies within the rope to face toward or away from the partner. It's a tense little game (like racing with an egg on a spoon), and we root for different couples or try to understand why some never seem to be able to adjust to each other. Is her ass too big? Does he let his spine cave in?

In "Walking on the Wall," Brown tricks gravity and our perception. She's had special tracks installed on the ceiling, close to two neighboring walls and parallel to those walls. Seven tracks—each with brown canvas sling suspended from ropes which can move along it. Each harness has ropes of a slightly different length. The dancers—one, two, three, seven at a time climb one or the other of two ladders stationed at the terminal points, choose a sling, slip into it. And walk on the wall. Really. They have to brace their feet against the wall and hold their bodies very straight. When they want to pass each other, one must step over another's ropes. The illusion is uncanny. Their shirts are brown like the slings, for camouflage, and some of them are excellent wall-walkers (no falling hair, drooping head or legs betray them). For dizzying moments at a time, you seem to be in a tower looking down on the foreshortened bodies of people promenading endlessly on two intersecting white streets. Sometimes you come down from the tower to watch the technique of it all— how they get into and out of the slings, how they pass, how they unstick a recalcitrant pulley, how they zoom around a corner. They go forward, backward, meet, separate, stand. After a while, wall-walking seems like something that you may once have been able to do. A long time ago.

The concert ends with "Skymap" (1969). The audience lies on the floor of the totally dark gallery and looks up. Brown's taped voice instructs us to try to make a map of the United States on the ceiling, putting in boundaries, lakes, capital cities. Words—the words that she speaks are to be our building material. She talks lovingly and quietly of words, the way animal words like "horse" will trot out to take their places. She gabbles the Lord's Prayer, apologizes, says that we need the words because there are a lot of mountain ranges to be filled in. She keeps talking, sweetly, wittily—sometimes giving instructions or reminders, sometimes reading diaries or shopping lists, but most often just saying the names of towns, lakes, rivers, cities, mountains. And the words that you haven't thought of since geography class or your last trip across the country call up pleasant nostalgias, child's dreams of a continent. Listening to her comfortable voice, you see the relief of cottonwood trees after miles of desert, or growling cascades, or steeples, or white front porches with rocking chairs, or crickets and honeysuckle at night, or roads and railroads. And I'm not sure whether you go home happy or sad.

Brown Climbs Again

The Village Voice, October 28, 1971

Admirers of Trisha Brown pack the NYU gym so full that I begin planning how I'll get out if there's a fire. A lot of people who admire Trisha Brown bring their children to admire her too. But what the children really like is sliding, screaming, falling on the slick floor, and making paper airplanes to sail. They provide the entractes, and sometimes more.

Brown is still into hanging and the peculiar perspective that she can give her audience by hanging. "Planes" is a calm and beautiful climb by Brown, Carmen Beuchat, and Penelope. They climb in black-fronted, white-backed (or the reverse) suits; they climb on a rectangular white "wall" with evenly spaced holes in it. There is backing so that the holes are not visible as holes. Framed in the light from a film projector, the three women ascend and descend the wall, cross it and recross it. They move so smoothly and skillfully that you can hardly see their hands grip the holes or their feet stand in them. The illusion works. You begin to see them as if from above; they are on their hands and knees crawling over the geometrical white terrain. Only, because they are really vertical and clinging to a wall, they can move with a fluidity that they couldn't achieve if they were crawling on the floor. So sometimes they remind you of the life trapped in a drop of water on a microscope slide, and, like that life, their purpose is as mysterious as their activity is clear.

Trisha Brown's solo, "Accumulation," begins with simple rotating arm gestures based on pointing (thumbing, actually). She's standing in one place facing the audience, gradually increasing a gentle sway of knees and hips. She adds a few careful gestures bit by bit; they're all of a piece with the original ones. She's very accurate about what she's doing, but beautifully relaxed—a watched kettle building up steam so slowly that each new ripple and bubble becomes immensely significant.

"Rummage Sale and the Floor of the Forest" is a big happy mess

118

composed of two peculiarly related elements. One is Trisha Brown and Carmen Beuchat up on a low-hanging grid of ropes climbing into and through the clothing that has been threaded along the ropes. The other is a rummage sale going on right underneath them, so close that one shopper could ask Trisha Brown's upside-down head the price of a tie. The group in charge of hawking the heaps of old clothing attracts a crowd under the grid by their helter-skelter selling techniques and crazy prices. There is, in fact, no sensible relationship between goods and prices: a fairly nice sweater sells for 10 cents, a dilapidated skirt for $1, and so on. The excited, haggling bazaar makes and dissipates itself, and many of those shopping take no notice of the clothes-climbers above. The snake charmer who shares a booth with the rug-seller. The recycling of our detritus. Who knows what it is?

A few others try climbing on the grid, and when the children fall asleep or get heavy or fall down so often that they cry, the people go home. Wearing their new 10-cent sweaters.

This was the first time I had concentrated on Trisha Brown's dancing. I was so impressed by her fluidity that I failed to define the structure of "Accumulating Piece." As in subsequent Brown dances built on this form, she accumulated a sequence, movement by movement—always returning to the beginning after each addition (i.e., 1, 1-2, 1-2-3, 1-2-3-4, etc.). At a lecture demonstration at Connecticut College in the summer of 1975, Brown remarked that she had never again performed "Floor of the Forest" with a rummage sale going on underneath, since she had found to her dismay that art couldn't compete with bargains.

When Is Not Enough Too Much?

The Village Voice, April 7, 1975

Certain minimal dances loiter in my memory long after I've seen them. By minimal, I don't mean just dances that make a point of everyday behavior and any-old-movement, but dances tenanted by one plain, vivid movement image or dances in which a few sturdy patterns are repeated so many times that the viewers' muscles begin to flex in response.

When I got home from Lucinda Childs's concert at her bare white-walled loft with its new golden wood floor, I tried to do her "Reclining Rondo" as smoothly and flatly as Susan Brody, Judy Padow, and David Woodberry had performed it. I'd liked watching it and I liked doing it. Doing it emphasized the even, easy-going bending and stretching of the body as it moved through the carefully arranged pattern of sitting crouching, and lying. Watching it, I had, of course, seen also the ingenious permutations of patterns created by three bodies performing in unison and had sometimes tried to anticipate the changes of direction or spacing that the pattern's occasional asymmetries (e.g., a quarter roll right or left) would produce.

Childs's dances are very brainy. It's hard for me just to look at them. Watching her walking pieces like "Calico Mingling" or "Duplicate Suite," my mind is almost feverishly busy. It notes whether the patterns unroll in six or eight counts (Childs's dances usually are insistently metrical), and then tries to figure how the curving paths relate to the straight ones and whether one dancer is moving inexorably to the left. The separateness of the dancers is awesome and slightly chilling; they pace in their distinct and complicated orbits as cooly as planets—as if each were surrounded by his or her own atmosphere and force field.

In a new piece, "Congeries on Edges for Twenty Obliques," James Barth and Susan Brody join the three people who performed "Reclining Rondo." "Congeries" is another path dance, but this time, after they've established an eight-count walking pattern (with half-time and double-time variants), they begin to fill the phrase with more elaborate movement. At its fullest, it contains two different jumps, a spin in a squat, and a cartwheel; then it empties back to walking. Not all the dancers execute the pattern-so-far together; you see one, now three, now two, now five spring into the air. Watching an individual, you see a phrase with a climax; watching the group, you see a pattern of unpredictable but steady pops and thrusts rist out of the texture of the walk.

It pleases me that in "Reclining Rondo" and "Congeries" the dancers get tired. In the former, their bodies want to cuddle into comfortable positions and not move on; in the latter, they breathe hard and brace themselves for jumps. I respect Childs's insistence on neutrality, but don't find it pleasant. Watching her in her solo, "Particular Reel," I feel her gentle tenseness tweaking my own arm muscles and wonder again why she should want to erase from her body all indications of ebb and flow.

Lassie Between the Sheets

The Village Voice, October 3, 1974

Like most of James Cunningham's jig-saw puzzle dance(s), "Dancing with Maisie Paradocks" is indeed a maze strewn with paradoxes; although it doesn't lack for signposts, they invariably point in the wrong (right) direction. If "Maisie Paradocks" were a cartoon, the balloon over Little Orphan Annie's head would bristle with Red Ryder's words, and vice versa. The dance has some of the wild charm of Cunningham's early pieces and lots of the glossier wit of his more recent ones. He again presents the theme that meanders and romps and storms through most of his work—scrambling and unscrambling the message so dexterously and so continuously that it decodes itself easily in your brain. You could probably cram on "Maisie Paradocks" and pass a course in Cunningham Fundamentals.

Cunningham (paradoxically) appears to believe in the mystic male-female principal of Indian philosophy while railing at customs that decree one kind of behavior for men (biological males, that is) and another for women. A wisely innocent litany whispers through his works: we are all compounded of dark and light, of air and earth; we are the lamb and the lion that devours it; aren't we all "male" at times, "female" at others? So Cunningham and the dancers who work with him scamper and glide through his big, bright, occasionally self-conscious works—mixing and mismatching the sexes with childlike intentness. They put on costumes and masks that are as direct in their messages as signposts; they play scenes—talking or singing or dancing, or all three. The transformations never stop.

"Maisie," like most Cunningham dances, begins with a rite: the performers, dressed in white tunics, sit in a circle and hum. Later, pairs of dancers in white (whoever's not busy) swoop on from time to time like helpful angels to revive the fallen and assist them offstage. (The dance is full of battles.) A tall figure in orange pajamas, wearing a tiger mask and carrying a parasol slinks on. "I am Shiva," a taped voice intones quietly. But the scenes that this aggressive, sunny deity issues in are all pied. An insistently romping golden girl (it was Linda Tarnay under the tiger mask) tries to vamp a scuttling businessman who has the head of a rabbit (Ted Striggles). He shoots her. Cunningham appears as an untidy, dreamy Bride. Shadowy men whom she clings to absentmindedly drop unnoticed as, in a brilliant monologue, she/he recalls a childhood of movie-going spent in love with Lassie. Inept yelps from the top of the aisle. Lauren Persichetti scampers down to the stage in her collie suit. Man as Bride and Woman as Dog laugh and dance and make love in a tangle of fur and net. Next a tough little girl in a baseball suit (Barbara Ellman) collapses when the bicycle she's riding is hit by a car (crashing noises, flashing lights).

Shakti (female, dark, moon, etc.) with her frog head turns into Ted Striggles in military uniform, lunging and hissing, facing a thousand enemies, stuttering "trained to kill" even as he is clearly running down. His collapse onto a chair begins an hilarious parody of "Specter of the Rose" with the soldier as the dreamer and Cunningham as a winsome and scantily clad Carnation. However, he/she wears a fetchingly matronly cap and dexterously folds the soldier's socks into a ball before enticing him to barefoot revels. This ends sadly; at the drop of a leap, the soldier is back in his expectant crouch, and the specter flies away (out the window, of course.) Striggles turns back into the businessman, now a lecher in droopy BVDs. Looking like an unfunny Groucho Marx, he chases a large, helpless Playboy bunny (Tarnay again). She is rescued, whether she wants to be or not, by Wonder Woman (Ellman) who leads all the women into battle against businessman, the male-chauvanist sheriff (William Holcomb), and a tiny mustachioed strongman who turns out to be Lauren Persichetti. In typical Cunningham fashion, the silliness, the ferocity, and the shreds of plot dissolve into a light-footed dance; the dancers look sweet and easy and at home in their bodies. Both adroit and childlike in his dancethinking, Cunningham pulls the sticks and straw from our familiar scarecrows and prances on the debris. He's still afraid of the empty clothes though, and so are we.

Riding at Anchor on the Lawn?

The Village Voice, August 15, 1974

One of the nicest things about the last weekend of performances at the American Dance Festival was the quietness. The Connecticut College campus itself was quiet—the students were packing or had packed. On Sunday morning you could sit down for a minute on the grass where Nathan Clark had spread a pre-breakfast picnic of screwdrivers and toast the end of the summer.

Friday night we sat in the Arboretum at dusk waiting for Laura Dean's "Changing," watching the melancholy dying pond and lighting cigarettes to warn away mosquitoes. Suddenly—how long had we looked in another direction?—a woman stood on the lawn with her back to the pond. Two women. Three women. Their long dresses—one crimson, one peacock blue, one yellow—belled out stiffly; loose bodices hid everything but their faces and hands. The silk of their dresses resisted the wind and glowed mysteriously against the dark trees and lake. Pale Gainsborough ladies. Ancient dolls.

Suddenly . . . were two of them leaning toward the center? How slowly they must have tilted. A drum began to beat in the woods behind us—John Smead, but I never saw him. After a long time it became clear that the women were advancing toward us over the lawn. (Here people nudged each other incredulously.) You couldn't see the women's feet moving, nor did their bodies betray them with the slight side-to-side sway a walk usually engenders. They weren't *walking*, they were simply coming toward us—sailing very slowly and by infinitesimal degrees.

Chess figures moved by a hidden hand. Suddenly, they all fell forward onto their faces, breathed into the grass, rolled over, got up with their backs to us, and moved away. Quietly, slowly, invisibly. When they reached the broad steps leading down to the water, they floated down. Their feet disappeared, theirlegstheirhipstheircheststheirshoulderstheirheads. They had sunken into the earth. Several small children ran to look for them.

Disintegrating Hero

The Village Voice, October 16, 1969

Bill Dunas must be unique among bright young artists in that he doesn't have to worry whether his second work will live up to the promise shown by his first. This is because he never does a second work. The six (or is it seven?) dances that he's made over a two year period are really one piece. He built this dance, block by block, until he had over an hour of material; then in each subsequent performance he varied the order, added or subtracted parts, changed his appearance or performing attack, appended a new title. When Dunas topples his block structure and builds up a different one, those who have seen the previous versions are lightly bombarded with associations denied those who are seeing the dance for the first time. It's the same as if you had actually built a castle out of painted blocks, knocked it down after a while and built a new one, and then noticed that a specific block that was the chimney before is now the doorsill.

Dunas's dance is always a created autobiography of a man alone—horribly alone; he might be the last man on earth or the first man in space, so complete is his solitude. Each version has been increasingly painful to watch, because he has been gradually denying us the palliative of virtuosity—that is, of knowing that the strong young dancer's body really dominates the suffering and exhaustion it is manufacturing. Now we see him, seemingly actually wearing out before our eyes. Very little "dancing" and very little youth.

Seeing the latest installment, "Ajax," at the Cubiculo, I sensed an unnerving progression (if only in my own mind): the man we see has been getting older in each dance. Now he wears his hair parted in the middle, and his jaw is edged with budding mutton-chop whiskers. His body, held in such a way as to make it look slack and bottom-heavy, is dressed in cut-off winter underwear. Nobody's foxy grand-dad. In the last performance ("Wax"), Dunas added a run that turned into a gasping hobble. Now he starts with a hobble—around the perimeters of the

Cube like a mole lost in someone else's burrow. In "X" and "Express," he tried again and again to clamber out of the performing area via fire ladders or the wall itself; now he picks up a tangle of rope, looks up, and laughs until he chokes. He's older in another way too—hardened, cynical. Once he used to devour a slice of bread, drink a cup of water, smoke a cigarette with the singlemindedness of a child, or someone who has gone without for a long time, or someone who may not experience these things again. Now, in "Ajax," he eats his bread meditatively, drinks eying things over the rim of his glass, smokes as he follows a conversation in his mind or around him. Still alone, but watching others' eyes for confirmation of his existence. The dance is now permeated with the twitching fear of a cornered animal, but within an intellectual being. Dunas plays almost the entire dance in a crouch, a slack snarl on his face. When he speaks, civilization hides the terror: "They picked me to play the Yellow Rose of Texas," he says drily, "I wore a long yellow dress; they sang, and I skipped."

There has been another progression too. Whatever this man is struggling against has become increasingly internal. In his very first solo, "Gap," he seemed to be up against overwhelming outside forces beyond his control. By "Express," the forces seemed to be the actual environment that imprisoned him; one by one he pried up the trapdoors in the stage floor at Riverside Church and dropped inside. In "Wail," he appeared a stoic, passively enduring prisoner. In "Wax," the adversary was clearly his own body—or soul. He seemed to be running down, melting away. I probably won't fully understand "Ajax" until I see the next version. The invincible hero still struggles. Or almost invincible: the real (?) Ajax was invulnerable except for one spot in his armpit and one on his neck. (Is it a coincidence that Dunas's hero always announces mysteriously, "I had a lump on my neck."?) I say that I won't understand "Ajax" until I see the next version, but, brilliant as I feel the dance is, I can't help hoping that someday soon there won't be any need for a next version. I look forward to Bill Dunas's second dance.

When I interviewed Bill Dunas in 1976, he said that he never really wore himself out; he was using all his resources as an actor-dancer to create that illusion. He also said that he didn't deliberately set about to cause pain or discomfort to members of the audience, but that perhaps that was a side effect of trying to create images that would be powerful enough to stick with them.

From the Inside

The Village Voice, October 22, 1970

When I told Jeff Duncan that I wanted to write an article on his style—in honor or his Brooklyn Academy concerts—he said lightly, "If you figure out what it is, let me know." I thought later that very few contemporary choreographers start out with any idea of an individual style. They know what interests them, and the style follows.

Duncan is interested in people, singly and in humanity-hordes. This is probably why some years ago he chose to work with Anna Sokolow and why in certain of his own dances (particularly the humanity ones) her influence is visible.

His movement is partially a spin-off from his own tall, columnar body. He enjoys the feel of verticality—body pulled straight and high, arms hanging at the sides—and also the plunging away from it into falls and crouches. Sometimes the verticality is re-stated by alert drops to one knee or shoulder-stands. Thus the ground becomes charged in his dances: in his nature pieces, it is benevolent, magical; in his violent or unhappy pieces, it often appears to be jolting or shifting.

He tends to steer away from what might look gimmicky. Arms are unusually neutral—hanging down straight or maybe held out to the side—until they are needed for hanging on to something or, very occasionally, for a specific dramatic gesture. In most of his group dances he seems to avoid complex phrases of movement in favor of repeating chains (leaps, piques, turns) punctuated by encounters between dancers or single contrasting moments.

Before I ever performed in his dances, I was most impressed by a sensitivity he has for the flow of group energy. It has something to do with musicality too, I suppose. In his group works ("Statement" is one that appeared on the Brooklyn program), the changes in the flow and direction of energy are handled very sensitively and very theatrically as well. Just recently I noticed an interesting point: this energy is almost always the same for everyone within the group. They all feel it. Even though specific movements may be different, it is as if the same tide has them in its grip. This, I think, is what gives the humanity-hordes effect—a metaphor for the human condition that we all share.

To me, some of his most effective movement as movement has come in those dances in which he was concerned with the individual or with a very specific situation. For instance, in his "Winesburg Portraits," which I saw in 1964 and performed in in 1970, the movement for each of the character vignettes arises out of character and situation. Elmer Cowley, the kid who is considered "strange," performs stiff, twisting motions of his whole torso on a stationary base that expresses his locked-in feelings.

The minister uses his fingers wriggling at his mouth as a desperate sermon. A lonely wife clenches and reclenches her hands with a sharp, dry noise. In "Resonances" (1969), Duncan also achieved some memorable movement. The dance is a suite of delicate, gentle little pieces—mostly solos. They seem designed to capture some quality of the dancers who first performed them. One section takes advantage of Lenore Latimer's long legs, the odd vulnerability of her knee and ankle joints. Another is made for Aaron Osborne's soft kind of strength and alert spine. And so on.

"Diminishing Landscape," which I have always been in and never seen, has a first section that feels very distinctive because the movement arises out of a specific motivation—four people marching, covering ground together, with bodies poised for action and eyes focused on something outside them and all around them. Duncan's newest work, "The Glade," also owes some very beautiful moments to movement that arises from a specific situation. (The dance may be some sort of landmark: the first male love duet, the first homosexual dance with a happy ending.) The dance begins in near darkness, a huddle of bodies just visible in the center. One of Olivier Messaien's "Vingt Regards sur l'Enfant Jésus" is played (and beautifully, by Ilene Furman) in its entirety before any movement takes place. This prelude is stormy; then the music becomes very delicate, and the two men (Ross Parkes and Daniel Maloney) make their first gestures. Still tangled together, slow and trusting, they stretch their arms to clasp hands. One leans over the other; the first to rise gently tumbles the other over his back so that they stand up together. The two men are nearly naked, dressed in skillfully designed (by Leor C. Warner) scraps of leather that give the effect of outlining some of their muscles. I found this whole opening very beautiful to watch. The dance is brief—an idealized pas de deux of male love in the way that a ballet pas de deux is of a particular sort of male-female relationship. "The Glade" even emphasizes parts of the body that might be considered beautiful in such an affair—the curve of the buttocks or the muscles of the shoulders. The two men seem to have some doubts and occasionally dance as if the world is holding them at bay. At the end, a slide of a starry sky is projected on the backdrop, suggesting that they are embarking on a kind of cosmic voyage.

This article is a kind of first too. Although I am obliged much of the time to write about the work of friends, colleagues, and even people who taught me how to dance, this is the first time I've tried to write anything about a choreographer right after a concert of his in which I appeared as a performer. There are certain things I can't talk about. For instance, in "Vinculum," I feel a new spontaneity in Duncan's work, but I have no idea whether the work really appears free. Oh, well, I've always felt that this column should be called "Inside Dance."

Climbing in the Ghost Ship

The Village Voice, May 23, 1974

What Douglas Dunn has been doing at his loft almost every afternoon in April and May isn't called dancing: it's advertised as a performance exhibit. A pretty accurate title for a concrete, yet eerily ambiguous event.

To get to it, you take a subway, probably, then a walk, then a long upstairs climb. Neatly printed signs point the way. At the door of the loft, another sign tells you how to open the latch. Silence. In the tidy living area, an open book waits for visitors' names and a paper bag for their dollar bills. I suppose sometimes—Saturdays, maybe—there are a lot of people here chatting quietly in museum voices. There's someone else here now, though. A girl with a tangle of black hair and rather forlorn stocking-feet is sleeping, face down, on a mat on the floor. The nonwatching watchman.

Come on out, Doug, I know you're here. My adventurous, rambunctious little son makes a sharp right and starts to run and crawl and chatter his way through . . . my God, what is it? Dunn has filled the room with slatted wooden cubes about three or four feet square piled on top of each other. He must have been dragging in heavy-duty skids from building sites for months and months and nailing them together. The path through this hulking maze is narrow; the distance from the entrance to the window wall seems interminable.

Our talkative caravan winds back and forth: "Mommy you come on up here let's go this way you help me this way mommy you climb up it's dark in here." It is dark, except near the windows and in the middle where one spotlight beam pierces the slatted roof. Looking up at this beacon, I see two bare feet. Quick, climb up and out onto the roof of the structure. There's Douglas Dunn, lying on his back with his eyes closed. Folded blue towels cushion his neck and ankles. He's wearing a white shirt and trousers with red trunks over them. Around his ankles, wrists, and neck are tied small bandannas—navy blue or red. Thin red lipstick lines run out the corners of his eyes, his mouth. I stare; the baby simply refuses to notice and embarks on noisier and more perilous climbs. Beneath the tranced figure, we go back and forth in the maze. I think I may measure it or count the boxes, but I don't. How will anyone ever dismantle this labyrinth of dim, ragged wood?

My son and I help each other out to the antechamber, although we're clearly in separate worlds. He's just been clambering in a splendidly dangerous, splintery jungle gym; I've been stalking through the empty corridors of a Viking burial ship that encases the body of a solitary warrior. Both worlds were made by Douglas Dunn.

Gestures Printed on Space

The Village Voice, May 26, 1975

A solo concert is a tricky thing. A fine performer impresses you with his/her skill and versatility; a poor one makes you feel trapped, as if you were sharing a train compartment with a chattering, small-minded person. But Douglas Dunn produces another effect. I always feel that dancing is just something important and interesting that he does. Occasionally he does this publicly, and then I go to him to be danced for the way I might go to a priest to be shriven or a doctor to be healed.

He begins his new solo, "Gestures in Red," lying on his back on the pale, clean floor of Merce Cunningham's studio, beneath windows that display New York's light-studded sky. Slowly he scuds around the room on his back—pushing with his feet. He stops, raises his body into a half-sitting, half-reclining position and turns his head sideways to stare past us. Where have I seen that before? Suddenly I remember the Mayan stone men which archaeologists call Chac Mool; this is the squared-off position they wait in—the flattened curve of their bellies holding a bowl for sacrificial blood.

This whole first section seems to be about ways of moving backward. Dunn rolls back and inverts himself into shoulder stands. He runs backward and lets his weight pull him down into a skidding sit. He walks rather ceremoniously backward; occasionally he considers altering the direction of his big, deep steps and hovers on the verge of a new path the way a weather vane waits to sense the groove of the wind. At last, he runs forward and leaps suddenly and lightly onto one of the windowsills. And the lights go out.

During the entire next section of "Gestures in Red," he stays in one spot and moves his arms, head, torso. He has a curious adventure with his forearms: he crouches slightly, laying his arms along his thighs as if to hunker down and rest, but his arms keep slipping away and falling. He works on this casually over and over. It's fascinating to watch someone not doing something you know he could do had he not imposed some mysterious limitation on himself.

The third part is a foot dance. Dunn's feet are up to any number of tricks—sliding and inching along the floor, pulling his long, quiet body with them. We laugh: at times he looks so like an old hoofer dancing in his sleep. During this section and the last complicated, hard-to-follow, everything-in-it part, I'm constantly amazed by the dancing; it never turns out the way I expect, and the dynamic texture of it is far more variegated than that of most dance-work I see. Yet Dunn never looks as if he's doing anything arbitrary or clever. He makes the most stumbling, doubled-back-on-themselves movements appear to flow subtly into each other. Sometimes his long slim body looks gangling, almost awkward; sometimes he looks as watchful and uncertain as a wading bird; sometimes he looks poised and extremely elegant. But always he looks intelligent and interesting and like a man you could trust.

How to Risk All and Still Play Safe

The Village Voice, August 8, 1974

We know, don't we, that the dancers in the Louis Falco Company are all beautiful—that they have shapely bodies and movie faces? We know, too, that they're marvelous dancers. They stretch the dancing from the centers of their bodies and fling it out into space—often not any real or imagined place, but a frightening void. They stare at each other, or talk, or flop onto each other; yet their dancing—whether it is a Dionysiac frenzy of joy or a cosmic yowl of despair—seems unfocused. Their huge gestures, their blazing intensity never gets them anywhere. The lavishness with which they expend their energy can make you impatient as well as thrill you.

The more dances I see by Falco and Jennifer Muller (also one of the company's associate directors), the more I feel them to be concerned with human desperation. But Falco in works like "Sleepers," "Soap Opera," "Avenue," "Two Penny Portrait"; Muller in "Nostalgia," "Biography," and parts of her "Tub" don't deal with humanity as a whole, nor with concrete disasters like hunger or death. They explore the forms desperation takes in restless, chic society. They turn sex and the quest for identity into games—pleasant and unpleasant; characters in these dances often express the states of their souls through the clothes they put on or take off.

The characters are obsessed with their childhoods. They talk about them, move with the uncivilized violence of children. They may cuddle teddy bears ("Two Penny Portrait") or need to be rocked to sleep ("Sleepers"). Sometimes they use sex as a form of thumbsucking—something to snuggle into when they're too tired to do anything else.

Once, I thought I learned quite a lot about Juan Antonio from a dance called "Day of the Dead" which Erin Martin made with him and about him. But in Falco/Muller dramatic works, although the dancers call each other Louis, Jennifer, Juan, Georgiana, Matthew, Mary Jane, I have never learned from any of these dances how Louis or Jennifer or Juan or Georgiana or Matthew or Mary Jane feel about anything outside themselves. I've learned their names and a few statistics, and I've learned that they have the same basic greedy drives we all have, but I don't know specifically what they're like. In "Sleepers," Falco and Antonio often alternate in one of the roles; only the names and the inflections change. I didn't see Falco's latest work, and I'm sorry because it sounded interesting. I guess I just don't like to watch such enormously gifted people going around and around in the same track.

In Muller's "Biography," the choreographer and Mary Jane Eisenberg present us with an identity crisis. While their taped voices recite their vital statistics—which occasionally coincide—the two dance stormily alike. They're wearing trendy white suits, black boots, skullcaps. As the dance progresses, Muller tries to break away: "Mary Jane, we are *not* alike!" Eisenberg disagrees, hangs on as if her only hope of identity lay in staying with Muller. Taped memories of childhood hint at parental pressures to conform. At the end, the two look disproportionately shocked when Muller slowly removes their skullcaps to reveal that one has straight hair, and one has curls. What a puzzle. I don't for a single moment believe those two women are alike, any more than I'd believe that a variation in hair style could make them different. Even in the adolescent world of copycat looks, individuality is predicated on more complex matters. It moves me to see Eisenberg inch her leg a triumphant fraction higher than Muller's: she's found out what she has to do to hold her own on a stage full of superstars. Neither of the Falco company choreographers seems to want to deal with that specific kind of struggle.

Although Falco's "Two Penny Portrait" is one of the most decadent dances he's made, it's also one of the most vivid and succinct. In this duet, he was able, for the most part, to resist pouring out a virtuosic flood of dancing; he lets us see the characters stopping, wondering, changing their minds. He and Georgiana Holmes are blown and tumbled onto a stage littered with trashcans. He's wearing the pants to a tux; she has on what might be a bridesmaid's outfit, and she's carrying a teddy bear. They stagger about, colliding occasionally. She hangs perilously over his back, and he doesn't even know she is there. Finally they recognize each other—or, at least, acknowledge each other as ports in a possible storm—and clomp around gleefully together. But they're so unalive to reality that they don't even notice when they slip from each others' embraces, any more than they notice the garbage or the traffic noises. Scott and Zelda with the polish gone—reduced to their infantile, drunken rock-bottoms.

Muller's new "Speeds" gives the company a chance to show off its classy dancing with nothing in mind but exuberance and changes of speed. Some of it is lovely: a long line of dancers just walking; Eisenberg and Diamond very slowly folding around each other while a fast-dancing group swings and bounces beside them. (This is one of the few times Muller shows two speeds at once.) The dancers shout "Change!" now and then, and that's nice too—especially when the commands produce a change you can immediately perceive. It's exhilarating to see the Falco dancers just dance, as an alternative to playing those glamorous, dissatisfied people who bear their names.

Dancing In Fits

The Village Voice, June 13, 1974

The dancing of Viola Farber's people is passionately intense and as insistent as sirens, but fogbound. Their limbs flail and slash and punch the air around them; they collide with each other and startle into tender stares and gestures. They had, perhaps, been thinking of themselves as alone with the violent intricacies of the movement. "Dune" has hills and valleys—a strained calm: June Finch in a steady flow of slow balances for instance. A sudden whirlpool: Larry Clark whizzing through a turn that seems precariously out of balance in about five different ways. Alvin Lucier's taped voice—"I am sitting in a room"—becomes more distant until it drowns in its own resonance or the room's overtones and becomes a high ringing sound.

"Willi I" is Farber at her most violent. The dancers wear slick, wet-looking red jumpsuits; Lucier's score, "The Fires in the Minds of the Dancers," is wonderfully thunderous—it sounds like waves crashing down, like sirens and alarm bells. The dancers appear to be trying to impede each other's movements. Lifts, falls, and carries have a drastic look. Everything happens fast, but your eye remembers people clumped around a fallen body, people dropping from above; tangling with each other. The dancers (Clark, Finch, Susan Matheke, Ann Koren, Ande Peck, Jeff Slayton) are formidable, but Farber herself looks more appealingly human. They tend to seal themselves off in what often look like tantrums of dancing; she remains susceptible to the movement. She doesn't, in the usual sense, "motivate" the dancing; it might have been flung onto her body from outer space, but she allows it to change her from moment to moment.

Pull Together in These Distracted Times

The Village Voice, March 31, 1975

I spend two evenings at La Mama watching the superficially anarchic Grand Union and come away absurdly comforted—thinking that if I stuck my head out the window and yelled to the street below, "catch me," maybe, just maybe, someone would.

The Grand Union is, of course, Trisha Brown, Barbara Dilley, Douglas Dunn, David Gordon, Nancy Lewis, and Steve Paxton. And everything they do is thought up on the spot: the swingy, slouchy dancing and bright "routines;" the improbable group feats; the tender body-against-body work; the saucy one-liners and dead-pan dialogue; the singing; the clothes-play; the satirical, in-passing references to theater, dance, movie traditions.

It's easy to remember a Grand Union performance in terms of its highlights and its low points or to talk about one performance that "worked" and one that didn't. But I find that the most important thing the group's performing does is to articulate for us, in a particular way, the shifts of equilibrium, the spurts of directed tension, the changes of focus that we're all constantly engaged in—alone or in groups. The particular way the Grand Union does this emphasizes—I can't think of a pithier word—coping. I like to watch the way a Grand Union person will try to see through something he or she has started—patiently, at times gallantly, even though whatever it is may have become unwieldy or painful—but then finally, drop it without regret. I like the way they all help each other out of difficulties or lend their weight to accomplish some group purpose, or the way they fit themselves into something that may not be their bag. In the deepest and best sense of the word, they are polite—however vigorous, raunchy, aggressive or noisily eccentric they may allow themselves to get.

I've seen improvisational work in dance and in theater and been turned off by a lot of what I've seen. But although the Grand Union may at times become "self-indulgent" (a critic-ese expression usually meaning that the performers explored an event for longer than you wanted to watch them explore it), they avoid a lot of improv pitfalls. They don't try to top each other or break up each other's acts under the guise of providing contrast; they don't always play copycat as a means of arriving at group unity; they don't play the lout the way some actors do when improvising, making every word and gesture a potential for confrontation.

The Grand Union copes, not just with their possibly cumbersome tasks, but with the weight of our boredom. I don't mean that in low moments they start throwing themselves round to keep us entertained, but that they make us feel that we're all locked into this (this what?) together; we have as much a stake as they do in the turn of events. This art presents so vividly a semblance of the pattern made by our own daily indecisions and little triumphs that it's possible to watch almost on tenterhooks—applauding "wise" choices, lamenting lost "opportunities," waiting to see who is the early bird and who the worm.

The performers seem to have long, hungry memories. A phrase spoken, a gesture made during a Grand Union performance goes down in history, and may be repeated or developed much later in the evening by someone else. Everyone seems fiercely sensitive to these thematic possibilities. For instance, during the March 15 performance at La Mama, Lewis, doing some rather abandoned quasi-ballroom dancing (lifts and all) with Dunn, asked solicitously "Is this your first time?" A little later, when the two of them sauntered hand-in-hand up to a group of hard-working others, someone asked them, "Is this your first time here?" Yes, they admitted, and walked around taking in the sights.

Oh boy, memorable moments. Lewis standing for ages way at the back, up on a little stage, with a blue blanket over her head and finally (in a propitious silence) asking in her high quavery voice, "Am I doing anything important?" Everyone attempting to help Trisha Brown mount the business half of a broken stepladder, which was being held up on Paxton's feet (he lying on his back). David Gordon playing emcee to a rapidly burgeoning monster-virgin routine he has discovered ("And now ladies and gentlemen, the only known version in which a trio of virgins attacks a monster"). Dunn holding Paxton in a fireman's carry after a long fruitless drill with Trisha Brown as sergeant ("When I count to five, I want everyone to face your hometown"): Dunn to nobody in particular, "Is this what it feels like to be in the corps?" Paxton, some time later still draped over Dunn's shoulder, "Is this what it feels like to be a star?" Dilley and Dunn exploring a long and beautiful nuzzling sort of dance on the floor and then Dilley lying there shuddering with laughter while Dunn, as polite and attentive as a doctor in the jungle, squatted by her and attempted to tell her how he had mastered the problem of laughing during performance. The three women dancing with desperate grace in an elusive little follow spot. And more.

The March 15th performance was by any standards a brilliant one; all performers high on collaboration. The March 16th one kept getting snarled. For one thing, David Gordon arrived with a stick in his hand and wearing an elaborate costume that suggested a Biblical patriarch; this made for some grand comedy but also, of course, limited his flexibility for a while and determined the ways the others wanted to relate to him. Yet his decision to appear in the trappings of a mournful Bedouin was a perfectly valid and potentially potent Grand Union thing to do.

I've heard of people walking out during flagging moments in Grand Union performances. I couldn't bear to do that. I'd have to wait and see how they got out of their predicament. And whether it was a predicament or just a change in the weather.

What Is This Man Giving Us?

The Village Voice, September 27, 1973

I guess I've never seen Raymond Johnson dance alone before. I left the concert he shared with Ze'eva Cohen—the Cubiculo's first fall dance performance—with an overwhelming sense of eyes staring blackly at the audience. Whether by coincidence or design, the three solos he performed all had to do with a man's image of himself and the calculated way in which this image was offered to others. We played the others, and Johnson defied or cajoled or seduced us or threw us to the lions with almost unnerving coolness and intelligence.

He's a good dancer with an exceedingly straight spine and a brusque kind of strength. His face looks like an African mask, carved and rubbed into smoothness with oiled fingers. But this same face can look bleak, demoralized, very young. In the beginning of his solo, "Black Dance," he strides firmly in a circle, looking straight ahead, like someone who knows eyes are watching him, but is, God damn it, not going to look back. At the end of the dance, he's reclining like a lazy, but watchful lion; his minute, but arrogant beckoning gestures seem to say, *"you* come here!" to an invisible crowd, or perhaps, "Just give me all you've got, baby, and fast." In between, Johnson shows a series of moods and attitudes from coquettish to defiant, but he doesn't dwell on any of them. All his ideas are blended into one seamless dance, and the roles are so dexterously assumed and discarded that you're not even sure you've seen some of them.

He's also cool in his ridiculously titled "Tuesday's Tempered Terpsichore"—a short, minimal, slow-motion jive. To a blast from Count Basie, Johnson walks into a spotlight and slowly, decadently melts into dancing. Almost too cool to move, he makes each tiny jerk, each blase gesture quiver disdainfully off his spine. Sometimes he looks like a depraved windup toy; perhaps it used to say "fuck you," but that part of the mechanism is broken.

"Feathers," a solo made for Johnson by James Waring, is as fascinating and as inscrutable as most of Waring's pieces. "Feathers" is dedicated to Barbette, a trapeze artist of the '20s and '30s who wore women's clothes while performing and took off his wig for the curtain call to show he was a man. Johnson appears in a short, gleaming tunic patterned with horizontal bands, and a gilt crown that curls down from his brow and forward onto his cheeks like spitcurls. A l'Egyptienne. Something about the two-dimensional "archaic" attitudes make me think of the nymphs in Nijinsky's "L'Après Midi D'un Faun." Certain dance phrases are repeated over and over, as precise as the Mozart music that accompanies them. Johnson attacks the movements harshly, holds them for a savage pause, and then wilts. He leans backward extravagantly, threatening us with a fall into darkness from the height of a tightrope. He's strong, but curiously wistful. At times, his tilted chin and drooping waist seem to evoke the way a whole generation thought women ought to be.

This review has been edited. It originally contained some brief, complimentary remarks about Ze'eva Cohen whose solo program I had written about in detail several months earlier.

Roof-dancing

The Village Voice, June 18, 1970

I like walking around New York looking up at old loft buildings and office buildings and warehouses. Sometimes way up there above the racks, trucks, crates and new foyers, sprout Medusa heads, cherubs, improbable beasts, wreaths of sooty fruit and flowers. Cruder, but still fascinating, the roofs are often grotesque playgrounds. Girders, water towers, steps that lead to nowhere, little buildings housing mysteriously clicking equipment, railings, skylights, chimneys.

I walked, rode, hauled myself up to the roof of some ante-everything building at Broadway and 12th Street to see a preview of Elizabeth Keen's roof dance, "On Edge." We emerged from a dirty hell of a stairway into the air to be confronted by Laura Pawel, Davidson Lloyd, Ted Striggles—open-mouthed gargoyles tangled up on a higher level of roof. Snarling and hissing and clawing they descend a ladder, while Keen perilously shinnies down from the high water tower. They canter off to arched brick interstices in a beautiful and meaningless wall hanging up over Union Square. Three girls in jeans climb off girders and sit in chairs; we follow. They turn out to be a Baroque trio; we turn out to be the audience.

Keen and her gang swing out into individual arches. Together, they stretch into the little spaces—feeling how the body feels good there. They wedge themselves in—feet off the ground—like nocturnal animals in the crotches of trees. What are they anyway? People, I know. But also like gargoyles, cats, monkeys that gibber antagonism and the next minute stroke and groom each other. These days, Keen is playing around with the face as a part of the dance instrument, twisting it into hideously virtuosic positions. At first, the four of them in their bright multi-colored shirts and their crazy energy look out of place on the stern old roof. After a while, I accept them: this is where they live, these are the things they do.

Their snarling faces and their hostility are wild and funny. The reckless way they run up walls, throw legs over parapets 16 floors above death is insanely lovely. A couple of times Striggles and Pawel begin a friendly mating duet, and both times Lloyd lurches between them with an apple in his mouth.

Keen is enamoured of the special shapes and spaces on this roof—I can see that. It's the girders, ledges, ladders, arches that she likes. The plain old open space that all roofs have interests her less. It becomes mainly a neutral crouching place, or an area to chase each other through. I find myself wishing she'd use it more.

Finally the dancers begin to move slowly, one by one, onto the slanting girders and crossbeams under the water tower. We have to turn to the West to see them. The musicians, who have been playing all along, move on to a particularly affecting Baroque suite. The dancers, quietly helpful to each other now, climb under, over, and through the structure. They walk smoothly down the perilous slant of the girders. Why is it suddenly so moving? The sun begins to set behind them. They curl up in the iron branches and sleep.

The Shape of Things to Come and Gone

The Village Voice, October 4, 1973

Kenneth King, Amerika's only rope dancer, prophesied the horror of Watergate two years before it happened, at a Free Music Store concert. I wasn't there and I probably wouldn't have understood much—don't now. Understand only that Kenneth King alias Patrick Duncan, alias Zora A. Zash, alias Pontease Tyak is—like many of us these days—heartsick, but unlike most of us, he is fighting. My head is buried too deep in the sand to know whether he's tilting with real demons or with windmills. Or are windmills the real demons now?

If anyone could get on the wavelength of Joseph G. Devadese of the Inner Seercret Service while trance-turning, King could. He dances like an angel. I could believe him a medium for any message, could sense, but not decipher, any number of cryptic codes lying just under the fine skin of his dancing.

To go back—"Inadmissleable Evidentdance." It is the Ancient of Days, September 26, 1973, Washington Square Methodist Church. Candles and flowers on the altar and a framed photograph. I guess it's Nietzsche, but can't verify. Altar-right, behind the rail, a table of tape recorders, microphones, papers. It's getting late. Appears Pontease Tyak, custodian for the TransHimalyan Society for Interplanetary Research. He's hirsute, grizzled, all that. Dark glasses are the only fixed point in a field of gray hair. Slavic, and wheezingly, cacklingly self-congratulatory, he warms to . . . what subject? He reads to us at length from his "beloved Nietzsche" ("Also Spracht Zarathustra"). I've gotten fond of him. He peels off hat, hair, glasses, coat to reveal Kenneth in his springy shoes, tuxedo pants, suspenders, shirt, knotted bolero of rope, neat navy and white bandanna. Dressed for axe-tion.

He's grave and worried, believes the news media have deliberately suppressed news of this event. He switches on his taped voice to carry the conversational ball and marshals himself for dancing.

Oh, that voice. It talks for 10 minutes. Pops on the tape indicate that the reader took thought breaks, water breaks, dance breaks, pee breaks, sleep breaks. We're not so lucky; we must try to digest (I give up) on the run. King's deceptively exact words erect astonishing bridges that afford me no footing on the opposite shore, or balconies suspended over mist. "And thus . . . " says the voice triumphantly. Thus what? Why "thus"? "And now we must get down to the raw lean meat of it . . . " (a paraphrase), he announces, and spirals on. He admonishes himself for his word play (e.g., essencespionage), and then throws in a dazzling au revoir of a sentence studded with them. His voice stammers extra syllables into words, making technological monsters of them, "electrototechnotizing." I can't understand Nixonese. Now I can't understand his adversaries either? I get your point, Kenneth, but I don't get your point. I understand about Mesmex, the new energy resource (sort of) and about the Master Control Panel with its ability to synthesize all existing communications media, and more. I can believe that all those government agencies are trying to suppress its use by any old us (they'd have suppressed sliced bread, for Christ's sake), but I don't understand how it does away with banking and the two-party system (among other things). Name me some names: I share your nausea.

Meanwhile, the rope dancer dances. Oh, wonderfully. Every time I see Kenneth King, he looks lighter, more supple. I've never known anyone to skim the surface of things the way he does. The tiny motions of his shoulder, head, hands, the twistings of his long, thin, nicely-made body are very swift—as if he hopes to refract each changing current of air . . . OR . . . field messages from outer space. Lightly and easily, his dancing feints across the floor. A continuous volley of twisting skips, hops, and glides. Sometimes he springs straight up into the air. Odd hand gestures this time. Some like praying; often he lays a finger beside his nose.

The dancer takes breaks, too. Drinks liquid. Sits. Kneels, crouches, at the altar rail. Stands silhouetted against a bright doorway of stairs. He's proud of his dancer-disguise. Who would suspect a dancer of being a courier of inner state seercrets?

But he's also desperate, and seems desperately sad. The voice stops, and the dancer continues a while to "Let It Be" and another song. Then, he walks around in front of us, his voice (live) breathless, worried, and tired. He had thought that at this point a verbal exchange might be valuable, but isn't sure what a verbal exchange is. Pause. We're cudgeling what's left of our brains. He walks back to the safety of the table, the altar rail, and the electronic devices, and begins to leaf through his manuscript.

I run for my eatpeesleep break, so long in coming, thankful for the dancing, helpless to deal with the veiled warnings. I've had it with being talked at in secret languages; they come at me from all directions. But even if I don't always understand the message, Kenneth, I understand the message.

Kenneth King wrote to me shortly after this column was published saying that during performance he became aware of "the difficulty of following the linear exposition of the material and watching dancing." One of the few dancers concerned with the communication of complicated ideas, King said he supposed that the only real alternative was getting the material published. Some of it has appeared in print in the Winter 75-76 and Spring-Summer 76 issues of Eddy.

Take a Trip With Monk

The New York Times, January 14, 1974

Meredith Monk doesn't call her works dances any more. "Juice" (1969) was billed as a theater cantata, "Needlebrain Lloyd and the Systems Kid" (1970) as a live movie, "Vessel" (1971) as an opera epic, and "Education of the Girlchild" (1972-73) as an opera. Editors are never sure what kind of critic to send to one of her performances.

Actually, Monk has never seemed interested in working with movement alone, not even in the mid-sixties when she thought of herself, I guess, as a dancer and a choreographer. In the small, innovative pieces she made then—many of them were solos or duets—she experimented, just as she does now, with layering and juxtaposing motion, music, speech, film, environment, costumes, objects in such a way that they imbued each other with a mysterious significance possessed by none of them alone. Some of the effects that she achieved with simple equipment, meticulous planning, and the cooperation of friends were astonishing. For instance, in "16 Millimeter Earrings" (1966), a color film of her own face was projected onto a paper globe which she had put over her head: an alarming technological nightmare of alienation.

Some of Monk's early pieces struck me as intriguing, but highly private. Now she's found ways of objectifying her visions. For one thing, the visions don't all belong to her; they emerge also from the minds of those who perform with her. And she makes you aware of the timeless solidity of certain materials and acts: bread and the eating of it; water and the drinking of it; books and the reading of them; wood, stone, metal; labor, journeys, trials, summonses, histories, deaths, births. And dreams about all of these.

For the spectator, her works are journeys through a dense landscape of meticulously shaped events. Some of the inhabitants are dancers; some are not. They may wear overalls or slickers or velvet gowns or bathrobes. One may have big red boots on; another may have a white-painted face; women may wear mustaches. Some may perform by sawing wood, or, in her outdoor pieces, riding a horse or driving a bus. Certain everyday sights and sounds acquire a surreal edge because they're isolated from their usual context or performed with great deliberation and intensity. Other quite fantastic images become grounded in reality because of the straightforward way in which they're presented. Events can be as specific (and miraculous) as a woman shooting an arrow into the center of a target, or as miraculous (and specific) as the final hair-raising moment of "Vessel" when Monk, identified with Joan of Arc—wearing a derby, gray pants and T-shirt, with her hair in a score of braids and her arms and neck painted silver—begins an odd skittering little dance that carries her into the depths of a dark parking lot, where she disappears into the flame and sparks of a torch held by a man who is suddenly there, welding something.

Many of Monk's recent pieces have involved actual journeys through time and space for the audience. For instance, the first part of "Juice" took place in the Guggenheim Museum, the second part a week or so later at Barnard's Minor Latham Playhouse, and the third part later still at Monk's loft. The diminution in scale from the vast museum to the small loft also involved an intensification of focus, a zeroing in on intimate details, and a gradual lessening of formality. "Vessel," Monk's most stunning work, was also in three parts, and, as in "Juice," each of the three parts revealed new aspects and dimensions of the same characters and events, but "Vessel" grew larger and louder. It began in a long, dim tunnel of a loft, progressed to a bright theater (the Performing Garage) and ended in an immense parking lot. To see this extraordinary and cryptic mosaic of the life of Joan of Arc, members of the audience had to line up on rickety stairs, drink wine while they waited for a chartered bus which took them from the loft to the theater, and then walk several blocks through one of Manhattan's decaying warehouse districts to the lot where "Vessel" culminated in an extraordinary pageant.

The works which Monk created for specific sites were enormously complicated to produce—to say nothing of expensive—and hence almost unrepeatable. Perhaps that's why "Education of the Girlchild," which just finished a series of performances at a downtown loft and also at the Cathedral of St. John the Divine, is more portable. The piece—the opera —has evolved over a two-year period, during which time Monk and members of her group, the House, have performed it many times and in many different kinds of places.

While Monk first saw "Vessel" as a tapestry, in terms of textures, colors, shapes, "Education of the Girlchild" began with people and evolved into a kind of legend. The most prominent people are Monk and the five other women whom the program lists as Companions. They're all dressed in white clothes of varying styles, and in the beginning they're all sitting around a white table, around a lifetime of tables. They differ wonderfully in age, shape, weight, color and style—ranging from Lee Nagrin who is monumental in size, and soft but strong, to Lanny Harrison, who is rangy and swings through a lot of space when she moves, to Monk who is small, swift, and vulnerable. Every deliberate, unhurried act they perform is both clear and elusive in meaning. At some point, they stumble over another woman (Coco Pekelis) who is buried under a mound of cloth. Who is she, dressed in full Peruvian costume, cranky and old and as stiff as if she'd been buried for centuries? A distant relation? A long lost member of the tribe?

Some see "Education of the Girlchild" as an odyssey or an exodus, perhaps because of the several "journeys" the characters make, perhaps because of the way in which two interlocutors shroud areas the performers are leaving, and uncover or frame ones where they are going. In another way, the work could be construed as a biography of womankind, a myth of real and imagined lives. There is a part in which the Companions simply sit and weep; another in which Monk and Pekelis sit at a table and converse in soft, wordless singing, while the others gravely rearrange a baby Stonehenge of bricks, pondering each move as in a chess game. At one point they perform ambiguous ordeals, summoned by an Ancestress (Margo Lee Sherman) whose shuddering body seems possessed by the halting, garbled, guttural incantations she emits.

140

Monk herself, in the remarkable solo that comprises the second part of "Education. . . " weaves in voice and motion a portrait that could be a condensation of, or a heritage from, all the notable women in the first part. Her songandance also slides back in time from the platform where she begins—white-wigged, stiff, and ancient—down a long trail of muslin to a point where she becomes light, fluid, and sings in a windy, innocent voice.

Coming from a musical family, Monk has always made music. (She's cut one record and is working on another.) The music for this latest opera, like all her music, has a ritualistic quality, an Eastern flavor. She seems concerned with small intervals, with fragments of repeating melody. Often an organ, one of her favorite instruments, will play a particular tight, clustering pattern over and over with varying inflections, while her voice—formidable in the range of its pitch and texture—natters its own designs, nudging its way between tones, sobbing, laughing, sighing, snarling.

What dancing there is in Meredith Monk's works these days shows the same preoccupation with minute gradations of shape and energy. Her style takes unemphatic note of awkwardness and angularity, pointing up those small transitional moments that we usually notice only in still photographs of people moving. Her own dancing is light, sweet, full of tiny fidgety motions, yet her limbs have a flyaway sprawl. She makes you think of a puppet, or someone in a trance. In a way, the movement is like the scenery and costumes; they all look handmade—clumsy but beautiful. Childlike in their intrepidness and in their humor.

Since Monk rarely develops an idea linearly, the events in her works seem to me to be analogous to the fragments of a long-buried vase. They might, for the scientific mind, make a logical whole; for the poetic mind they might symbolize a whole. Yet many of the fragments are so lovely, so specific in hue that it almost doesn't matter what the mind of the spectator does with them. I hoard them myself.

Even the Bushes Are Not to be Trusted

The Village Voice, November 4, 1971

It would be foolish to speculate whether Meredith Monk's "Vessel" is more properly dance or music or theatre; any of the arts should be happy to claim it. However, to keep matters straight: Monk calls it "an opera epic."

"Vessel," like the earlier "Juice," is in three related parts, which happen in three different places. Also as in "Juice," the same, or closely related, characters and events appear in each of the three parts, but each time are constellated differently in regard to time or space. The six "House people" (Lanny Harrison, Daniel Ira Sverdlik, Signe Hammer, Monica Moseley, Mark Monstermaker, and Blondell Cummings) sit initially in a loft's living area, slowly and soberly performing minute, invisible chores with their hands; each at some time does a "turn" in another costume under a lightbulb which each switches on. (E.g., Monstermaker sheds his formal black suit and bowler hat and enters as a red-robed, fully crowned king or cardinal. He recites the first two lines of the Paternoster in French and flings a handful of coins on the ground.) These second costumes are what the house people wear for extended roles as "mountain people" in Part II. By Part III, they are dressed in black again, sitting in the little living room that has been assembled in a huge parking lot. This thematic use of material is everywhere in "Vessel": a man who plays an accordion in Part I strums a dulcimer in Part II, and formally gives way to a French-horn player in Part III.

Every act is a key to every other act. The work is like an immense jig-saw puzzle in which—as you begin it—you aren't sure which blue pieces are sky and which are lake (even the bushes are not to be trusted); only when you find blue-with-fish or blue-with-cloud can you know where you are. As you watch "Vessel" you find yourself sorting and bundling images in your mind against the moment when the proper place will open up for them. Some remain mysterious: you admire their grandeur and *know* that Meredith Monk knows where they belong.

The layers of subject matter are astonishing. One of the most important shaping ones is the life and death of Joan of Arc. Mixed with the specific hagiological fragments are bits seemingly related to broader-based religious ritual, plus elements from Monk's earlier pieces. For example, it is no coincidence that the camping pioneers (straight out of Monk's "Needlebrain Lloyd and the Systems Kid") cluster around fires and dance out with corn and that the last performance occurred on Hallowe'en, the ancient harvest festival once celebrated with bonfires. Also a figure with a huge flaming torch appears on the wall of the parking lot. Also at the very end of everything, Monk in her "Joan" costume (silver gray jeans and t-shirt, silver-paint on her hands, forearms, and in a helmet pattern around her face and neck), but with a Chaplinesque bowler hat on, dances all alone across the big, dark, now-empty lot—a very light, skittering dance, as if she were a dry leaf being blown, or a tiny puppet—and immolates herself in the flare and sparks of a welder's torch. Fire as ritual, as specific history, and as personal fantasy (the burning doll at the end of Monk's "16 millimeter earrings").

The changing spaces permit different ways of revealing the subject. "Vessel" progresses from private to public ("Juice" went the opposite way). The first part, "Overture: Open House," moves quietly and slowly, almost conversationally—except that there is no conversation. The people in black make small adjustments in position. Monk recites a key speech from Shaw's "St. Joan" twice; once she merely whispers it.

Part II, "Handmade Mountain," happens at the Performing Garage where unbleached muslin has been draped over the existing scaffolding and platforms to make little grottoes in which the mountain people perform their particular tasks with real props (e.g., the king reads, the necromancer mixes fluids, the peasant or gypsy woman cooks in an iron pot). They also communicate across to each other in musical calls. The pace is more "theatrical" at the Garage. And the atmosphere is that of a court—both regal and judicial. There is a wonderfully sinister, and silly, row of courtiers in flowered robes posing and chattering high up on one side of the scaffolding. There is a pallid juggler and a bit of buffoonery between an idiotic king and queen (excellently done by Ping Chong and Lanny Harrison). It was a brilliant idea to have Joan's inquisitor, Bishop Cauchon, played by two people, a man and a woman. They take turns tossing insane questions and statements into space ("Let's dispense with the business and get down to formalities," or "Is there any more baked Alaska?"). Martin Gleitsman is deadly, mellow-voiced, and professional; Coco Pekelis hisses her lines, narrowing her eyes and composing her face into a sneer after each delivery.

Part III, "Existent Lot," is like a field of battle, a public square. Some occurrences are magnified by the space; others, like the group in the living room, compressed by it, lost in it. The two figures in headpieces who spar briefly with rakes in Part I have become two armies advancing from opposite sides of the parking lot. In Part I, a waterfall is the long and false hair unrolled from a disembodied gray head; in Part II, a waterfall is a line of people in blue and gray jeans and shirts tumbling slowly from the scaffolding, somersaulting across the white-draped floor and looping back up another ladder; in Part III, a waterfall emerges from a group of Hallowe'en revelers who wind through a crowd of still figures dispensing ears of corn.

It is impossible to describe the richness of Monk's conception—visually, aurally, and intellectually. So much happens in depth as well as in a linear manner that the printed word cannot in any way convey the experience. Many of the sounds and images are startlingly beautiful: Lanny Harrison begins the whole thing as a disembodied voice, outlining in a marvelous kind of sprechstimme the delivery to certain persons of directions and messages and maps (hidden inside a nut, etc.); a dark woman and a fair man, both naked from the waist up, sitting at a kitchen table side by side (reminiscent of the couple in "Blueprint"); Monk, dimly lit, her hair hanging in a score of tiny plaits, playing the electric organ, and wheedling strange sounds from the back of her throat; the mountain people ritualistically making salads—no sound but the crisp tearing of fresh lettuce leaves; a group far away in the parking lot waving and swaying in front of a wall, the shadow of a leafless tree huge behind them and swaying too; three people in pale clothing illuminated in the porticoes of the church across the street from the parking lot, waving slowly. There are motorcycles and buses and children playing and a Spanish dancer and many visions and revelations that interlock, that unlock. A treasure hunt that you pursue but needn't fathom because of all the prizes along the way.

The Stillness of Rudy Perez

Art in America, May–June 1971

In the summer of 1952, at Black Mountain College, John Cage engineered a now-famous theater event. Above the collage of simultaneously performed dance, poetry, piano music and recorded music were suspended some of Robert Rauschenberg's all-white paintings. It is probably no coincidence that shortly thereafter Cage produced his ultimate exploration of silence, *4' 33"*, during which the performer sat motionless before the piano—opening and closing the lid to indicate sections. In 1957, Paul Taylor, who had met Cage while dancing with Merce Cunningham, presented a duet in which he and his partner remained immobile for the duration of the dance.

These rigorous experiments did not have to be repeated; the point had been made. Without silence we could have no conception of sound; without stillness, no understanding of motion; and no knowledge of color if black or white didn't exist. Therefore, an art form that contained ample amounts of the complement (or antithesis) of its prime element would be not only richer, but more lifelike. Stillness was once—for the most part—what happened before a dance started or after it was over. Now it is often stressed within the work.

Rudy Perez has made some very interesting experiments with stillness in dance. Where others—Merce Cunningham, for instance—pit stillness against bursts of virtuoso movement, Perez shades it into minimal movement and back again. His brand of stillness is not so much the temporary absence of movement as the charged potential for it. For example, his "Topload/Offprint" begins with three figures in colored Mao suits (vermilion, wine, navy) sitting on chairs that are facing the audience, but arranged in an evenly spaced diagonal. They sit for what seems an eternity. You feel that a current is passing through their bodies, but is somehow being shortcircuited before it can force them into action. They look ready to explode. Finally, when Perez is ready (long after you may be), he rises to a standing pose as alert and immobile as his sitting one.

The others begin to move—their frozen positions reminiscent of the way the projected slides that precede the dance click quickly into view and hold for a second. In the soft, summery photographs, wind, light and ocean have the same arrested motion as the dancers' bodies.

Perez doesn't cast all of his dances in this move-hold-move-hold rhythm. He also uses time in huge gulps—developing gestures in meticulous slow motion. Repetition fixes the images that he wants you to hang onto. Paradoxically, the slower-than-normal speed with which he performs certain actions has the effect of condensing time for the spectator.

His movement could justly be called minimal, but in no way is it casual or natural. Everything unnecessary is stripped from his work, and the bare bones are polished until they gleam. In "Countdown," a solo, the very slow and stylized gesture of a man lifting a lighted cigarette to his lips becomes immensely important. Perez moves the bodies of his dancers through clean-lined, emblematic positions. Pointing with one outstretched arm, crouching as if to begin a race, marching, bending slowly into the floor: these are some of his motto themes. Straight lines are the rule; curves in both body and path are a luxury. When, in "Transit," Perez enters on a pair of roller skates and swoops scallops a-round Barbara Roan and Anthony La Giglia, the effect is of a sudden and surprising freedom. Fast dancing and out-of-control dancing are also rarities, used to make a particular point.

Perez himself is of medium height—lean, but with a large frame and heavy muscles. Built organically on his own body, his movement is deliberately heavy, yet he rarely allows his weight to drop. He moves as if he had the density of iron, places himself carefully, does not yield easily to gravity. This may be one of the reasons that his work, for me, has affinities with the primary structures of contemporary sculpture. The resemblance also has something to do with his strong, unadorned designs in space and the bright, unshaded colors and blocklike cut of his costumes.

Physical contact is something else that Perez uses seldom, and then for special emphasis. His dancers intersect; they coinhabit the space. But rarely do they touch each other. "Arcade," for instance, begins with a group marching toward the audience in babysteps, while a bravura march contrasts with their inching progress. As the dance ends, they are slowly embracing each other. After the aridity of the dance, that last moment on the stage is tremendously moving.

Perez's dances *are* often moving—full of repressed emotion. Just as his immobility suggests a terrific lust for motion, so his masklike face and unemotive postures suggest an ache for the release of tears or laughter. He relinquishes little of his tension. Instead, he allows music, sounds, films, slides to present the freedom that he cannot attain. His mimimal gestures in "Countdown" are accompanied by Madeleine Gray's wildly beautiful singing of a couple of Auvergnois folk songs. In "Fieldgoal," the dancer's awkward and inhibited movements are accompanied by phrases from Gounod's "Sanctus." At the end of "Topload/Offprint," the Mamas and the Papas are singing their lungs out, while Anthony La Giglia slowly tips the chair on which he is sitting until it is lying on its side, and he is still sitting on it—lying on his side, too.

Since Perez began choreographing in 1963, he has always had admirers. But I can remember in 1967, when I first saw his work, talking to people who were baffled by what he was doing. Nothing happened, they complained, and hinted darkly that the reason he moved so little was that he wasn't a well-trained dancer. Hardly a fair criticism, and disproved now anyway. In the past three years, he has improved greatly as a dancer, but he continues to work in his own way—whether with a large group or with the original trio which consisted of himself, Roan, and La Giglia.

Audiences have begun to stop straining against the bounds he imposes. They realize that they are indeed watching something, instead of the prologue to it. Critics have begun to praise his work—often finding his dances a stylish and tasteful relief to the excesses of others. Suddenly he has a following. His is not a direction for all dance to take, but a quiet, private and ultimately fascinating path.

Who's That Under Your Skirt, Dear?

The Village Voice, March 22, 1976

"If they weren't so young and beautiful, it would be *gross*," said the man in front of me at the Brooklyn Academy's spiffed-up Playhouse, while the guy behind me cheered and clapped and hugged his girl and asked her for the hundredth time if she didn't think this was the greatest. We had been watching "Ocellus," in which the four men of Pilobolus curl and stretch and slide and somersault slowly over each other until the entire four-man organism has rolled from one side of the stage up to the other. True, the company is spectacular. True too, it's possible to notice that occasionally, in order for the group to build some new and complicated structure, one man has to maneuver his face into another's crotch.

However, you rarely see them this way, because they don't want you to. Pilobolus is a highly flexible creature with many appendages—Robert Morgan Barnett, Alison Chase, Martha Clarke, Moses Pendleton, Michael Tracy, Jonathan Wolken. In its early works like "Ocellus" (1972), the company delighted simply in showing the entrancing inkblot shapes it could build, or in using kinetic humor to caricature societies or social habits (as in the 1971 "Walklyndon"). These days, I sense the company trying to use its gymnastic skills to give psychological or mythic dimensions to drama. The new "Untitled" is a bizarre nightmare depicted literally. ("I dreamed I was at a party, and all of a sudden I noticed a head under my skirt; I went on talking and tried to pretend nothing was wrong, but . . . ") Two shy, slightly awkward women in long white dresses and straw hats glide around the stage. All of a sudden they, like Alice, have shot up into the air to display long bare legs. (They are, of course, sitting on others' shoulders.) Unlike Alice, these pretty giantesses take no notice of their height; they reconnoiter like wading birds, settling down all white and fluffy and then rising up again onto these big-striding legs. Two men wearing identical boaters and summer whites, greet the huge damsels imperturbably and leave. But, as if their advent has aroused dangerous yearnings, the women sprout bulbous stomachs and give birth to naked men. In a beautiful sequence, the women dance with these dream lovers they have spawned; the men seem half asleep and are tenderly nudged into caresses. But then they are left—sort of in cold storage—lying on their backs with their knees bent and their heads held off the floor. The other men return and dance with the now normal-sized women, but not for long. The women again put the naked men under their skirts and shoot up (out of reach?). Things become even more bizarre: The clothed men fight; the women drop their skirts over *them* and leave them inert on the floor too; for a second, one woman attempts to catch the other *woman* in her skirt. The dance ends with the two women using the clothed men as rocking chairs and making polite chit-chatting gestures.

"Untitled" is a disturbing, often very poignant expression of sexual fantasies in a repressed turn-of-the-century society; it also makes some unpleasant remarks about woman-as-devourer-of-man. When Pilobolus uses its highly original style to "say something", it's clear that the messages it's best suited to deliver are humorous ones, or fantastic ones, or cruel ones. Since shape-making is such an important feature of Pilobolus's dances, not only does the dynamic tend to be always slow and controlled, but the stage picture is often a flat one—as if there were a single "best angle" for every position. In "Untitled," the company creates a deeper, less artificial space, but can't quite escape the fact that the style is founded upon a spectacular gimmick, and audiences respond to the virtuosity and the oddity more than to the ideas.

The Story of a Woman Who . . .

The Village Voice, April 12, 1973

Like Martha Graham, Yvonne Rainer now seems hell-bent on exorcising demons. Unlike Graham, Rainer tries to achieve this by a precise barrage of words—printed and spoken—and movements and poses carefully emptied of the passions that produced them. In her new work, "This is the story of a woman who . . . ," there is none of the stylish muscular strife which Graham uses for the flailing of neuroses, public and private. By a kind of alteration or deprivation of motor intensity, Rainer succeeds not only in objectifying her own emotions, but also in creating an oppressive, repressive image of the discrepancies between thought, emotion, behavior, and art.

"This is the story of a woman who . . . " is an autobiographical fragment. It deals (I'm being very general now) with a deteriorating relationship between a man and a woman who is a dancer. Rainer is the woman. John Erdman is the man. Shirley Soffer speaks for Rainer and sometimes for herself. The principal fact that emerges about Rainer is that she is a woman tormented by doubts—about her work, her feelings, everything; and she examines these doubts relentlessly. I kept thinking of peeling onions: sometimes you want so badly to arrive at the best, whitest, quintessential onion that you keep peeling until it's all gone, and you're left with nothing but the parings. (Autobiography is catching.)

Rainer begins the dance with her solo "Inner Appearances" (1972). A green eye-shade covers her eyes, but reveals her mouth. Her short, bristly bobbed hair also curtains her much of the time. She hums monotonously, vacuums slowly; and all the while projected, typed 3x5s present us with the vigorous activity of her brain. One card tells us that the character "reveals her characteristic dissembling." Yes.

Another card mentions the powerful clarity of cliché. And cliché becomes one of Rainer's tools for putting the proper distance between herself and her fears. The barren white stage of the Theatre for the New City contains a shabby bed and mattress at floor level, some chairs, a suitcase of props. Soffer at a mike begins to read about the anger, jealousy, lust, growing lack of understanding or tenderness between Rainer and Erdman. Mostly as Rainer sees it. She speaks almost entirely in clichés (people have "changes of heart," can't "take things lying down"—terms like that). Meanwhile Rainer and Erdman go through a series of frozen attitudes that do not relate specifically to the text. The poses congeal suddenly or melt into each other. They arrest the two talking, reaching, avoiding, watching, etc., and they're marvelously designed to suggest a gesture, a facial expression caught by a camera at an extremely awkward transitional moment. Implication of the trajectory of a movement projected into utter stillness.

A fact—curious, disturbing, fascinating: the deeper you get into the piece, the more you assume you are learning about Rainer, because of all the information, heard and seen, that you're being given via movement, words, family photos, films. It seems so specific. And later you realize that you know very little. The words and the action have been edited in such a way that they could apply to many things, many people. Illusion of intimacy. We can only guess some of the extremes of passion that this relationship elicited. Once, for instance, Erdman casually lays a gun on the bed beside Rainer; another time, he picks it up and lets it drop, although the words say that he pointed it at her.

The atmosphere of the dance is spartan, clinical, but at the same time rich with potential mess. When Erdman and Rainer fight, they do so in a series of slow-motion attacks—clearly violent in aim, but controlled in execution. They bend heads back, smash faces, twist arms, knee groins, bring to the ground. They alternate emitting terrible prolonged gasps, screams, moans that are meticulously realistic, but sometimes the attacker makes the sound, sometimes the victim. Throughout, Soffer shuffles a pile of papers into order. As with everything in the dance, some element of reality has been displaced—either space, sequence, intensity—so that a distancing occurs between you and Rainer, between Rainer and Erdman, between Rainer and her fears.

In one part, Erdman and Rainer sit side by side on chairs, while Soffer stands to tell her (Yvonne's) dream. The two smile covertly, whisper, behave as if Soffer were doing something wrong and embarrassing but for some reason they have to be polite. From overhead a light falls, dangles drastically from its cord, and goes out. Rainer eyes it without change of expression.

The eyes of a lover watching you transform you into a performer. Pleasurable and wearying too. As if to heighten this illusion, Rainer performs her "Three Satie Spoons" (1961) for Erdman and us. A fine dance. The cards tell us it bothered her that he said nothing about it. This whole work seems unbelievably courageous when you learn that the two performers continued to work toward this performance while the events we are told/not told about were occurring. I don't know the original plan, but she did teach him her stoic, complex path dance "Walk She Said" from "Grand Union Dreams" and "Trio A" from "The Mind Is a Muscle." "Trio A" is usually done in loose canon, but this time the performers are greatly separated from each other in time. They mark it first, then do it fully; the marking has the effect of making its casual style in performance look more emphatic than it might normally.

"This is the story of a woman who . . . " is probably most impressive to those who know Rainer well, but I think it matters only that you know she is important as an artist. Knowing that, you feel depressed, infuriated that she's spending so much brain-time on this love affair. Yet her attempts—not to make art about it but to objectify it into art —are touching and admirable. Perhaps even more so because you sense her reticence, moral fastidiousness, intelligence, and wit—qualities that are not normally brought to bear on confessional art. Anyway, this is emphatically not a work about letting it all hang out; it's a work about someone who can't.

After "Trio A," a repeat of a pale filmed beachscape. The white typing whispers "I've always liked ocean endings."

This is one of the most peculiar articles I've ever written. Perhaps pride ought to have stopped me from including it, but in some ways I think it a good description of the work.

Under the influence of Rainer's earlier, factual style, the powerful sincerity of her performing, and the fact that in the work, she performed her own early solo, "Three Satie Spoons," I confused the roles Rainer and Erdman were playing with the real Rainer and Erdman in an extremely misleading way. Rainer, polite but properly outraged, informed me what I ought to have sensed; she was emphatically not making a piece of "confessional art" out of an actual affair with Erdman. "Do you think that I am such an exhibitionist or so insensitive that I would expose myself and an ex-lover and all the gory details before a public (or private, for that matter) audience?" She pointed out that at least four women were described in the piece, only one of them her, and three men, none of them Erdman.

The letter which Yvonne Rainer wrote to me clarified her current stance:

> *Since making "Grand Union Dreams" (1971), I have been involved with finding ways to use performers as something other than demonstrators of behavioral and kinetic phenomena. We are no longer ourselves; we are becoming stand-ins for personae, protagonists in a novel, characters sustaining a narrative. To carry out these transformations demands the use of certain devices that have traditionally been the the domain of fiction and the theater of dramatic illusion, many of which tend to blur the distinctions between illusions and reality.*

I also wonder at myself caring whether "Rainer" spent "brain-time on this love affair." Rainer spent brain-time on a love affair, and the result was an extraordinary work of art.

Merrily Onto the Black Grass

The Village Voice, August 17, 1972

Connecticut College's summer faculty, like Rudy Perez, June Lewis, Margaret Beals, Walter Nicks, usually present their companies and/or their students or maybe just themselves in some kind of performance before the summer is over. You never know whether you'll find them dancing in a gym or one of the three auditoriums or the streets of New London or the lawn. On August 2, 1972, at 8:23 p.m., Don Redlich presented a group of his students, Lavina Hovinga, and his assistant Billy Siegenfeld in "She Often Goes for a Walk Just After Sunset," an unusually beautiful and unrepeatable event that nevertheless left an indelible track on the night, the lawn, many minds.

We waited in the dusk on the terrace of the brazenly new concrete and glass Cummings Art Center. A single long diagonal beam of light sang along the grass of the Great Lawn. Then, far, far away across the lawn, a speck of a figure in white came down the steps of one of the college's old stone buildings and strolled toward us: Lavina Hovinga, delicately punching the lawn with the tip of her parasol at each stride, sauntering into a sudden wind that blew at her long white dress and the brim of her straw hat. A thunderstorm was waiting. Suddenly a horde of figures in dark clothes (leotards, tights, blue jeans, sweaters) came leaping and whooping after her from the bushes. She paused in the center of the light beam, and by twos and threes the wild people ran and dived into a circular shoal around her. Not in pursuit? In the small space remaining between her and the fallen bodies the gentlewoman fastidiously picked out a circular path; she seemed to be nudging them gently with her feet or parasol. They rolled out in a wave, spread over the lawn—small, dark figures making hyena cries bounce off the stone buildings. Once, by hidden signal, they rocked stiffly from side to side, feet apart, arms held up squarely, looking in the deepening night like cave drawings come to life. Sometimes they ran through the light, but most of them were barely visible. I remember that "Nelly Bly" emerged sweetly from the taped collage of sounds and music.

When the lady continued her stroll to and along a small cliff at the edge of the lawn, the wild people leaped after her and plunged raucously over the edge. But as she started across the lawn directly in the path of the beam, they appeared single file behind her at a slight distance—a group of rambunctious pets suddenly docile and ready to heel. I loved them then. They caught up with her under a wind-whipped tree and let out with a last howl before trotting away. The lady descended a stone staircase into a square sunken courtyard with a small circle of lawn and a clump of birches set into the middle of the pavement. She looked curiously at the contemporary sculptured objects that decorate the court; she seemed now out of her own time—as if she were a figure from Connecticut College of 75 years ago. The stone buildings would have been there, so would the lawn, but not this new place. She passed on to the rectangular arch opening on the lower lawn, and stood there for a long time with her back to us, her dress billowing out. Watched from the terrace above, the scene had the clarity and the mystery of a Magritte.

Suddenly the dark people came snuffling and hopping through the arch, Billy Siegenfeld first, waggling his ass dog-like, keeping close to the ground. The courtyard seemed unfamiliar to these people too; they didn't like the look of the statues. While the lady sat calmly on a stone bench under the birches, the mob went on a binge of irrational passion— rubbing themselves against the more phallic of the sculptures, screaming curses at us and each other. A boy, crucified against a long welded statue, sang an old pop tune; the woman who made a pietà with his fallen body said enthusiastically, *"All my men wear English Leather."* The vocal craziness turned into a running, slamming-into-walls kind of craziness. The dancers all this time were being grandly free with their bodies and their psyches, playing self-indulgence with considerable discipline and verve. The lady made a foray to a corner of the courtyard and raised her umbrella; the young people (all 32 of them) huddled close to their protectress, and together they advanced onto the circle of grass. Rain began to fall on them—not the real rain we were expecting, but water from a concealed hose. As if released from some purgatory of drought or heat, the animal-people yelped and rolled and tore off their shirts and hugged each other. During their watery bacchanal, the lady moved quickly and quietly away and up the staircase. At the top, she lifted her skirts, hoisted a shapely leg over the back of a motorcycle behind a man in a helmet and goggles, and in a blast of music and engine noise they tore off across the lawn with the others in pursuit. Hi Nelly, ho ho Nelly. And the spotlight went crazy, and the real rain didn't come, and I went weeping rather merrily out onto the black grass.

A Birthday Party

March 1, 1976

All those people who stood out in the damp night of lower Broadway wanting to see Sara Rudner's solo concert, "Some 'Yes' and More"— was it because they, like me, think of her as The Compleat Dancer (complete: having all the customary skills; undivided; uncompromised; lacking nothing; entire; full; perfect in kind and quality)? After you've seen her dance, as generously as she did that night, you don't really need to see anyone else dance for quite a long time.

She doesn't show anything that is posed or decorative or self-consciously "beautiful" or "interesting," but she uses richly and with superb control all the vital elements of dancing—time, space, weight, shape, and so on. Even though her dancing has subtle gradations most dancers never achieve (and some don't even know about), she dances unaffectedly and with pleasure.

Even the small first section of her hour's dance is amazing. She comes into Lucinda Child's full-to-bursting loft, puts two paper cups of water and some Kleenex on the radiator, and starts to walk. She's wearing a black Chinese jacket of padded silk and white pants and shoes; a pair of woolier pants that she has on underneath flaunt their red hems. (I always like the way she looks: her strong, small, quiet body, her frizz of black hair, her pretty, blunt face with its alert, sober, but potentially mischievous expression.) So, anyway, she walks. Circles, figure eights. She casts matter-of-fact (inquisitive?) glances at points high on the wall. Without obvious stylization, she puts crescendos and descrescendos into her walk, subtly alters how her weight falls onto the front foot. Here's this woman just walking around looking at the room, and, on the sly, she's giving you the unexpurgated history of the walk.

That walk might have been more seminal than I'm prepared to admit, because I have a hunch that throughout her variations on something, Rudner was working with a carefully restricted roster of movement, only we didn't fully realize it, either because she manipulated it so brainily, or performed it with so many different shadings.

It's a marathon—full of the twisting and spiraling, the slam-bang footdancing, the loose-jointed leg gestures, the silky complexities that are Rudner's heritage from about eight years of working with Twyla Tharp. Rudner takes off her jacket and twitches her black jersey into place. She breathes deeply, mops her face, and drinks water between sections. She luxuriates in movements that deposit her on the floor. But she's always game for more: the deepness, the resilience, the trueness of her dancing never falters.

At first she looks at us from time to time and holds up her hands to tell us this is, say, section five-fingers-plus-one; later I think I detect those signals too, but after 12 or so she stops stopping. Here are some of the events I remember. A lickety-split progress across the floor, full of false starts, and go-back-to-your-marks; rolls with her body folding and sprawling indolently; a section in which she stands still while her arms dive and snake around her and end up, wrists together, in front of her, forcing her body back (fleetingly: the end of another Perils of Sara episode); Rudner standing almost on the toetips of her shoes, backed up against the wall, staring at a point in space. Did she really put that arm stuff on top of an equally complicated foot phrase? Probably. Did she really transfer that arm phrase to her legs? It's possible. I know she takes some tumbling falls and later repeats them creakily, bit by bit, groping for the floor like an old person.

The repetitions and variations give subliminal comfort. We're aware that all this spontaneous-looking dancing is firmly anchored to some form or other. Our eyes register visual rhymes. The silence of the hot crowd is staggering; the walls could fall on us before we'd notice.

She's into a quiet section. She says a few names, and her slow generous bending and folding motions acquire the significance, almost, of a bow, an expression of gratitude, an homage. She's drinking her last few drops of water, back to us, when with consummate timing, she pours the rest over her head and startles into dancing. (It's like coming upon a deer: you could swear that your footfall was the first step of its run.)

Grinning, she yells inaudibly into the clapping and the cheering, "Thank you for coming. It's my birthday!" So after all the clapping stops, someone shouts, "Happy birthday, Sara," and we clap some more. And then the elated, the dumbfounded, the wet-eyed fall down with the elevator. Many happy returns, Sara. What a celebration.

Rudner did not begin this evening's dancing by walking. She began by swinging her arms quite violently to the sides and across and behind her body and allowing this to pull her into turns. It was like a limbering-up preamble to the walk.

All Decked Out in Dire Intentions

The Village Voice, June 20, 1974

Gus Solomons, Jr. has taken this big plunge, and I hadn't even noticed. He's always been prolific and gracefully accommodating—could produce a dance for anywhere any time, but he's also been a witty maverick. I've liked the combination of suaveness and violence in his dances; I remember the way he sketched himself during a solo as if it were no more than a bit of trendy game-playing, and then slashed the drawing to pieces with his pencil. Or the way he tap-danced (wearing his blackness imperturbably, like a costume) while we listened to a newscast of the bombing of Pearl Harbor. I liked solos we had to accompany by rustling our programs, or dances he never even showed up for, just left taped insinuations about our inevitable audiencedance.

Solomons has been doing group pieces for quite a while. And now suddenly I notice that Solomons the choreographer is in the service of something called The Solomons Company; and for this touring unit he must make dances that travel well. He has decided, apparently, to go the whole hog, to make a program in which components like wit and seriousness, dancing and drama, complexity and comprehensibility are carefully balanced. He is concerned with showing off his dancers and with having them spell each other so tidily that there are no unwieldy pauses between numbers. I understand what he's doing; I don't think he's losing any integrity by doing so; I imagine he's got the skill to pull it off. Only, during this transition period for Solomons the choreographer, I feel bereft of Gus's old sardonic, stonily sporty choreographic profile, and can't yet grasp a new identity.

What has this pretty solo for Randall Faxon to do with either Randall Faxon or Gus Solomons? In 'Stoneflesh,'' why do the muscle men in glittering jockstraps keep leaving the finely constructed, deliberate, unflashy dancing they're doing to streak across the stage in diagonals of fancy leaps like something out of "Etudes"? The dance has so much impressive dancing that could be serious, lively, and friendly; why the dancers' hunted, Béjartian stares at the audience and the miniscule eye-grabbing ball baskets?

Why the brilliant colored lights (designed by Ruis Woertendyke)? In "Stoneflesh," the dancers often have one bicep outlined in green light, the other in dayglo pink, while amber beams streak across their bellies. The stage looks like one of those luscious record jackets favored by the acid rock set.

At its ATL concerts, the Solomons Company presented several works new to New York, but seasoned by touring. "A Shred 'of Prior Note" is a quartet that breaks down into duets—Valerie Hammer with Ben Dolphin, Randall Faxon with Douglas Nielson. The feeling is one of passion and alienation, and the Hammer-Dolphin duet has many interestingly obdurate, frozen-looking lifts and supports. There are oddly light touches, though, like a man and a woman prancing lightly around, side by side, arms about each others' waists. "Molehill" is mysterious, and as flat in space as a cardboard Punch and Judy show. Solomons in ragged clothes drags his way in babysteps across the stage, bent over to suggest he's ascending a mountain. In the second part ("Plateau"), Santa Aloi and Ruedi Brack sit stiffly on chairs and stare through us. He is in white military dress uniform, she's wearing a tutu. They move, as does Solomons, like figures on some puzzling music box. They rarely look at each other, although they abruptly edge closer to each other, then apart, and once he imitates her awkward ballerina poses—first accurately, then garishly. At the end, Solomons trudges across again.

It struck me at some point that Solomons (a magnificent giraffe of a dancer whose compact torso often looks about to rip apart from the lashing power accumulated by his long arms and legs) and his dancers haven't yet found a performing style to fit their new dramatic dances. They're used to staring coolly past their own dancing, or reacting to each other with minimum spontaneous emotion. Some of them seem to find it hard to warm up on stage and work at it overeagerly. In Solomons' bright gamedance "Par/tournament," they now never stop their vocal egging-on of each contestant.

It's interesting in light of their rather unbending demeanor that Solomons structured his most interesting new piece. "Yesterday," as a series of solos, with himself as a man looking back on his past, speaking Ethan Ayer's poetry in mellifluous, highly stylized Dylan Thomas tones. Ben Dolphin, leaping and twisting, represents the hero as a boy, I guess; and Ruedi Brack, helmeted, given to striking square heroic postures and doggedly repeating his dance themes, shows us the narrator (I think) as a young man naively idealistic, off to battle waving banners. Santa Aloi, narrow and rigid on a wooden bench, patters out a dance of repression and frustration. Randall Faxon is the swirling goddess—earth or moon, it doesn't matter—who expresses a luminous acceptance of destiny. I'm only playing; I don't really know what the dance is about. But I noticed in this dance that Solomons was allowing his ideas to pull the dancers bodies into expressive shapes and rhythms.

I'll have to get used to this new Gus Solomons. In honor of the old one.

Since this was written, Gus Solomons hasn't presented any more programs of this sort—at least not in New York. He seems to have become interested in widening and deepening his earlier ideas instead of trading them in.

Persevering Toward the Light

The Village Voice, March 17, 1975

Once, some time ago, Kei Takei was having trouble with her visa. People wrote letters to the Department of Immigration, praising her work, trying to convey how unusual and beautiful it was. Nothing seemed to work. Finally, we discovered what was wrong. We weren't using the magic words, "exceptional ability," or something like that. (Your child, madam, shows exceptional ability in Clay Modeling, but performs disappointingly in the Sandbox.)

I don't know whether to be disappointed or relieved that there were no immigration officials in the audience at Brooklyn Academy's LePercq Space a couple of Sundays ago to take in (or try to) the awesome spectacle of Takei's complete "Light" (Parts I, II, III, IV, V, VI, VII, VIII, and IX). The event lasted almost seven hours, with generous food breaks, and it was an important seven hours to me—hours in my life, hours out of my life, hours for my life.

Takei has been making and showing sections of "Light" since 1969. Most of them are strong and plain—a few actions, stunningly simple, cluster and swim about some mysterious guiding principle, some half-guessed truth. Put together in this giant structure, each section shimmers with new import. The whole dance now seems to embody man's dogged, almost blind determination to keep going—to rise after every fall even when rising becomes an impossibility, to keep dancing even when his limbs are bound, to create what is constantly being destroyed, to obtain the unobtainable. But because of the ingenuity and almost painterly beauty of Takei's structures, "Light" is not simply grim. It can appall you, delight you, and move you to tears. Takei's ideas may sound related to those of Samuel Beckett, but the pristine strength and deliberateness of her work strike me as unmistakably Eastern. And the mystery. I think of certain Japanese poems: every phrase is simple, every word is clear, yet at every reading new meanings branch from them.

I had never before thought about the title, "Light," but after seven hours spent with the work, it seemed a useful key. Takei often uses blackouts within a section, and these periods of darkness elongate your sense of passing time and unchanging activity. From light to light. Nearly everything in the dance is white—objects, sets, the bulky cotton kimonos and/or loose pants that everyone wears. But, also, you can think of each section as expressing a feeling about light. In each of the first four parts, Takei sets up contrasts between those who are at home with "light" and those who stay in "darkness," between those who can't "see" and those who can. For instance, in Part II, a woman advances slowly toward us in a straight line, her eyes fixed on a light. Around her in diminishing circles, two other women toil, bent under huge packs, making a monotonous rite out of swinging, dropping arm gestures. At the end, their path curls in behind her, and—still unseeing—they follow her. Or take Part IV: running in with piles of big white cardboard pieces, Carmen Beuchat proceeds to put together a jigsaw puzzle that will fill a white frame (perhaps 15 feet square) laid on the floor. The other people may use only the rapidly shrinking areas of dark floor. These people, like visions that inhabit darkness, are often bizarre; a couple of the women scurry around twirling umbrellas, and for a while John de Marco struts like a chicken. They're pathetically docile, though; Beuchat easily shoos them out of the way with her cardboard pieces. She treats them like big pets that might just turn nasty and hurries to complete the puzzle. One more piece, and they're crowded unprotestingly into a small corner. Blackout. When the lights come on, they're nowhere in sight.

In Parts V and VI, all the people seem to be caught between the polarities of light and darkness. First, Takei, Maldwyn Pate, and Lloyd Ritter cling together. They struggle to stand, hanging on each other; they brace themselves stoically until fatigue forces them to slide to the floor. They rise again in another intricate system of support. And again, And . . . The hordes of people in Part VII vary the themes of Part V. People advance laboriously through space with other people clinging to them, dragged along by them, pulling them down. Those who can, rise; and bodies are sucked up from the floor as if by capillary action to cluster on them. Self-pity and grief play no part: the people labor on as dumbly as ploughhorses. You don't know whether to cheer for them or scream at them to give up.

In Part VII, a cheerful, crude—and cruel—little play, light becomes a metaphor for fecundity and creation. Takei, hitting the floor with a cane, barking orders, is The Crippled Choreographer forcing her dancers into absurd and painful maneuvers; she is also God creating the firmament. Women sow and reap a starfield of white balloons.

In some of the sub-sections of Part VIII, light becomes a private adversary. It transfixes Joan Schwartz, licks at her, keeps her wiggling in an endless excruciating dance. It tantalizes Mal Pate, luring him down what must be a dangerous path; over and over he dives out into space, grabs at the air, and crashes to the floor. Deformed and abused, light somehow *becomes* the pile of lumpy garments that Takei greedily decks herself with—sticking her head through legholes and her legs through armholes—until she's barely able to move, although she's still sttempting to skitter gleefully around.

The newest part of "Light" is lucid, orderly, reasoned. The incredible set is a huge open spiral binder with one page flying up the back wall, and the other pages extending toward the audience. Wow. A young man pitches white cloth balls through a hole in the raised page ("One white cloth call for white milk" etc.). When he has lobbed about 15 balls, he helps roll one page up. Another man takes his place, but a little nearer the binding, and throws more balls. (There are four ball-throwers in all.) Each throwing accompanies different activities by the dancers who crawl in through the huge hoops of the binder. Page Three is a parade, or perhaps a forced march. A group of men and a group of women march along the square perimeter of the book; at each new round, they add something to their walk. Stamp, stamp, toe-in, tiptoe, shuffle, shuffle, bend, straight . . . it gets quite complicated both to watch and to listen to. And, all the time, rice spills from holes in the packs they wear and makes its own brown record of their track. "One white cloth ball for white canvas!" At the end, the lights go out, and one more ball is thrown and called. In the darkness.

Kei Takei, Maldwyn Pate, Lloyd Ritter, Amy Berkman, Elsi Mirandi,

Joan Schwartz, Wendy Osserman, John de Marco, Abel, Richmond Johnstone, John Parton, Barbara Mitsueda—these, in no particular order, were most prominent among the many vital and valiant performers in "Light".

"Exceptional ability . . . " by all means. That too.

Sure to Surprise

The New York Times, February 18, 1973

Twyla Tharp makes a piece for the Spring season of the City Center Joffrey Ballet, and the dance world is astonished. The idea of one of the most important and obstreperously radical young dancer-choreographers hooking up with a ballet company is unusual, but then, both Tharp and the Joffrey like to be first at things.

If you ask Tharp why she decided on this venture, you get a lot of answers, all interesting and none—not even: "Didn't you know I've always wanted to write a classical ballet?"—implausible. For one thing, Tharp wants to work with a lot of bodies, claiming, for instance, that to make three-part counterpoint clear she has to double or triple each part; otherwise the audience will think one part is being improvised.

Tharp, who as a child studied music energetically, in addition to downing large mother-organized doses of ballettoetapacrobaticbaton, forms her choreographic structures meticulously. She does occasionally give dancers leeway with the shape, timing, or spatial dimensions of her movement, but they always know where they're heading.

If the dances look improvised at times, it's because the movement—which is what Tharp's dances are all about—looks so complex, so spontaneous that you can hardly believe that someone taught it to someone else. Her phrases are composed of many small, rapid, fluent motions. At any given moment, a dancer may be sustaining one kind of rhythm and dynamic in the feet, another in the head, another in the torso or arms. And nothing is end-stopped; there are no poses for the spectator's eye to rest on. Sometimes you feel as if the dancing were a palpable thing, like a garment that the dancers are twisting, sliding into or shrugging delicately out of.

The changes in speed, energy, direction can be dazzling, but for all the loose-jointedness and slammed-into passages, the dancing has a kind of elegant ambiguity and restraint. Part of this may be due to the company's performing style. Tharp herself, Sara Rudner, Rose Marie Wright, Kenneth Rinker, Isabel Garcia-Lorca, Nina Wiener—all handle their dancing with superb ease and skill, but they don't impose attitudes on it. Instead, they allow what they're doing to absorb, amuse, exasperate them.

They have a lot of concentrating to do. Sometimes, the dancers are all doing something different; the next instant they're in unison; then they slide apart into canon. Material from one dancer's solo may reappear embedded in a later section, subtly altered. Space is used unconventionally, dangerously. Neat formations tend to splatter off, clump up, dive through other formations. Dancers often look as if they're trying to invade each others' territories, even trip each other up.

Audiences of many kinds love the Tharp dancers these days. Perhaps this has something to do with the fact that the latest works, "Eight Jelly Rolls," "The Bix Pieces," "The Raggedy Dances," have used pop (or once-pop) music and hinted superbly at pop dance styles. Perhaps it's the engaging combination of offhand performing and terrific dancing. Perhaps Twyla Tharp, still in her early thirties, is getting better and better at what she wants to do.

But still, right from the start, when she left Paul Taylor's company in 1965 and began to work on her own, she's always made interesting dances, and she's always found audiences that liked them, although she didn't make it easy for her public in the early days. Some of her pieces were highly conceptual. In the maddeningly brilliant "Re-Moves" (1966), three dancers made a journey of slow, flat, precise dancing around a huge square wall placed in the middle of the Judson Church. The audience sat on three sides, which meant that no one could see the performers all the time and, consequently, few saw the same dance. You spent a lot of time waiting for the dancers to reappear.

Tharp liked slowness and stillness then, as I remember—bold poses, deadpan stares and big, deliberate movement. Some of the material was very simple, as if she needed to be sure you could recognize it if you saw it again. The dancers, all women, performed with an almost belligerent objectivity, giving the impression that they wanted to come by admirers the hard way, without resorting to seductive—or even friendly—demeanor, although they always looked very glamorous in the chic, spare costumes designed by Twyla's then-husband, artist Robert Huot.

There have been many subtle changes in Tharp's style, in the look of her dances. Around 1968, you could notice a lot of big leg movements flung into the air and allowed to trail casually away. For a while, she augmented her company with hordes of student-dancers; the works looked healthy and athletic—no special costumes or lighting. And for a while, music was out, although Tharp says, "We always worked with music; we just didn't let the audience hear it."

Although Tharp's dances are mostly about dancing they are also intermittently about how dances get made. For example, in New York, "Excess, Idle, Surplus" (1968) was accompanied by a tape of the dancers' voices arguing about how to reconstruct the original choreography, while the onstage dancers often fumbled or stopped dead in perplexity. The last section of the 1972 "The Bix Pieces" was in part a witty and moving lecture demonstration of how the dance was made. In "Group Activities" (1969), 10 women danced over a grid of adhesive tape, occasionally asking a timekeeper for the count—as if they wanted to make the complicated space-time ratios of the dance highly visible. Tharp at her brainiest.

Some of the dances, like "Re-Moves," have a lot to do with how people perceive dance. One 1969 work, premiered at the Wadsworth Atheneum in Hartford, strewed dancing through much of the building—cueing performers and aiding spectators by means of closed circuit TV. The New York performance of the beautiful "Medley" (1969) occurred in Central Park near dusk; toward the end, the vision of those watching had to accommodate to distance and darkness as 50 or so dancers spread over what seemed like miles of grass into the approaching night.

It's difficult to keep up with Twyla Tharp. Her dances are often premiered in out of the way places or such unusual spaces that they can't be repeated. Even her works for prescenium stage don't stay in repertory for long. It's not that she disapproves of her past—she wouldn't mind televising works, or teaching them to a second company, or putting on a retrospective, if time and money permitted—it's just that she and her company don't like performing a dance over and over. They reach a peak, maybe after 10 performances, and then they want to move on to something new. That's what excites them, and if the studio is big and clean and the dancers are getting paid, so much the better. A few weeks ago, Tharp was happy as a clam because she'd been able to work on the new ballet, "Deuce Coupe," from 9 A.M. to 9 P.M.

It's possible that Tharp wanted to produce this particular dance with the Joffrey company because of the challenge of working with (or against) the expectations of an unfamiliar audience which may be baffled, delighted, or infuriated by a brand of virtuosity different from the pose-oriented beauty of most ballets. In setting her work to what amounts to a retrospective of Beach Boy hits, she has created another challenge for herself: after all, the Joffrey is the home of "Astarte," the first so-called rock ballet.

Tharp herself and her own company of five will perform along with a group of Joffrey dancers in "Deuce Coupe" this season. Yes, Tharp is putting some of the Joffrey dancers on pointe. And yes, it's bound to be surprising. In the wonderfully written speech that accompanied the last part of "The Bix Pieces," Tharp asked, "Can anything be new, original, private?" Maybe not. But she has ways of putting things together that makes them look like nothing you've seen before, even if you've seen them a million times.

Dancing to Beat the Band

The Village Voice, March 8, 1973

Oh Twyla, what have you done? Finally stunned me into wordlessness, I think. Here I sit, staring at the rows of mint-green letters on my Hermes, wondering how I can possibly hit them into sentences that will suggest the liveliness, the complexity, the marvelous ease of "Deuce Coupe."

As everyone probably knows by now, "Deuce Coupe" is the ballet that Twyla Tharp has just produced with the City Center Joffrey company. It's done to a selection of Beach Boy hits from the past 10 years. Tharp and her company, for the time being, are dancing in it, along with 14 members of the Joffrey.

Calling the ballet "Deuce Coupe" (a Beach Boy title too) was appropriate. It's a real double-doored affair in which ballet steps and steps based on social dance styles of the '60s banter gently with each other or go their separate, often simultaneous ways. This is not a simple matter of the Joffrey kids doing classical ballet while Twyla and her people frug and boogaloo. They're all in it together. I mean, suddenly you notice Beatriz Rodriguez in a clot of Tharp women—doing that silk-ribbon ripple of the spine with great finesse. Or Larry Grenier, making a brief, lazy trio with Kenneth Rinker and Nina Wiener of the Tharp company. And right near the end of everything, Tharp, alone in an upstage corner, begins the same soft, lyrical phrase with which Rebecca Wright and William Whitener open the ballet.

Erika Goodman—dressed in white, more relaxed and glamorous than I've ever seen her look—acts as a stylistic reference point. Throughout almost the entire ballet, she works her way through steps from a ballet glossary, leaping past, and into, obliviously wiggling hordes. Occasionally the force of the others' dancing seems to crumple her or knock her from the stage. She becomes a kind of testament to the dancer's discipline and endurance.

But in the end, "Deuce Coupe" doesn't contrast ballet with rock-dancing; it points out their kinship. Tharp's ballet style doesn't show you a lot of poses or long, sharply drawn body lines. It makes you aware of those elastic little traveling steps—like pas de basque, glissade, coupé. The dancers look open and soft doing it—arms, head, torso free to glide and twist on top of the easily springing feet. Not that the balletic movement is all peaceful. Rebecca Wright and William Whitener execute some rapid turns—whipped by one extended leg and a contracting and expanding torso—that are terrifically exciting. Once I noticed a phrase that Glenn White was doing very beautifully, and I was wiped out by the combination of intricacy and nonchalant elegance—both in the choreography and in his dancing.

Tharp's approach to rock is like her approach to jazz. None of the dancing in "Deuce Coupe" looks anything like adapted Broadway-style stuff that often passes for up-to-the-minute pop in the ballet world (e.g., Fernand Nault's choreography for "Tommy"). Tharp shows you loose, scrambling legs, shrugging shoulders and hips, rolling heads. Sometimes the dancing is tight and fast, abrasive; sometimes it's lolling, lost in space, falling apart. Even in music as straightforward as the Beach Boys' stuff, there's a lot of ambiguity.

"Deuce Coupe" uses 14 cuts, some of them very short. There are a few repeats, and David Horowitz made variations on the finale, "Cuddle Up." Maybe the dance is too long; maybe it isn't. Maybe it's just so much richer and livelier than a lot of the dances I see that I can scarcely take it all in. The gentle, happy beginning with Wright, Whitener, and Goodman segues through a sprightly trio passage for White, Starr Danias, and Henry Berg into a long juicy canon with all the dancers strutting and shuffling and hip-shaking onto the stage one by one in a long line—looking very wise-ass pleased about it all. From then on, the stage often looks like a crowded dance floor on which people are sometimes dreamy, sometimes aggressive. The dancers dash in and out, drift past, butt their way through. Pardon me. Get outa my dreams. There's no such thing as a number bracketed in important pauses; the dancing is an unstoppable flood.

Twyla and Gary Chryst jackknife in, feet barely touching the floor. Their bodies jabber at each other in the air. Some kind of crazy happy contest. Tharp *smiling* on stage? In "Alley Oop" a bunch of dancers slouch about while Goodman completes the passage from Pas de cheval to Repetition. They're not doing the Monkey; this is full-size ape-dancing—pensively lewd. Small Tharp skitters through in the wake of big Rose Marie Wright ("Long Tall Texan"). Splat, Tharp's down. Wright walks over her into the wings, and Tharp follows still importuning. Five of the dancers mime musicians dragging on preperformance joints, then begin slowly jerking their way along in a clump. The gestures of their limbs speed up crazily, although they don't seem to cover ground any faster. They exit, looking as if the friction of their feet on the floor had built up enough static electricity to blow the place up. Sara Rudner's little solo is a long shudder of self-absorbed sexuality. Yet, even with the infinitesimal vibrations from her shaking hips and shoulders, the inviting opening and closing of one probing leg, she looks elegant. Just the sheer dancepower of it is tremendously moving.

Much of the dancing is witty or just happy. Some is equivocal. Once Chryst, Grenier, Rudner, and Tharp dance close together—arms bodies, hips swinging with the cozy love ballad, but their heads keep twisting so their eyes never meet. The kids in "Catch a Wave" slide exuberantly over the floor, but the girls who line up for "Don't Go Near the Water"

look positively schizzy—arms swimming directionless, heads averted—
and they finish by writhing and twisting as if trying to climb out of
their skins.

There's canon, fugue, counterpoint, and what-not in "Deuce Coupe,"
but they're hard to see because of the breezy look of the dancing and
some of the haphazard space patterns. Still, it seemed to me that in the
long, lyrical, swirling finale, I saw little muted flashes of almost everything I'd seen before, and that felt somehow reassuring.

Everything about "Deuce Coupe" looked fine to me, except for
some of the lighting. The women's orange dresses (by Scott Barrie)—
each cut slightly differently from every other—move nicely and are ex-
chic beachy without being gimmicky. The boys wear red trousers and
tropical shirts, but not blazing ones. A group of guys from United
Graffiti Artists do their impudent stuff with spray paint on a rolling
white paper backdrop, and by the time the ballet is over, they've achieved
something like the outside of a Seventh Avenue express train. Only more.
The casting of "Deuce Coupe" is weird. I got the feeling that whoever
showed up for a rehearsal was put in a section, and the injured, the too
busy, the tardy ended up with less dancing. I kind of liked barely seeing
some of them; I knew we were at the same party. All the dancers are
fine. Some are better than others, but I'm not naming names. I don't
want to exclude anybody. Boy is it nice to see *people* up there dancing.

*This article, of course, refers to the original, the irreplaceable "Deuce
Coupe," not to "Deuce Coupe II," the streamlined version which Tharp
"customized" for the Joffrey dancers.*

Enter the Dancers, Rippling Fastidiously

The Village Voice, November 2, 1972

Over at the Anta Theatre, Twyla Tharp's "The Raggedy Dances" deliberately, delicately probes into pop styles and the decadence behind the
figure of the public entertainer. Joel Sachs plays seven Scott Joplin
piano rags, also one by Bill Bolcom called "Graceful Ghost" (1970), also
Mozart's variations on "Ah, vous dirai-je, Maman." There is indeed a
graceful ghost in the pit; the playing is quiet, limpid—an echo of something that was louder and merrier in New Orleans, a premonition of the
Mozartian elegance that ends the work.

The dancers in sleek, chic individual outfits by Kermit Love slide
kinkily in and out of the music, in and out of our sight. They surprise
us by becoming suddenly forceful, jab their weight at the floor. They

twist and shudder lightly as if something were crawling on their spines. Sara Rudner and Rose Marie Wright make many spattering crosses— wrangling amicably for a slice of moving territory. There are a lot of false entrances, near-collisions. "If it's in my way, I'll dance with it." Many of the sections are duets or double duets. Two figures subtly slipping in and out of phase with each other. One of these duets (for Tharp and Nina Wiener) is very distant, both in space and in texture. Each woman dances as if she were absorbed in a private tune she was humming. You notice, barely, that each possesses a part of the other's dance and shows it to you in her own way. Another duet, for Rose Marie Wright and Kenneth Rinker, is a tangle of coincidental ballroom clutches. Just when you tire of the jaggedness, everyone struts out some unison.

Tharp, in a purple bikini, solos as a stripper. All her gestures are small, self-absorbed. She does a creditable belly dance; leans her head back to brush her shoulders with short, bristly hair; wiggles her spine. She dances for a long time, looking with every passing minute smaller, lonelier, tireder. A stripper seen through the wrong end of a telescope, more concerned with scratching some sly private itch than with ingratiating herself with an audience.

Rudner and Wright wrap up "The Raggedy Dances" with a beautiful display of dancing. Everything they do with the Mozart looks and sounds immensely clever. You can almost imagine the music skidding over the floor like a flock of beautiful birds that they, grinning and concentrating fiercely, must step in and out of without damaging a single feather.

Tharp, in an interview, mentioned that her solo in "Raggedy Dances," called "The Entertainer," had a lot to do with the performer's dilemma. Many of the most gifted dancers seem to have a reticence about "performing"; perhaps they're afraid of cheapening the movement by over-emphasis or obscuring it by imposing the flash of their personalities on it.

The Dance Behind the Dance

The Village Voice, March 29, 1973

In the middle of his dance, "Changing Your Mind," Dan Wagoner does just that and takes us all by surprise. In the beginning, Mirjam Berns, Karen Levey, Sally Hess, and Judith Moss are strutting and kicking and jerking and bending and stamping around the stage of the Exchange

Theatre. Just doing typical Wagoner movement, which is a bit like slangy Cunningham done very fast and at a feverish level of intensity. I worry about the floor getting bruised. (Sorry, Wagoner was here last week; we have to let the floor recover before we allow any more dancing.) As usual, the dancers occasionally touch each other with absent-minded palsiness, as if they're mothers with 10 kids and only a second to spare for each. Come to think of it, Wagoner's dances are like busy households in which the occupants are constantly running back and forth between uncompleted chores. As usual, too, there's a lot of amiable panting and sweating. George Montgomery reads numbers from the New York Times, as he announced he would before the dance began. Later he switches to stories, chosen at random.

But one story is a plant (you realize only later). You hear "Monroe Administration" and then something about a young Indian brave and his sweetheart performing a dance before a great crowd, before committing suicide to protest a life of poverty and degradation. And suddenly Wagoner is no longer creating a spate of vigorous, happy dancing that bears no relation to Montgomery's words, he is showing us the dance behind the dance those Indians did. He has changed his mind about a lot of things. He and Emmy Devine wear tan outfits subtly fringed like buckskin. She carries a big bag. They dance to night noises. Much of the movement is non-specific—Wagoner stuff with a wary look and a reduced speed. But occasionally he stamps in a special questioning way or makes stiff ceremonious gestures. Once she lies down and makes a seat for him with her upraised feet. When he lifts her, her body looks desperate—clinging or stretching out. They dig into her bag, and a flash-light inside it makes their faces blaze; they streak each others' face with paint. Finally, they look at each other very carefully and . . . well . . . they die. I guess. It's very subtle. And very beautiful.

The third section is a dialogue between Wagoner and Montgomery about changing your mind. A rapid, thoughtful, complicated talk that fades with the dimming of the lights. At one point Wagoner talks about really changing your mind—exchanging it for someone else's—and wonders at what point it really will have happened. Can you retain a percentage of your own mind and still have changed? That's just part of what this dance is all about.

Life Pageant

The Village Voice, May 28, 1970

I couldn't make either performance of Robert Wilson's "The Life and Times of Sigmund Freud" so I went to the dress rehearsal, which was an event in itself—the work shot through and veiled over with glimpses of its own procedures and preparations. At a dress rehearsal, you are constantly aware of potential and actual as the one approaches or draws back from the other.

"Freud" is unlike anything I've ever seen. It's billed, as I remember, as a dance-drama: dance maybe as in "dance of life," drama as in the "human drama." Wilson works as a visual artist, arranging, combining and separating various realities in the stage space—an orchestrator of daily bodies and objects. Many of the realities that he deals with are simple—a man walking, a woman sitting, a boy lighting candles, but, viewed against each other, they become complex, charged with a special radiance. Other events are extraordinary, astonishing—like the four furred, clawed, floor-to-ceiling legs of an immense cat which stalk across the front of the stage in Act II.

There are what seem like hundreds of performers in "Freud"—children-men-women-animals of all ages-sizes-shapes. At the dress rehearsal, many of them were still getting to know each other. (High agitated calls: "Where's Jesse?" "Who's Jesse?" Or a woman crying "Hey, E. Z!" and a man telling her, "Her names's S. K.") Objects, lights, people often refused to function properly. As in every dress rehearsal, the quiet continuing event was surrounded with babble from time to time. It was fascinating to huddle in the middle and compare the scope, the tumult of the undertaking with the small intent activities ebbing and flowing on the stage.

Act I is an act of passage. The stage is divided into equal horizontal zones, each with its own discrete reality from moment to moment. The stage floor is covered with sand that sprays curling into the air when people pass through it. I can't begin to describe the people who pass through it. Here are some of them: Three bare-breasted people in tan levis who perform a gentle canon of movement exercises; a beautiful Negress in a severe black dress who does not pass, but sits in a chair with a stuffed raven on her wrist; a giant turtle (papier-maché manned by a little boy); an old woman alternately stretching and making cradles of her arms in some kind of extravagant elegy of loss; two people in bear suits; Kenneth King in a white suit stuffed to make him look very fat, prize-fight-dancing through; a runner passing continuously back and forth in the most upstage layer; numberless unremarkable, remarkable people. There are some astonishing events too: a snake-charmer is

167

pulled into the flies by a rope, and, in return, a life-sized angel dummy with disintegrating cotton wings descends. A pair of feet tight-rope across on a batten high above the stage. At the end of the act, hordes of identically dressed "mammies" dance weavingly through—men, women, and a tiny child. Some are real blacks, some burnt-cork blacks, but they are all padded fore and aft like cliché Aunt Jemimas.

Act II is more an act of assembling and accumulating, and the layers of space acquire more scalloped contours. The scene is like a dark living room in some shabby rooming house. People sit and smoke; three standing men move pieces on a table in an arcane game; a woman somersaults in and carries on a chatty monologue, plays the piano ("Oh, E minor! That always sends chills up my spine."); one large woman sits in a miked chair whose every creak is beautifully amplified; a camel sticks its head in the door and retreats. Toward the end, almost everyone piles up on and around a ladder while armloads of hay are brought in; Wilson does a loose-limbed Aunt Jemima dance; the people walk off in a line; finally a mysterious figure (The King of Spain) who has been sitting, almost invisible, in a high-backed chair facing upstage rises and turns. He has a gigantic, bearded, wild-eyed humpty-dumpty of a head. Astonishment and terror at this messiah. The curtain falls.

Act III has a ritual quality—a Nativity that has been fractured and whose parts are floating tantalizingly about the stage like pieces of a jigsaw puzzle skidding away from your ordering hand. It seemed to me that the front part of the stage—a vast straw-heaped cave—was like one layer, while many layers were sometimes crowded into the sunny strip of beach visible outside the cave's mouth. Inside the cave, the King of Spain sits, the old woman (suggesting a shepherd, a Joseph) sits. Wild animals enter one by one; they are people in beautifully realistic suits and heads. Outside the cave, the changing scene has a surreal clarity, a violence of light. Bare-breasted people do something gently ritualistic with a real baaing lamb in front of a female figure with streaming false blond hair. Later those figures on the beach become a costumed panoply. By that time, vertical bars have fallen very slowly one at a time, slamming into the floor, gradually making the cave into a cage. Finally Freud enters (he has made three previous entrances, one in each act) and sits at a table on a chair that has slowly been lowered from above. He writes while the animals cluster about him and a little boy curled up on the floor whimpers (like a newborn baby? like a monkey?). Freud's young woman companion enters and stands over him; she has come in quickly, naturally, as if to say "Lunch is ready. Can you come now?" A white scroll of cloth rises from the pit, a suspended square of glass falls and shatters, the curtain falls.

I can describe these events, cannot get across the effect they have when viewed together. I cannot quite evoke the mysterious beauty of some of them. The unity, the inexplicably mythic dimensions of the work come from the way figures and events appear and reappear in the acts—sometimes in full focus, sometimes very briefly. There is always a runner. There is always a rope: in the first act it undulates upstage; in the other acts it is pulled out of things—the King, the haystack, the bears. The bars descend in each act, but their importance is clear only in the last. A tall, melancholy man with a fan, who crawls through the sand in Act I, drags lovesick through Act II wearing a walrus head. In Act III, he is in complete walrus suit, but still carries his fan and now walks upright.

There are many more events: Audrey Monk speaks an introduction; there are activities in intermission—wordless yowling, high screaming songs. I forgot the tumbleweeds that whisk across the stage in the very beginning. Oh, well . . . What I am trying to convey is the density and the gentle, surprising beauty of "The Life and Times of Sigmund Freud." The pace of each activity is tremendously slow and weighted, but new ideas are introduced with carefully theatrical timing. It is as if Wilson has encouraged each special individual to perform his part in his own way, but then surrounded them with supernatural happenings, crowned them with haloes, put ravens on their wrists and lambs in their arms. So it is like some pageant of living, studded with symbols from Christian mythology, pondered and observed by a tender and venerable Freud.

Quiet Please, a Berry is Breaking

The Village Voice, May 4, 1972

Everything that happens in Robert Wilson's plays is something you should have known but probably forgot. All glory to our collective unconscious. "Overture for Ka Mountain and Guardenia Terrace, a story about a family and some people changing" didn't begin in a theatre but in his loft building. He takes you into his world (from 6 a.m. to 9 a.m. or from 6 p.m. to 9 p.m. and lunch and exhibits in between), and his world is everything you see there. It is the chopped, unbranching birch grove in the hallway; it is the tryptych biographies of performers, overlaid with photographs, graffiti, cabalistic signs—beautiful as unburied temple tablets; it is the doweled, fresh wood pyramid with the layered cityscapes on glass deep within its heart; it is the onion that is slowly peeled away to nothingness by the slim black fingers that belong to the beautiful black child/woman in the white Edwardian gown; it is the matter-of-factness of two children in white sailor hats who change the props. It is a world in which the daily miracles of stone, wood, fire, water, birth and growth and death are celebrated in many ways—hidden and accessible.

Everything grows up as if Wilson and his collaborators had scattered handfuls of seed which would burgeon into the right event at the right time. For instance, there are sea seeds that produce surprising flowers: Edwin Denby in a distant corner looking like an ancient mariner buffeted by a storm; a man and a boy rowing on the balcony rail; a sea captain holding a model ship; ancient maps hanging in the hall; an engulfing wave of fabric; a boy/woman musing beside an anchor. Miracles are everyday happenings. A large woman in black velvet marked with silver triangles stares from the doorway of the pyramid at a dead pine branch on a pile of stones and it bursts into flame. Later a cardboard city catches fire while a mountaineer violinist plays with beautiful intensity a small range of notes clustering around one tone, and a girl trickles water from a pitcher to a bowl. Flamingos dance up through slits on the floor, and elephant heads unfold from the pyramid, which is really a ziggurat maybe, is the Tower of Babel because of the holocaust of tongues that someone speaks from underneath it, directs at it from the balcony. "Quiet please, a berry is breaking." While Edwin Denby reads, a girl with his white hair, blue shirt, brown sweater stands behind him, reading over his shoulder.

From the tragedy of a pile of dead soldiers to the comedy of Edwin Denby frightened up a ladder by a firmly roaring lion/man while he continues to read aloud from Nijinsky's diary about vegetarianism and love of animals, to the hominess of a big woman talking about Iowa or Wilson's grandmother recalling her life in a faded but sweetly vigorous voice, to the ritual of a dervish, to the mad violence of the lunge with which Wilson lays withered gladioli across a table, to . . . I expected the heavens to open, and maybe they did.

In far retrospect I can sometimes ponder and evaluate Wilson's works. I can say now that I liked "The Life and Times of Sigmund Freud" better than "Deafman Glance." But the pieces are trance-begun, and they leave me in a trance for a long time.

Ancient Traditions and Miscellaneous Festivals

Bird Dancing

The Village Voice, August 27, 1970

I may be the only dance person in New York who had never seen Les Ballets Africains. Nobody had ever described the company to me, or I would have made the scene a lot sooner. It is not—as one might be forgiven for thinking—a ballet company working out of Guinea, but neither is it a cultural variety show of ethnic and folk dances. It's . . . well, it's hard to describe; perhaps you could think of it as a terrific example of happy, popular theatre. Les Ballets Africains has certain things in common with Eastern forms of dance-drama, but is less tidy. Oh boy, is it less tidy. A packed stage is the general rule with everybody dancing and/or singing, speaking, making noises, playing instruments, and playing their parts to the hilt. Often your eye picks three girls out of the dazzling throng. They seem to be moving in a somewhat similar manner: by God, yes, it's a dance number.

Interesting to compare the company to the Moiseyev. With the Russians, the neat, cleanly punctuated line and circle dances lend themselves to stylized stage patterns. The choreography looks as if it were planned for Madison Square Garden—as if everything you needed to see could be seen from a block away. But the Africans have made tribal dancing an integral part of their story dances; the difference between dancers and singers or onlookers is looser. People fade in and out of a singing, arguing, drumming mob, catching your attention the way a brightly colored fish does when he swims to the front of the aquarium for a minute. The effect is both primitive and immensely subtle. The two artistic directors Hamidou Bangoura and Italo Zambo know their stuff: the comedy is really funny, the tragedy is really sad (or temporarily sad; nobody seems to want to be tragic for very long). The numbers are staged, often very theatrical, but they're not phony.

The stories are cheerful blends of history, legend, and current political feeling. One is about Soundiata Keita, "the lion king" (c. 1200-1255), a cripple whose mother had exiled him and given the throne to her other son. When the brother abdicates out of fear of a powerful war lord who collects caravan routes, Soundiata with immense difficulty learns to walk, gathers an army, and saves his people. Another story concerns M'Balia Camara, a brave woman who organizes the women of the village of Tondon, and encourages the men to throw off the yoke of servitude (in this case, a cruel, if comical, native chief who is under the thumb of the ruling colonial power). In the middle of the fight, the bad guy kills the heroine, but the dance ends in triumphant festivities anyway.

Then, there's a sly little tale of the rivalry of a tall, elegant guitar player and a short, cocky flute player for a girl who, in the end, prefers to stay with her runty old protector because she likes to baby him. The action is accomplished by some adroit upstaging of each other and some beautifully explicit vocal noises—trilling, grunting, howling, wailing, laughing, etc.

The only non-story dance, "Night of the Cora," has a group of girls in colored turbans and silk robes (rectangles with holes for head and hands) who sing while bending and swaying like bright flowers around the strolling cora player. (The cora is a long-necked stringed instrument played standing with the bowl resting against the player's stomach.)

The most spectacular ballet concerns an initiation rite that is almost profaned by a hot-eyed young man and one of the girls. They are given a working-over in the forest by the Koma (the master of the ceremony) and his two henchmen, while the (supposedly) invisible gods dance in and out. Among these gods are Naadians, skipping on stilts the height of a man; Gnamou, a fellow with lots of horns on the back of his head and a snout like an alligator; a couple of little guys who look like walking heads of Simpson lettuce. In the dark forest, the guardians of morality fling the hapless couple around like rag dolls, but ultimately forgive them.

It's all vastly entertaining. Interesting how African dancers make you aware of the beauty of the body's joints. Rarely do they lift an arm, move a torso, as one unit. The elbows rise, the lower arms follow limply, the wrists snap back. Or, the body pulls back, and at the last moment the neck whips back and completes an arch. You notice knees too—lifting high to engineer that soft, flat slap of foot on floor. Sometimes, I think that primeval Africans must have been very impressed by wading birds.

The rhythmic relation of dancing to music is very subtle. So is the musical relation between the drums and the more melodic instruments like thumb pianos, pipes, and so on. Everything has "rhythm," but bodies and arms float and snap in delicate counter-rhythms to the slapping feet, the way those instruments weave around the drums (except that some of the African drums can play melodies too). Often quite long pauses and silences occur. The excellent dancer who portrays the Koma has a great way of making strong, terse movement statements and then freezing into fierce immobility.

What I think of as "African" movement is fleshed out, jazzed up with acrobatics, tumbling tricks, international favorites like barrel turns, funny crab walks, and individual virtuoso stunts. It all works because of the beautiful, unbelievable energy and strength and commitment of

174

the performers. When the actor playing the crippled king takes his first steps, you believe. When M'Balia Camara grieves for her people, you believe. The way you believe, and don't believe, a puppet show or a fairy tale or a myth. Some of the performers are better singers or more powerful dancers than others, but everybody is tingling with life. I can't tell you any names. All are listed; none is singled out. You have to salute them as a company, to thank them as a company.

Spanish Gems with Faults

The Village Voice, December 30, 1971

Spanish dance, Europe's richest traditional form, can be innocent, light-hearted, elegant, sensual. The different regions of Spain produce springy couple dances—like the jota aragonese with its squared-off arm positions and clacking castanets, or grave circle dances like the sardana of Catalonia, or classical 18th century court dances like the pavanne, or the Flamenco dances of Andalusia, and many more. Flamenco is perhaps the most exotic—reminiscent of the dance of North India in which the dancer also maintains a taut carriage and uses rhythmic foot-stamping and slowly circling wrist gestures. Flamenco is also fiercely affirmative; its powerful sexuality is like an assault on death.

Many Flamenco dancers overplay this sexuality—especially, I suspect, for American audiences. Often the performer manages to convey by his shrugging shoulders, thrusting hips, hot-eyed stares, that he can hardly wait to get off stage to jump into bed with somebody . . . anybody. Of course, this can be terrifically exciting, but it can also be vulgar and even funny.

Mariano Parra's company is decidedly not vulgar nor is it funny. Jerane Michel, Barbara Martos, Parra, and his sisters Ines and Mariana perform a variety of Spanish dance styles with skill and elegance. They put on a good show. You can admire the controlled fire of tall, slim Jerane Michel, or the spacious way small Mariana uses her arms, or Ines's long, pliable body, or Barbara Martos's beautiful vehemence with the floor. Parra himself is tall and slender and performs with a certain hauteur. He likes stopping suddenly in stretched-out lunges. His heelwork has a marvelous clarity, and he's subtle with the castanets. The voice of Dominico Cara, the guitars of Guillermo Montes and Emilio Prados (the latter played two solos), the piano accompaniment of Sandra Owen added a lot of zip to the program that I saw at the Fashion Institute.

Well, so the company is elegant, tastful, skilled—all that. And I admire Parra for not permitting excessive camping around. Yet in many numbers, I found the dancing a bit pale—as if the performers were not getting any emotional feedback from their dancing (or if they were, were controlling it masterfully). They seem so anxious to present each little step as a polished gem, distinct from its neighbors, that the dancing loses its impetus, its flow. Spanish dancers that I have admired the most (Luisillo, for example, or Roberto Ximenez) have a way of making a chain of small repeated movements appear to grow more powerful— louder, almost. It's as if the steps formed a swelling wave; the dancer who rides the wave must exert more and more authority in order to quell it, in order to avoid being lost. It's a very subtle thing, and I'm probably explaining it badly. Anyhow, Parra's dancers, for the most part, release their energy in even spurts. The sudden stops do make interesting punctuation, but no movement, no phrase seems more important than any other. So the effect is always attractive and agreeable, but not often profoundly exciting.

Because the dancers are best at light, purling passages, I especially liked Parra's elegant "Playeras" and "Evocación," a quiet dance for Parra, Martos, and the two Parra girls. This last was choreographed by La Meri, and its small canonic passages along a diagonal line are very pretty. (I like these even though I'm not a fan of solo piano Albéniz, Granados, and de Falla. I'm reminded of salon art and wish someone would use Scarlatti or Soler, or *something* beside those sweet old chestnuts.) Jerane Michel did a fine "La Caña." And Parra made an interesting "Romanza Gitana" for the company.

This last intrigued me, not only because I liked the choreography, but because it exemplified the hierarchy of casting within the company. Barbara Martos and Ines and Mariano Parra are almost always featured as a trio. Mariano Parra dances with the three of them together (except in one zapateado) or by himself or with Jerane Michel. In "Romanza Gitana," the three act like a sisterly bodyguard to escort him on and later to separate him from Michel. Parra is the only man in the company, so I found myself wishing that he'd occasionally deploy the dancers he has in a more surprising way. Inevitably, Parra's dance personna emerges (for those given to daydreaming irreverently, like me) as a conscientious man too busy supporting his three sisters to make out with the girl of his dreams.

To Keep the World Turning

The Village Voice, November 30, 1972

"You're a regular whirling dervish," my grandmother used to say, not always appreciatively, when I would spin as fast as I could—shutting my eyes to get dizzy quicker—until I tumbled into a shrieking heap. I thought that real dervishes could probably do what I did much faster, maybe with a few jumps thrown in and possibly—but I wasn't sure about this—biting on knives. The woman who stormed out of an exhibition of dervish dancing at the Brooklyn Academy muttering "The Emperor has no clothes" may have had a similar childhood.

Certainly I would have preferred to see the ceremony of the Mevlevi in a church, rather than on a stage where I'm accustomed to watch theatrically-paced virtuosic dancing. However, I can't really fault something for being boring when it wasn't conceived as entertainment. And, in some strange way, my impression of what happened in the Turkish ritual has become stronger with the passing of time.

First, a group of musicians played. Drums, wooden flutes, a zither, a tiny fiddle (it looks like a rebec and is bowed, absurdly, in an upright position resting on the musician's lap). The music is sparse and decorous. Perhaps because some of the instruments have a limited range, the players embroider many melismas around a few central tones. The gently beating drum maintains an even pace, a dry tone.

The actual ceremony begins with a long vocal "eulogy." The singer too plays out throatfuls of notes that cluster around a given tone. Sometimes he squeezes out his voice; sometimes it emerges fatter and sweeter. After a flute improvisation, the nine dancers (semazen) walk several circular processionals, turning to bow to each other as they pass a piece of red cloth that lies on the ground at one end of the circle. They're sober but relaxed in their tall, almost conical brown hats, black robes over white ones. They don't bother much about walking on the beat. I've forgotten just when they remove their outer robes, but they're all in their full-skirted white gowns when they begin to whirl. As each man passes the old man who stands by the red cloth, he simply makes his walking begin to turn. He turns to the left, evenly and gently; his right foot crosses over, slightly toed-in, and his left foot pivots to accommodate to the new direction. You become very aware of that right foot lifting to generate a revolution, which in turn makes it necessary to lift the right foot again. Each man holds his right hand with the palm facing upward to receive Divine Grace; his left palm faces downward to transmit it to the earth. His turning body is the mill that accomplishes this priestly transformation. The dervishes can make their turning travel or stay in one spot. They whirl with their eyes closed, as if concentrating on some central inner spot. They show you only this continuum, this steady spinning flow.

They pause to mark off the four, no five, different "dances" that look the same but represent—*are*—different stages of heightened consciousness for the dancers. When they stop, their belled-out skirts twist the other way and then subside. The men form a casual circle; sometimes they are paired off, pressing slightly against each other for support before they begin again.

The old leader joins the last dance, turning gravely and a little stiffly. After more musical improvisation and a hymn of thanksgiving, the mystical word "HUUuu . u . . u . . . " is expelled, and you feel that this midwinter whirling ceremony ending with this utterance of the name for The One is perhaps sufficient to keep the earth itself turning for another year, whether that is its real purpose or not.

Dancing the Darkness Away

The Village Voice, December 27, 1973

The man sitting next to me at the top of the bleachers in the Barnard gym was obviously not a member of the English Country Dance Society. As we watched a huge, hot, jolly crowd of people working its way through the longways dance, "A Trip to Paris," he said, "It's such an anachronism—I mean, I never would have believed that there were this many people in New York who'd do this kind of thing."

I remember thinking the same thing years ago when I attended one of the society's regular sessions, but the annual Christmas party really knocks the message home. Here were these people of all ages and sizes come together, not just for each other's company—although they plainly enjoyed that—and not for the cookies and Hawaiian Punch—although they consumed buckets of both, but because they love these dances.

Most of the dances are those whose fiddle tunes were written down by John Playford in the 17th century. The tunes, pretty and fresh and sprightly, found their way into a lot of important English music—Purcell orchestrated some of them. The dances have little fancy footwork; their beauty lies in the complex patterns the dancers must weave with their turns and passes and circles. Each is set up in a particular way: longways, square sets, sets of five couples, sets of three couples, and so on. Most of them are couple dances, but an occasional one may have more unusual groupings. "Walpole Cottage," for example, has a circle of alternately facing sets, each of which consists of one man and two women. The names are terrific: "Parson's Farewell," "Hole in the Wall," "Mr. Isaac's Maggot."

The Christmas Festival featured country dances for everyone, a few complicated ones ("for those who know it," said the program firmly) and three American square dances. A lively little ensemble played the tunes, and Director Genevieve Shimer (I believe it was she) and Director Emeritus May Gadd talked the dances in hearty, unflappable British voices.

In spite of party fervor, the people were wonderfully industrious about their dancing—the awkward teenagers being given helpful shoves by their elders, the elderly show-offs, the worried ones, the ones with so little sense of space they went clear through their own sets and into the next one down, the hoppers and stampers, the cool stylists. Most of all, I liked watching May Gadd, who is small, round, and white-haired, execute the requisite "jaunty walk" for "A Trip to Paris"—maintaining a smooth glide underneath a hint of a bounce, twisting slightly to eye her partner with her whole body as he passed. Properly done, the dances have a charming sobriety, a sturdy, country cleverness.

I arrived at Barnard as the first interlude was ending—just in time to see the Morris dance, the "Nutting Girl Jig." A large group of the men, all wearing white shirts and trousers and black hats trimmed with holly, resplendent with red ribbons and bells, capered and pranced in a circle with skill and spirit. There are no drums or cymbals, the dancers' feet and bells prick out the rhythms against the supple and lively solo violin. Big jumps that spend one of their three counts in the air soar surprisingly out of the one-stamp-to-a-beat texture.

The second interlude featured the Uckfuss Mummers' Play and "The High Walbiggen," a sword dance. The play, like most of its kind, features sweetly inept rhymes and rowdy comedy, with contemporary colloquialisms grafted oddly onto the remnants of an ancient rite concerning the death and resurrection of a vegetation god, the spirit of the year. The brief Uckfuss play begins with Father Christmas as a kind of narrator. St. George as a loud and pompous hero, and Simon Simple, the fool. To St. George is opposed the King of Egypt and his son and champion, Bold Slasher. In a tight circle of onlookers, St. George and Bold Slasher fight. In good school pageant tradition, the latter falls with the hero's sword grasped firmly under his arm. With stirringly simple eloquence, the King of Egypt laments his dead son, "Alas, you've broken his tool and ended his life." After much horseplay with a giant pill, the doctor, a genial quack ("I have a bottle under my belt that makes young girls feel better than they ever felt") resurrects the dead. Then the Tommy and the Betty (a man and a man-woman) lead on the sword dancers.

In the last mumming I saw, the sword dance was the means of killing. this time it was pure exhibition. Five men carrying the special flat and flexible swords keep up a lively jigging step, holding their own swords with the right hand, the tip of another with their left. By a series of complicated knotting passes over and under each others' arms, they make the swords into a locked star pattern that one of them can lift and display to the audience. There are many ingenious ways in which they achieve the star; one, for example, involves three of the men backflipping the other two over the swords. It's fast and intricate and unbelievably thrilling.

Two boys of about 16 were sitting next to me with their mouths hanging open, and everyone applauded each pattern breathlessly. At the end, the sword dancers—again of all ages, men who'd been dancing all evening—were cheered loud and long by their friends. By all of us. It was an occasion for both laughing and unobtrusive weeping because of the beauty of the dance itself, of the trouble the men had taken to learn it, the skill they had achieved, and the love which they and their audience had for dancing. And the pride in it. What they were doing didn't involve any kind of remote virtuousity, but a degree of excellence —greater than, but no different from—that of everyone who was there to dance that night. It made up for a lot of dancing that doesn't get done in America. And if spring comes, I'll have to write them a thank you note.

As Genevieve Shimer pointed out to me in a very friendly letter, the correct name for this group is the Country Dance and Song Society of America. Its members also do a lot of American dances—squares of all kinds, New England contras, play-party games, and so on.

Dancing on Air—Is That Flying?

The Village Voice, December 16, 1974

The dance world has its quota of superstars and vociferously ardent fans, but balletomanes are prim compared to the crowd that squeezes into Madison Square Garden to see the Soviet Gymnastics Team. Hordes of what must be novice gymnasts splash coke onto the aisles, pound up and down stairs during intermission, searching for rumored vendors of Olga Korbut t-shirts; in concerted cheers, their shrill voices rise above the noises of the crowd: "YAY, OLGA!" Do they perhaps imagine that some day we—the sportsfans, the pros, the reporters, the lovers of spectacle—will be watching *them* instead of these very young Russians with very big titles? That *they* will be the bright specks shooting across the far-away ring, the golden youths who defy not just bars and rings and hurdles, but the super-obstacles of gravity, mortality, and human frailty?

Ludmilla Turischeva, Honored Master of Sports, Absolute Champion USSR, Europe, 20th Olympiad, and the World is missing from the line-up, so Olga Korbut is the undisputed star of the show. And it is a show. Instead of the hushed voices of TV sportscasters with their speculations about who's going to get the number of points necessary to beat whom and why, we hear an announcer whose fervent voice seems designed to bring the distant serious figures working in the ring into dazzling close-up. He not only shapes our attention with his superlatives, he plays on our feelings: "She broke your hearts in Munich . . ."—the invisible voice is warm and trembly.

Korbut hardly needs the hype; because she is a phenomenon, with her violently over-arched back, her wispy yellow hair, her gleeful attack, her routines that are almost impudently innovative. She seems to enjoy playing with speed changes: on the uneven parallel bars, she's as light and quick as a mosquito; on the balance beam, she teases out certain stunts as slowly as she dares: for example, resting her chin on the beam, she arches until her toes touch the beam beyond her head.

The various gymnastic events sanctioned for international competitions look like elaborate developments of skills once needed in warfare —dexterity, balance, strength, well-aimed impetus. Watching the steady pull of arms, the rapid changes of support from feet to heand, the swing and thrust and flight of bodies, you imagine ancient battles, Hollywood-flavored, with men vaulting onto horses, scaling walls, swinging into besieged towns on ropes.

Even the "modern rhythmic gymnasts," Galina Shafrova and Lud-milla Yevetushenka (substituting for injured Galina Shugureva), who dance nimbly under, over, and around whatever hand object they are manipulating—a ball, a streamer, a hoop—give you the illusion that they're dealing with something volatile or sharp-edged. Even the feats that the acrobatic couple, Galina and Yuri Saveliev, toss almost casually out of their mildly flirtatious dancing—she stands on one leg on his up-stretched palm and leans slowly backward—strike me as hyperstylizations of "If you stand on my shoulders, you can reach the parapet."

Perhaps it's this direct and inherently combative element of gym-nastics that makes some of the occasionally interspersed "dance steps" look odd. Certainly ballet has done a lot for gymnasts. These Soviet athletes have long, unbunchy muscles, and little unnecessary tension in their shoulders and chests. They have a lot of finesse: no unpointed feet break the arrowy line of their flight. But the actual dance move-ments and poses used—mostly in the women's floor exercises and the balance beam routines—to provide contrast, link stunts, and embellish pauses for breath come from some grand and mannered world of 19th century ballet. They contrast strangely with the straightforward speedi-ness of backflips and somersaults. It's almost endearing to see these super-athletes of the 20th century moving as if their model were a ballerina of heroic dimensions like Maya Plisetskaya, or some improbably dainty soubrette. And the grandiose salon music they dance to can make even an intricate and intriguingly designed floor routine like Rusika Sikharalidze's look gushing.

Because gymnasts understand so well the shapes their bodies have to make, they adapt easily to the exigencies of balletic line. But because they must always emphasize strength, or impetus pushed to its maximum, it may be hard for them to dance with fluidity or ease. Their fingers are always tense, as if ready to grip a bar at a moment's notice. Their pointy-toed strut is almost a travesty of that of a child ballet student. They press out or fling every move, so that there's less dynamic vitality in their "dancing" than in their gymnastics. Even beautifully smooth Elvira Saadi can't make a grand jeté on a balance beam look anything but jarring, since knees and ankles lock on landing to provide optimum security.

But gymnasts doing what they do best are thrilling to watch. A performer tears toward the vaulting horse, coils his body to spring, blossoms into some unexpected shape as he rebounds from the horse. As with a rocket, the beginning gives no hint of the end. I love the work with the rings too—the gymnast's legs swinging up to relieve the arms' endurance tests, his slow pressing into a cross, his sudden shooting to a handstand. Our announcer calls the horizontal bar a "hairy-chested event," but compared with the rings, it looks all ease—the man's body swinging through long arcs and circles arrested in perfect verticality at the top. And the women's flights on the uneven parallel bars are perhaps the strangest and most terrifying of all—because of the nonstopping speed and the way they arch from one bar and jacknife around another to rebound. I think of threads spooling in and winding off and reversing paths around the wheels of some rapid and fantastic machine. Best of all, I like mid-air twists—Viktor Klimenko executes a high-twisting handspring from the horse, Vladimir Marchenko dismounts from the parallel bars with a full-twisting back somersault, Nelli Kim manages a midflight half turn on the uneven parallel bars. It's easy to understand why judges give points for twisting: so many gymnastic exercises involve establishing a plane and working within it, as every kid who's mastered cartwheels knows. A twist can throw the body through several planes; you wonder how the guy will ever reorient himself to land cleanly.

Everything is accomplished so easily that after a while you could almost forget how difficult these events are. Nina Dronova tears toward a vault, thinks better of it, and her stop wrenches you. So does someone's hand slipping from a bar, or Korbut's momentary waver on the balance beam. Golden champion Nikolai Andrianov attempts a triple somersault as his dismount from the horizontal bar. By the third somersault, he's barely off the ground; he gets his legs under him, but then sprawls chin to the mat. I wonder if we watch for these slips—not to see suffering or failure, but to remind us that these are *our* supermen, that they are, after all, human like us.

This article was originally commissioned by some adventurous editors at Sports Illustrated, *and rejected in horror by the Managing Editor. Not enough point-keeping and tough comparisons perhaps . . .*

Boy, They Must Be Cold

The Village Voice, September 12, 1974

Who is the New York Dance Festival for? Any old lovers with nothing better to do? Dancers on late summer lay-off catching up with work of friends and rivals? Bargain hunters? Dance freaks? Maybe everyone who makes the scene at the Delacorte is a dance freak of one kind or another: Black, Beautiful, and Sullen as Hell, who freezes out the usher and one whole row of people and then turns to jelly, screeching "Look at George go!" when George Faison (or George Faison Universal Dance Experience) lets loose with a lickety-split leap; Old, Fierce, White, and Shabby who stands beady-eyed in the aisle watching for un-pegged-down seats, ready to bare claws and beak against leggy young dancers in the 7:50 dash of the no-reservations set.

At the Delacorte, acclaim is seldom widespread. Five (?) staunch pairs of hands applaud Dennis Wayne's solemn entrance in Richard Wagner's pas de deux, "Youth." (By the end, the house is warm with approval: Bonnie Mathis is on pointe and very lovely, and we can all empathize with guys who like each other but, despite perfectly matched pirouettes, can't quite get together.) When Ze'eva Cohen bravely appears in Rudy Perez's almost immobile "Countdown," three impeccable dark clawmarks of makeup on one cheek, a woman mutters concernedly "How'd she get her face so dirty?" Heavy, polite sighs punctuate Cliff Keuter's "Visit," perhaps because the choreography, and the four lovely women performing it, keep avoiding the climactic moments they have induced. I mean, are they beautiful, edgy creatures fighting and playing and loving each other in a perpetually-pink sci-fi dusk or are they just dancers obediently reiterating themes? When Ze'eva Cohen performs (wonderfully) "Escape" from Anna Sokolow's "Rooms," conoscenti approvingly situate the solo in its place in the dance; a few chuckle as if they thought Cohen were some mawkish, out-of-date creature instead of a gifted performer playing a lonely woman who is dreaming extravagantly; the rest applaud the skill and effort, accept the offering, but wait for the flash and sparkle of Faison or the liberated ballet of Dennis Wayne's Dance Repertory Theatre.

This company of Wayne's is composed mostly of Joffrey dancers, when the Joffrey isn't working, but only Wayne and Mathis are appearing at the Delacorte. "Youth," a relic of the old Harkness company, is an odd vehicle for them. Wayne is an ardent, vigorous sort of dancer, and in the icy wind that's blowing in clear weather his knees and ankles look unresilient: he has trouble sinking from the smooth, slow, balancing steps that move the dance along. Wagner's pas de deux has a couple of striking lifts, but the dancers must perform a curious mixture of yearning gestures and ballet steps that are as perfectly placed and planned-for as class exercises. Norman Walker's "Lazarus" is a meaty vehicle for Wayne, who stumbles backward onto the stage, rosy bare buttocks peeking boldly from under his flimsy grave-wrappings. Death has ruined his clothes, but not impaired his pirouettes, thank God. Throughout the solo, Walker's dramatic sense wars disturbingly with his love of beauty and virtuosity, and, as a result, Wayne often looks stylishly grotesque, but never completely bewildered or out-of-control. When he stumbles, his falls arc pleasingly to earth. This Lazarus passes through many states —terror, confusion, pain remembered, lust for life; finally with inexorable magnetism, the grave drags him back. This draws many bravoes, especially from a man who's spent the whole evening saying, "God, they must be cold!" or "She's really cold, I'll bet." For certifiable bravery in the face of coldness, Wayne in his white loincloth carries the day: "Now that's COLD for you."

George Faison's dancers, in his "Reflections of a Lady," wear lots of clothes, make many clever costume changes. They portray the dreams, memories, visions of reality that haunt a despairing Billie Holiday. Since I last saw Faison's work he's gotten more skillful at what he's trying to do (inching in on Ailey's market may be part of it). He's slicker about the way he maneuvers choruses of savagely strutting dancers, more savvy about the uses of stage space. "Reflections of a Lady" is not exactly a dramatic piece *about* Billie Holiday; it's a suite of dances relating to the neighborhoods in Holiday's life, the climates of her songs. (Ironically, Holiday gets no collaborative credit for her taped voice—"Tape collage, George Faison.") What holds the dance together is the figure of Billie wandering through, joining in, breaking away. Another potent force is Hope Clarke's performance in the central role. She has extraordinary theater goodlooks—big eyes and mouth in a broad, beautifully shaped face. Her every expression is clear, and her acting wonderfully honest and intelligent.

Some of Faison's dances are flashy, compressed, and symmetrical. You feel as if you might be watching them on a giant television set.

Others are bitter—Clarke trying to smile ("Smilin' Again") in a world of fixed smiles, white evening gowns, and dinner jackets and finding that her mouth doesn't like making that smile. A few are witty—Clarke trying politely to get the attention of a stony-backed judge (Faison in robe, holding gavel) while Holiday sings "Take All of Me."

Faison's dancers tear the place up. They're all terrific—vivid and scornful and blazing with dance power. They can do all the tricky semi-ballet Faison requires plus the Blackdance hip swings, speedymean direction changes, struts, and slides. What I like about them is that they let their bodies change character: the prettiest and neatest of them can slouch and stumble and hobble as junkies, whores, scrubwomen if necessary. Even when the characters are super-slick clichés, the dancers' transcendent honesty can grab you and hold you.

It's no surprise that the park audience is wild about the George Faison Universal Dance Experience, but how interesting that Katherine Litz's famous old solo, "The Fall of the Leaf," should be instantly recognized for the funny/sad classic it is, and laughed at and loved. Litz's comic sense is subtle, but it's also clear and wise, and her body tells no lies on stage: maybe that's why most people like her. Here she is, a lady of uncertain age and very certain refinement, wearing an elegant gown of autumnal red and a big ruffle of a hat. She is both the reluctant leaf itself and the poetic soul undone by every hint of the onset of winter. We howl at the occasional small, sharp, pained gestures that punctuate her wellbred swaying, at the puzzled, but resigned look on her face, at her pattering little walk. She sets her jaw and doesn't give up, even as she tugs the hat (it has no crown) down around her chest, then—ever obedient to some urgent dictate of The Scheme of Things—around her knees. By the time she leaves, the hat is around one ankle, but she, hobbling slightly, is so brave and dignified that you almost hate to notice what's making you laugh so hard.

Theatre of Giants

The Village Voice, December 3, 1970

Maybe it's because Western Europe copped out when it came to ritual dance theatre that I get so excited by examples of it from other countries. I'm not alone. The audience assembled at Hunter last Friday night to see the company of the Kerala Kalamandalum perform the Kathakali version of the "Ramayana" seemed deeply excited and cheered loudly after the performance (condensed from the possible 12 hours it might have run in India to an acceptable Western three and a half).

I have yet to read a completely satisfactory account of the origins of Kathakali. In its present form it can be traced back to the 17th century and a company owned by a poet-prince of Calicut. However, the style was clearly not his brain-child; he made use of, combined, and further refined some much older traditions of South Indian theatre and dance. Some of the positions used in Kathakali can be seen in medieval art work, and some of its traditions date back to the famous treatise of the 2nd century B. C., the "Natya Sastra."

Kathakali can be taken on several levels. It is meant to be popular theatre, depicting the body of Indian religious mythology in a colorful and comprehensible way. Yet the way the great performers embellish their roles by improvising around the simple chanted text gives the balletomanes and scholars a more complex experience.

The dramas were designed for courtyard performance. Usually a huge oil lamp provides the illumination. (At Hunter, a small lamp was used as a symbol of this.) The actors may be visible to you, but a scene does not start until two assistants drop a rectangular silk curtain from in front of the performers. Certain characters (mainly demons or animals) have a battle with the curtain first—peering over it, shaking it from side to side. The costumes and makeup are overpowering if you've never seen them before: the huge headdresses with bits of mirror flashing on them, the starchy white skirts, the knee bells, the heavy long-sleeved jackets, the jewels, the white neck scarves with the ruffled ends that contain mirrors, the white rice paste beards, the painted faces (green for heroes, green with red for demons with a touch of nobility, black and red for monkeys, etc.).

A conch shell is blown eerily in the distance to signal the start of the performance. Except for that, there are no blown or plucked instruments in a Kathakali performance. It's all percussion—two kinds of drum, gong, cymbals, a squeeze box to provide a drone. Two singers chant the text of the play. The dancers illumine the text with gestures that have specific meaning (about 24 basic hand positions that can combine to produce a large vocabulary), facial expressions, and body attitudes. Certain demonic, animalistic, or primitive characters are allowed to howl and shriek (which can be frightening or comical). There are also passages of pure dance, and footwork to accompany descriptive passages.

The dance style is so extraordinary that it is hard to describe clearly. The performers spend a lot of time in a deep second position plié with the knees rotated outward; the feet, however, turn forward or even inward and are clubbed. The dancer actually stands on the outside edges of his feet. Most of the footwork moves through this splayed position. Not only are the lines of the body squared, but often the patterns move in a square, showing you the movement from four angles. Although head, arms, hands, and feet perform independently much of the time, sometimes in dance passages the whole upper body rolls or sways from the waist—head held still or doing a follow-through snap. The effect is beautiful, but it can also suggest great power or a kind of pomposity. I found that it was almost necessary to sit close or use field glasses in order to get the full impact of the facial expressions. V. M. Govindan, playing Ravana, the demon-king, made rapid and minute rotations of his eyeballs that were truly terrifying. The two rather ignoble monkeys, Bali and Sugriva, (Padmanabhan Nair and Nelliyode Vasudevan Namboodiri) had round fangs attached inside their upper lips which they could pop in and out during their very funny battle—first a real combat, later a seated war in which they flung howls and lice at each other.

Even from a distance, however, the whole thing is impressive. You can sit on the edge of your seat while Hanuman, the white monkey (Ramakutty Nair), fights an evil counsellor with flaming torches. You can be moved when the heroic bird, Jatayu (Sankaran Namboodiri), lies dying with one wing cut off, and Rama and his brother Lakshmana kneel to stroke his feathers. You can admire the skill of Kunchu Nair, an actor of great renown in India, as he shows you Rama stalking through the forest, attempting to catch a young deer for his wife, Sita. You see clearly the stalking, the coaxing, the repeated flight of the deer, Rama's increasing vexation that finally leads him into shooting the deer; it doesn't matter at all that you don't understand the meaning of the specific gestures.

Someone who hadn't seen any of the plays the Kerala Kalamandalum company (reputedly the best Kathakali troupe in India) was performing here asked me if the evening seemed long or if I was bored at times. Strangely, although I was very tired, and the theatre was overheated, it took me only the first scene to get onto the right wave-length. If you can accept the fact that each play contains not only action, but description of that action or plans for it, you can relax and stop that inner pressure which we in the West have in relation to the theatre—that is, to get on with the plot as quickly as possible.

The Dancer as Divinity

The Village Voice, August 26, 1971

Some of India's major classical dance styles—Bharata Natyam, for example—are solo forms. Properly speaking, there can be no chorus of milkmaids for Krishna to dance with, no duets for Shiva and Parvati, no armed conflicts as there are in the Kathakali theatre. Yet these soloists perform not only pure dance, but poems with elaborate glosses and variant stanzas, and complicated dramas in which they play all the parts.

Ritha Devi danced at Jacob's Pillow again this summer, and as I said last summer, I would travel farther than that to see her, expecially since when she is in the U.S. she gives relatively few concerts. She performs in the Kuchipudi and Odissi styles, both of which are closely related to Bharata Natyam, but with subtle distinctions. Both styles slip into the carved, frontally oriented poses of bas reliefs; both, of course, use rhythmic foorwork, mudras, stylized facial expressions. However, Odissi and Kuchipudi seem to mix more curves and loops with the angles formed by knee, ankle, thigh, elbow, head. Odissi in particular has an equivocal, almost languid look because of the beautiful S-shaped countercurves of hip and rib cage. It makes you think of the happily copulating gods on those famous temples where divinity is a sweet, reassuringly sensual power.

Ritha Devi specializes, it seems, in dramatic dances. She is a tiny, pretty woman—almost doll-like in her paint and her silks. When you first see her, she seems so compact, so charming that you wonder what she will do with the massive themes she tackles.

This summer's Pillow program eases her formidable strength out to you slowly. She begins with a "shabdam" (a poem dance—an exploration of perhaps one corner of a dramatic event). In it, she is a court dancer enticing her king with small gifts and elegant praise. She is quick, willful, arching briefly away from him and then swaying back. The focus of the dance makes you, the audience, the recipient of these promises.

So, she finishes this one. It's difficult, but it deals with one character and one mood. After a second's pause, she's back on stage with a different kind of dramatic dance, also in the Kuchipudi style. She is the child Krishna playing with his ball. When an unlucky toss lands it in the river, he dives after it, and in the process of recovering the ball overcomes the evil serpent, Kaliya, who poisons the river water. This simple tale slowly opens out to reveal the power and importance of the god, and it ends with a whole catalog of Krishna dance walks. Some of these I hadn't seen before: the taut little jump with both big toes locked together, the walk with the toenail of the gesture leg dragging a semi-circle on the floor, the strange footwork executed while standing on—and propelling—a large brass plate. Ritha Devi manages it all. She is the child Krishna—innocent, almost awkward as he dives. She is the serpent. She is the redoubtable god. She is the tireless dancer showing you how to recognize him.

Her final dance, "Dashavatari," is Odissi. In it, she becomes in rapid succession all of the different incarnations of Vishnu. He is the Preserver of the Hindu trinity, the once and future king who appears when mankind most needs him and who will appear again, riding a white horse and wielding a sword.

The dancer shows/becomes the fish, the boar, the man-lion. In between each new incarnation, she is humanity pleading for divine aid. Some of the god's avatars are men and warriors; the movement that reveals them is in a broad, strong style. The dancer settles into deep, wide knee-bends, stretching her arm and body back to lift the axe, the plough, the bow. Like most of these Indian solo dramas the dance is a rich mixture of narrating, cataloging, acting, dancing. The performer moves from depicting to becoming to commenting to praising. The process of transformation is as informal as it is mysterious.

Ritha Devi's dances are quite long: I don't thing that any concessions have been made to Western concepts of theatrical time. I like the length. Absorbed completely in the shape of what she is doing, she hordes power at the center of her dancing, and only when she has absolutely finished can she bestow it on you—as if it were fabric tied off and snapped from the loom on which it was made.

Kill Them All!

The Village Voice, February 17, 1975

Even if I hadn't read the Asia Society's lucid program notes about Chhau, the masked dance of Purulia, I think I would have guessed from the dancing that this part of West Bengal is hot and dry, that the land is rocky and hard to cultivate, and that fierce beasts still roam the forests.

The style is not simply virile, it's ferocious. You can't see the faces of the all-male performers, only their glossy masks, but their bodies always look vigilant, battle-ready. They stride or strut along imaginary paths on the stage—knees bent, arms swinging, spine straight, head turning from side to side. Many, many times in the course of an evening, dancers stamp one foot in front of them and take off in a rapid jumped turn; during preparation, turn, and landing they hold their bodies in a tense crouch, sometimes in a squat. Whap, whap. Are they trying to beat grain out of stubborn ground?

The music that accompanies their dancing is played on a dry, woody flute, an immense drum that is hit with two thick sticks, and a smaller drum that the player slings around him. The musicians, who also chant plot elements, are as combative as the dancers: sometimes they seem to be luring them onto the stage or goading them on in their endeavors.

Apparently, the earliest dances of Purulia were all war dances. Later, to please helpful Hindu rulers, the dances were embedded in stories from the Ramayana and the Mahabharata. The eight Chhau dancers performing at Carnegie Hall must have presented an anthology of their fiercest fights and contests. Ganesh, the elephant-headed god, and Kartik, the god who rides a peacock, (marvelously suggested by the performer's costume which includes a feathertail and a bird head on his groin) fight a demon one by one and are defeated. Durga, their mother, arrives and gives the demon a good thrashing. Three good kings and the demon king, Ravana, attempt to lift the bow of Shiva and win the hand of a valuable maiden, and no amount of grunting and wrenching does the trick; the great Rama lifts the bow, but then has to fight a Shiva devotee. Krishna, relaxing in the woods, is accidentally shot by a hunter and dies in twitching convulsions that lift his entire body off the ground. Finally, Abhimanyu, the son of Arjuna, has to fight seven warriors simultaneously.

Sounds harsh, doesn't it? Well, I suppose it is. But it's never grisly. The actors are too brisk, the fights too formal for that. (Combats are designated by rapid advances and retreats, the flourishing of weapons, spins and jumps, and the participants' fierce attentiveness to each other.) A few scenes are lyrical, almost languid—Krishna executing a melancholy dance soliloquy after battle—but most get down to business (i.e., fighting) quickly. The bow-lifting contest is one of the most human of the excerpts offered. King No. 1 (Kshirod Sing Mura) approaches the sacred bow with awe and hesitation at first; King No. 2 (Jagru Mahato, a particularly fine dancer, very loose and bold) strides in cockily, a know-it-all; King No. 3 (Gambhir Sing Mura) takes a look at the two stalwarts who've been defeated and begins to worry about his own prowess.

And you see all this despite the masks. In fact, the strong, agile, expressive bodies contrast poignantly with those frozen faces and glittering crowns. A demon appears forever snarling, in triumph as in death; a king—his small, pretty, sharp features crowded together in the center of his face, (the way they are on those American china-headed dolls)— looks as placid when he is surrounded by adversaries as he does strolling through the forest.

The Chhau style of Purulia hadn't been seen outside Bengal until 1969. The man who "discovered" it in 1961, Asutosh Bhattacharyya, directed this group. There are reputedly two troupes to nearly every village, and, I guess, when the men aren't dancing or preparing for a dance, they're fighting the soil and hoping the rains will come.

The Fine Art of Bloodsucking

The Village Voice, December 31, 1970

If I ever had a program for "Vampyro Freako," I've lost it. That might, in any case, be fitting, because I lost my way several times trying to find 83 Leonard Street where Ellen Klein's Ecole de Mime is located. I also had to shed a few of my preconceptions about mime before I could enjoy myself (which I most certainly did).

Most of Klein's troupe of adults and children do not perform with the cleanness or economy of gesture that we (or I) associate with classical mime. What they do is more like a hugely expanded and stylized version of actors' sense memory exercises. They use their bodies in a loose and zany way—swaying on a base of spraddled legs and bent knees.

"Vampyro Freako" is a happy, fiercely energetic mess of people, slides, props, and taped music going through a series of scenes loosely linked together by their common idea: the delights of bloodsucking. Everyone has a beautiful and horrendous makeup; almost everyone has tap shoes on (high-heeled silver shoes with the ties missing, saddle shoes: you can nail taps to anything). The children are especially gleeful— swigging blood from a bar at a vampire cocktail party, dying horribly from poisoned drinks (poisoned blood?) in a harem scene. Strap-hanging in a subway they are suddenly moved to sink their teeth in the nearest neck. This requires skill and cooperation, since the victim of the moment must be prepared to sink to the floor in direct ratio to the amount of bloodsucking that is being inflicted on him.

Everybody on stage moves all the time. There is no such thing as holding still for the main event. In one gory adult scene, a dental patient is sucked all but bloodless by a sinister dentist and his black-lipped nurse who bounces up and down merrily on the anaesthetized patient. No doubt the enraptured three-year-olds in the audience thought nothing of it: "Ride a cock (sic) horse to Banbury Cross." Every bared neck offers a challenge to every greedy fang. Demons win hands down over angels. Even a dead, well-crucified Christ wiggles his nailed-together feet when some hard-tapping demons with peculiar red wattles strut in to rock music. Good taste you can forget; what is Holy Communion but legal blood-drinking, after all? For some reason, a slice of bread, a carrot, and some other food (I can't remember what) elect to do a bit of mild tap-dancing together. One (nine years old maybe) has endearingly wrinkled and grubby tights.

So it's a recital of some far-out neighborhood kids that somebody (Ellen Klein, I guess) had the wit to organize. I suspect that ideas were contributed by everyone. "We did it!" shrieked the baby vampires from backstage after the event. "You were really terrific," said some friendly parents to a little girl with a red face, black lips, sequined eyes, and driblets of fake blood running down her chin, "really, you were."

Hanging Up Over the Fair

The Village Voice, September 19, 1974

The 134th annual Barrington Fair is a maze of balloons, draft beer, hot fried food, immense fuzzy prizes, grimy Ferris Wheels that break down and leave you queasily suspended above the noisy crowd. In sheds on the periphery wait the sweet-faced heifers and coddled rams waiting to be judged; the bulbous, polished vegetables; the jams and cakes.

But the Fair's opening is to be graced by visiting royalty—Lipizzan stallions. "Not," says the ad hastily and in minuscule print, "affiliated with the Spanish Riding School or Austrian Government." Equine renegades? No, probably just a little touring company bred from the horses the grateful Austrian government gave Patton in return for rescuing their animals during the war.

Thousands of us crowd around the track. Nothing is quite ready. Behind a parked van of understudies, four men in red livery and cocked hats warm up their horses. You can see flashes of white tails and prancing hooves.

Finally they appear, bold and white—a child's dream of noble horses —strutting to a Handel fanfare. Compared to race horses with their lean, edgy bodies, these horses seem immense and solid. Their training has shaped them into massive baroque curves. Although the riders' hands appear kind on the bridle, the reins are short, and the horses hold their chins in, making their necks look even thicker and more deeply arched.

I can't imagine them lazing. I wish I could imagine them covering ground. What are they like offstage when their manes aren't braided and their plumy tails curried? They rarely make a mistake in the tasteful program of pas de deux, de trois, de quatre, pas seul. Two can step sideways, keeping heads or tails toward each other in mirror image. They can pirouette by walking in tight circles. They can pace together with subtle alterations in gait. They can stand on their hind legs for a moment in a jubilant-looking salutation. The bravest and strongest, with the star-rider (authentically Austrian) not mounted, but walking cajolingly beside him, demonstrates curvets, or cabrioles. His front feet lift, and just before they touch ground, both back legs kick out, rocking the horse back and forth. The landing must be a shock. We cheer, and our horse—the handsomest, the best—suddenly doubles his front legs under and kneels in a bow.

I cry the way I cry at parades—laughing at myself for crying. I cry too for the miles and years that separate the courts of Vienna from Great Barrington, Massachusetts. And I cry for the fine, big, doubtless happy horses who've been taught to restrain all lust for distance to mince elegantly, printing many steps onto a short stretch of track.

And yet they do nothing truly inimical to horses; watching them, you see only a slight—disturbing, but beautiful—deformation of their nature. They make me think of bonsai, of topiary gardens, of radishes cut into the shape of roses. And I think idly of women dancing on pointe and how they would look to a Houyhnhnm. Then I decide I'd better stop thinking and have some popcorncottoncandyhotdoglemonade so I'll have something worth being sick with when those cars start whirling.

From the top of the Ferris Wheel (stuck, of course), I see that the track has been taken over by Hurricane hell drivers.

Index